# Electronic Document
# Imaging Systems
## Design, Evaluation, and Implementation

## William Saffady

**Meckler**

**Westport • London • Melbourne**

**Library of Congress Cataloging-in-Publication Data**

Saffady, William, 1944-
    Electronic document imaging systems : design, evaluation, and
implementation / William Saffady.
        p.   cm.
    Includes bibliographical references and index.
    ISBN 0-88736-840-9 (alk. paper) : $
    1. Business records--Management--Data processing. 2. Document
imaging systems.  3. Information storage and retrieval systems-
-Business.  I. Title.
HF5736.S18   1993
651.8--dc20
                                            92-36182
                                              CIP


**British Library Cataloguing-in-Publication Data**

Saffady, William
    Electronic Document Imaging Systems:
    Design, Evaluation and Implementation
    I. Title
    006.4

    ISBN 0-88736-840-9

Meckler Publishing, the publishing division of Meckler Corporation,
    11 Ferry Lane West, Westport, CT 06880.
Meckler Ltd., Artillery House, Artillery Row, London SW1P 1RT, UK.
Meckler, GPO 61A, Melbourne, Victoria, Australia 3001

Printed on acid free paper.
Printed in the United States of America.

# Contents

# Preface

This book deals with computer-based information systems that convert documents to electronic, digitally-coded images for retrieval, display, printing, or other purposes. Such systems offer a widely publicized, potentially effective alternative to paper-based filing systems and microfilm technology for documents maintained by corporations, government agencies, not-for-profit institutions, and other organizations. This book is intended for information systems analysts, records managers, office automation specialists, and other information processing professionals who have document management responsibilities and want a systematic introduction to and explanation of electronic document imaging concepts and technology. The book describes and discusses the most important components and methodologies associated with electronic document imaging implementations. It emphasizes characteristics and capabilities of electronic document imaging technology that are important for system selection, implementation, and operation. The book is divided into five chapters:

- Chapter One defines essential terms and delineates the scope of electronic document imaging technology, differentiating the systems discussed in this book from other document management technologies (such as facsimile and microimage transmission) that incorporate electronic imaging components but do not offer a completely computerized approach to document storage and retrieval. It provides a brief history of electronic document imaging and discusses the most common motives for the implementation of electronic document imaging systems, emphasizing their advantages over paper-based filing systems and microfilm technology. The chapter concludes with an overview of components and worksteps in electronic document imaging installations.

- Chapter Two discusses input procedures and devices in electronic document imaging implementations. It begins with a lengthy discussion of document indexing concepts and the role of index data bases in electronic document imaging systems. Document digitization is explained and the characteristics and capabilities of document scanners described in detail. The chapter concludes with a discussion of data entry methodologies, including auto-indexing approaches.

- Chapter Three covers image storage concepts, devices, and media. It delineates factors which determine image storage requirements for specific types of documents. For many users, electronic document imaging systems are closely identified with optical disks, the most widely utilized media for document image storage; often, the phrases "electronic document imaging system" and "optical disk system" are used synonymously. Chapter Three describes and discusses the characteristics, advantages, and limitations of optical storage peripherals and media for electronic document imaging implementations. Similar treatment is provided for magnetic storage devices and media.

- Chapter Four deals with retrieval procedures and equipment. It outlines retrieval capabilities supported by electronic document imaging systems. Topical coverage includes workflow implementations, as well as computer-output laser disk (COLD) methodologies for retrieval of computer-generated, page-formatted reports. The chapter provides detailed descriptions of retrieval workstation components, including image displays and printers. Microfilm output and image transmission options are also considered.

- Chapter Five examines widely discussed issues and concerns associated with electronic document imaging technology. It considers records management problems posed by the limited stability of image storage media and the dependence of recorded images on specific hardware and software components for their continued retrievability. The legal status of electronic document images is reviewed. The potential for integration of electronic document imaging with other document storage and retrieval technologies is considered. The chapter closes with a lengthy discussion of electronic document imaging costs and cost justification.

Where pertinent, the narrative discussion is supported by tables and illustrations that complement or supplement points raised in the text. While the coverage of topics treated in individual chapters is often detailed, it is not exhaustive. As with any publication, some subjects are inevitably treated more briefly than certain readers might like. Where more detailed information about particular topics is desired, references to books, articles, and technical reports are incorporated into the narrative discussion as suggestions for additional reading. A bibliography is included at the end of each chapter.

Companies that offer specific electronic document imaging hardware and software are noted at various points in the book. Mention of such companies is for purposes of illustration only and does not imply endorsement of their products; nor does the omission of specific companies imply lack of merit in their offerings. To assist readers interested in obtaining additional information about available products, an appendix provides names and addresses of some companies that manufacture and/or market electronic document imaging systems and components.

This book reflects the state-of-the-art in electronic document imaging in late 1992. Recognizing that no published discussion of a developing technology can be completely up to date, individual chapters emphasize fundamental aspects of electronic document imaging and the categorization of system components and methodologies. While continuing product developments will affect specific facts presented here, the book's overall conceptual presentation should retain its utility and readers should be able to relate new electronic document imaging developments to those described here.

*William Saffady*
*School of Information Science and Policy*
*State University of New York at Albany*

*Chapter One*

# An Introduction to Document Imaging Systems

A document imaging system is an integrated configuration of hardware and/or software components that produces pictorial copies (images) of office files, reports, publications, and other source documents for storage, retrieval, dissemination, or other purposes. This broad definition encompasses technologies and devices with widely varying characteristics and capabilities. Familiar examples of document imaging products include photocopiers, which make full-size or near-size reproductions of documents, and micrographic systems, which record source documents as miniaturized images on microfilm, microfiche, or other microforms. Such widely encountered imaging devices typically employ photographic technologies for document recording. As such, they fall outside the scope of this book which covers systems that record and store document images in electronic formats on optical or magnetic media for reference purposes. While most photocopiers and micrographic products incorporate electronic components, and some newer models employ digital imaging techniques to facilitate document reproduction, they do not store documents in electronic formats.

The storage of document images in electronic formats for reference purposes similarly distinguishes the systems discussed in this book from other products, such as facsimile transceivers and desktop publishing systems, which generate and process electronic document images. While such products may incorporate electronic recording and storage components, they invariably store document images as a means to an end rather than as a primary objective. Facsimile transceivers, for example, are communication rather than storage devices. They generate electronic images of paper documents for transmission to compatible equipment; where storage facilities are provided (an increasing number of fax machines feature internal memories, for example) they typically serve as a temporary repository for document images that will eventually be forwarded to their intended destination. Similarly, the electronic document images generated and manipulated by desktop publishing systems are principally intended for incorporation into other documents. While the images may be retained in electronic form for later reuse, storage for reference purposes is not intended.

As noted above, the systems described in this book convert source documents to electronic images for storage on optical or magnetic media. The electronic images are typically produced by scanners that digitize source documents for computer processing and storage. Less commonly, video cameras may convert source documents to analog electronic images. In most electronic document imaging applications, the source documents are paper or paper-like records; examples of the latter include the vellum or polyester sheets used for engineering drawings, overhead transparencies, and certain artwork. In some cases, however, input to an electronic document imaging system consists of photographic or electronic images that were produced from paper records by a previously implemented document imaging system. As an example, document images recorded on microfilm may be scanned for conversion to an electronic format; alternatively, images created by a given electronic document imaging system may be converted to a format required by the system of a different vendor. Such image-to-image conversions are likely to become increasingly commonplace as the installed base of document imaging systems matures and users seek replacements for them.

Regardless of input source, electronic document imaging systems maintain a computer database which serves as an index to stored images. The index typically resides on magnetic disks. It is searched to determine the locations of document images that meet specified retrieval parameters. Depending on application requirements, images may be displayed, printed, or distributed in support of particular retrieval operations. Electronic document imaging is one of two approaches to document storage and retrieval that rely completely on electronic storage technology. The other approach (variously described as text storage and retrieval, full-text retrieval, text data management, or text information management) is a computer application that stores the contents of documents as character-coded text rather than as images. Each letter of the alphabet, numeric digit, punctuation mark, or other character is represented by a sequence of bits defined by a predetermined coding scheme, such as the American Standard Code for Information Interchange (ASCII) or the Extended Binary Coded Decimal Interchange Code (EBCDIC). In many cases, the documents originate as files generated by word processing or electronic messaging programs; alternatively, the contents of paper-source documents may be converted to computer-processible, character-coded form via keystroking or optical character recognition (OCR).

Like electronic document imaging systems, text storage and retrieval systems include computer hardware and software components which capture, process, and store the textual content of documents. Their significant advantages include very compact storage of textual information and the ability to retrieve documents by the words or phrases that they contain. Unlike electronic document imaging technology, however, text storage and retrieval systems do not preserve the appearance of source documents. They are consequently unsuitable for document storage applications where significant information is conveyed by signatures, logos, typographic characteristics, or other visual elements. As discussed later in this book, text storage and retrieval capabilities can be combined with electronic document imaging components to address this limitation.

## History

While electronic document imaging is often described as a new and innovative information management technology, its underlying concepts are well established, and document processing products based on them have been available for several decades. A widely cited article by Bush (1945), for example, delineated the advantages of automated document storage and retrieval based on image-oriented technologies. Among the earliest examples of imaging products, business-oriented facsimile transceivers date from the 1960s, and fax machines for special applications were available prior to that time. While facsimile technology generally falls outside the scope of this book, the scanners utilized as input devices by electronic document imaging systems closely resemble facsimile transceivers in concept, design, and operation. Many electronic document imaging systems employ image compression methodologies that were originally developed for facsimile applications. An increasing number of electronic document imaging configurations incorporate fax modems for long-distance transmission of retrieved document images. Some electronic document imaging systems also support fax machines as remote input devices, but, while it incorporates electronic imaging concepts and components, facsimile is principally a communication technology. The following discussion provides a brief developmental review of electronic technologies and systems for document image storage and retrieval.

### Video-based Systems

The earliest electronic imaging systems intended specifically for document storage and retrieval relied on a combination of computer and video technologies. Such examples as the Ampex Videofile and Infodetics System 2000 were introduced in the late 1960s and early 1970s. They employed specially designed video cameras to record documents as analog images on videotapes that were packaged on reels or in cassettes. Like their modern successors, such early electronic document imaging systems relied on computer-maintained databases to index and locate recorded images. Given the serial access limitations inherently associated with tape storage, however, retrieval proved unacceptably slow for many applications. Because some of their hardware components were custom-developed, costs were high.

It is consequently not surprising that few videotape-based document imaging systems were installed; none remain in use, and their brief period of commercial availability is seldom recalled in historical surveys of automated document storage and retrieval technology. Their modern successors, electronic document imaging systems that utilize magnetic tape media originally developed for video recording, employ digital rather than analog imaging technologies. They are described in later chapters. Conceptually, however, video-based systems introduced in the 1960s and 1970s offered attractive capabilities that anticipated the features of modern document imaging products. Their database management software supported flexible document indexing and powerful image retrieval capabilities. Intended as "paperless" alternatives to conventional document management methodologies, they featured specially designed video monitors for the display of retrieved document images. They also incorporated printers for high-volume document replication as well as on-demand production of reference copies. Document images could be transmitted to remote workstations, although transmission speed and convenience were limited by the comparatively primitive data communications infrastructure of the 1960s and early 1970s. As an optional feature, the Ampex Videofile supported a video-to-microfilm converter which offered a more stable alternative to magnetic tape for long-term document storage.

*Microfacsimile*

A second, somewhat more successful group of early electronic document imaging systems (sometimes described as microfacsimile, microimage transmission, videomicrographic, or electronic micrographic systems) combined facsimile capabilities with microfilm storage of miniaturized document images. Conventional facsimile equipment is designed to transmit electronic images of paper documents to compatible equipment; microfacsimile systems, as their name implies, can transmit images from microforms. This can be simply accomplished, of course, by using a reader/printer to produce paper enlargements of microform images for input to an ordinary facsimile machine, but that method can prove time consuming and labor intensive in applications where large numbers of microimages are involved. As an additional constraint, reader/printer copies may lack the sharpness and contrast required for satisfactory facsimile reproduction. A true microfacsimile system permits direct scanning of source document or COM-generated microimages recorded on roll microfilm, microfiche, aperture cards, or other microforms. It converts such images to an electronic format suitable for transmission to remote display or printing devices. The technology is discussed by Barrett (1974), Barrett and Farbrother (1977), Costigan and Burger (1982), Horder (1980), Meyers (1970), Penniman and Tressel (1975), and Walter (1979, 1982).

Microimage transmission concepts are more than four decades old. Experimental microfacsimile systems were demonstrated in the late 1950s. The initial operational installations, implemented in the early to mid-1960s, were custom-developed for large corporations and government agencies. Examples are described by Knudson and Marcus (1972), Overhage and Reintjes (1974), and Costigan (1971, 1978). While such customized implementations demonstrated the technical feasibility of scanning and transmitting microimages, none of them led to commercially viable products. Through the mid-1970s, the limited performance, unreliability, and relatively high cost of conventional facsimile equipment did little to stimulate interest in related document imaging technologies. While prototype microfacsimile products were routinely demonstrated at information management conferences and related trade shows, prospective customers were often confused about the technology's viability and availability.

As a significant constraint, the potential market for microfacsimile systems has historically been limited by the ease with which microforms can be copied for distribution to remote locations in anticipation of reference; as an alternative to maintaining a centralized collection of microimages to be transmitted to remote workstations on demand, microform collections can be inexpensively duplicated for decentralized storage at multiple locations. As a further impediment to microfacsimile's acceptance, the information processing industry obscured the importance of microfacsimile and other document-oriented technologies by emphasizing computer-based data-oriented storage and retrieval systems in the early to mid-1970s. At that time, many information management profes-

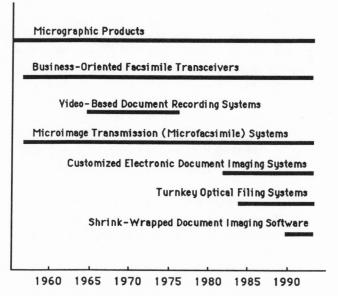

*Figure 1–1. Commercial availability of selected document imaging technologies.*

sionals regarded documents as transitional information carriers which would soon be replaced by computer databases, a point of view which argued against the implementation of complex image-oriented storage and retrieval systems.

During the late 1970s and early 1980s, however, some significant changes in information processing technology and information management practices led to renewed interest in microimage transmission. In particular, an intense interest in the productivity of office workers promoted increased awareness of the importance of documents as information carriers, accompanied by a growing concern about the time wasted in document retrieval and dissemination. A number of information specialists, accustomed to centralized data processing operations, advocated similar centralization of document storage, retrieval, and distribution activities. At the same time, significant improvements in conventional facsimile products—especially the introduction of sub-minute digital transceivers and of compatibility standards—promoted user awareness and acceptance of document transmission technologies. New developments in communications technology (including the proliferation of terrestrial microwave, satellite, and coaxial cable facilities) created the infrastruc-

ture of broadband linkages required for high-speed, high-volume microimage transmission. Finally, the growing size of many microform files increased the cost of conventional duplication and distribution in some large-scale installations.

During the late 1970s, a number of ambitious microfacsimile systems were custom-developed by systems integrators and information management consulting firms for large-scale document storage and retrieval applications in corporations and government agencies. They were invariably implemented in the context of a computer-assisted retrieval (CAR) system which employed a computer database as an index to document images recorded on microforms. Examples are described by Fain and Gruener (1979), Felton (1979), French (1981), Hopkins (1977, 1982), Peck (1983), and Wilkins (1982). Their micrographic hardware components typically included an automated microform selector which eliminated manual handling of 16mm microfilm, microfiche, or aperture cards. Retrieved images were scanned for transmission to remote workstations where they were displayed on video monitors, printed on paper, or, in rare instances, recorded on microfilm. Widely publicized in conference papers and information management publications, such systems were praised as leading-edge solutions to document storage and retrieval problems. By the early 1980s, more than a dozen companies offered microfacsimile systems or components. Examples included Access Corporation, Antone Systems, Infodetics, Integrated Automation, Omex Corporation, Planning Research Corporation, Ragen Information Systems, Rank Cintel, and TERA Corporation. During the same period, several vendors of computer-assisted microfilm retrieval systems introduced microimage transmission as an optional capability. Some implementations featured robotic retrievers for 16mm microfilm cartridges, microfiche, or other microforms. On instructions from a host computer, a specified microform was automatically extracted from a storage receptacle and mounted into a scanning mechanism.

When optical disk-based document imaging systems became commercially available in the early to mid-1980s, however, microfacsimile ceased to be viewed as a state-of-the-art technology, and customer interest quickly shifted to the new products. While no vendor currently promotes micro-facsimile as its core technology, microfacsimile components can be effectively incorporated into sophisticated electronic document imaging installations described later in this book. In such implementations, document images may be recorded on either microforms or electronic media. Backfiles, for example, may be stored on microfilm, while newly received documents are recorded as electronic images on optical disks. A single index provides integrated access to images in both formats. When retrieved, microform images are converted to electronic formats for display or printing in a manner identical with images recorded on optical disks. The source of the images is transparent to the requestor. If desired, microimages can be transferred to optical disks following conversion to electronic form. Such integrated implementations are described more fully in Chapter Five.

### Optical Disk-based Systems

While they employ electronic document imaging concepts and components, microfacsimile systems do not actually store documents in electronic formats. Instead, electronic images are generated from microphotographic images when requested by retrieval operations. Microfacsimile systems are hybrid products that combine computer and photographic technologies. During the late 1970s and early 1980s, there was considerable discussion of true electronic document storage and retrieval systems as completely computerized alternatives to such hybrid implementations. Seeking high-performance replacements for paper files and microfilm technology, some system developers and information specialists experimented with the text-oriented, character-coded approaches to document management described above. Others, however, advocated electronic imaging for its ability to capture a document's appearance as well as its content; as their principal advantage, image-oriented technologies can accommodate documents with signatures, illustrations, and other significant graphic elements ignored by text-oriented systems. During the 1970s, several vendors demonstrated systems that recorded electronic document images on magnetic media, but such products were not successful. Magnetic disk drives lacked the capaci-

ty required for high-volume document image storage; as removable media, magnetic tapes offered sufficient capacity for imaging applications where offline storage was acceptable, but their retrieval speed was limited by serial access characteristics. Optical disks, which were just beginning the transition from laboratory prototypes to commercial availability, offered an appropriate combination of direct access capability and high storage capacity.

As discussed by Horder (1981), Mole (1981), Schipma (1981), Schwerin (1984), Walter (1982a), and others, early attention focused on read-only optical videodiscs, the first optical storage product to be successfully commercialized. Broadly defined, a videodisc stores television images on a platter-shaped medium resembling a phonograph record. The images, which are recorded in analog rather than digital form, may be generated by video cameras or transferred from previously recorded video sources, such as videotapes. Read-only optical videodiscs themselves are produced by a mastering process in multiple copies from customer-supplied information. Recorded information is represented by microscopic pits with varying reflectivity characteristics which can be read by lasers. The technology is explained by Clemens (1982), Isailovic (1985), Kloosterboer and Lippits (1986), Lippits and Melis (1986), and Van Rijsewijk et al. (1982). Other types of videodiscs, which were never suggested for document recording, employed non-optical recording and playback technologies.

A 12-inch read-only optical videodisc—the most popular size—can store the equivalent of 54,000 television frames on each of two sides. When utilized for feature films or in interactive training applications, each side offers thirty to sixty minutes of full-motion video programming. If desired, however, videodisc images can be treated as a series of still frames which can be individually addressed and displayed, either manually or under computer control. If each frame contains the image of one letter-size page, a double-sided videodisc can store the equivalent of ten four-drawer filing cabinets. In addition to high-media capacity, proponents of read-only optical videodisc systems for document image storage have cited the advantages of media durability that permits relatively casual handling, the availability of inexpensive

*Figure 1-2a. The 12-inch read-only optical videodisc became commercially available in the early 1980s as a storage medium for full-motion video and still-frame images.*

players which can operate under computer control to quickly access specified video images, and relatively low unit costs in electronic publishing and similar applications where mastering charges and related preparation costs can be spread over multiple copies.

As potential disadvantages for document imaging implementations, the economics of mastering and replication favor applications which require multiple copies of read-only optical videodiscs for sale or distribution, while delays inherent in off-premises production can pose significant problems for applications with stringent turnaround time requirements or where new information must be added to previously created media at frequent intervals. Those impediments are at least partially addressed by videodisc recorders, which became commercially available in the early 1980s. As their name implies, such devices support the direct recording of video images on platter-shaped optical media. Capable of accepting input from video cameras, videotapes, read-only optical videodiscs, or other video sources, they

eliminate delays associated with mastering and permit the use of videodisc technology in applications where only one copy of a disc is required.

Whether read-only or recordable technology is employed, however, limited image quality is a formidable barrier to the successful implementation of videodisc-based document imaging systems. Specifically, the television signal formats employed by optical videodisc systems do not provide sufficient detail for consistently legible reproduction of the typewritten or typeset textual information contained in most office documents and publications. In their North American and Japanese implementations, videodisc systems conform to television signal standards defined by the National Television Systems Committee (NTSC). Such standards specify television frames consisting of 525 horizontal scan lines. Videodisc systems sold in Europe, Asia, and other parts of the world conform to PAL and SECAM standards, which specify television frames comprised of 625 scan lines. As described in later chapters, systems designed specifically for electronic document im-

*Figure 1–2b. Kodak photo CD player and disc, one of the latest CD technologies to arrive on the market. (Courtesy: Kodak)*

aging routinely support scanning formats with 2,000 lines per page, and some implementations support twice that number. Since the late 1980s, various Japanese companies have demonstrated videodisc recorders and related products based on high definition television (HDTV) formats which provide more than 1,000 lines per frame. While such enhanced television recording devices may be appropriate for electronic document imaging, their utility for such purposes has not been established; in any case, they were not generally available at the time of this writing.

While they are inappropriate for textual documents, conventional videodisc image formats based on NTSC, PAL, and SECAM television standards are suitable for storage and retrieval of visual materials, an application that is of considerable interest to museum curators, librarians, and others responsible for photographic archives, as well as large collections of artistic reproductions, medical illustrations, and other pictorial documents. Widely publicized examples of videodisc systems that store pictorial materials include the Videodisc Catalogue produced by the National Gallery of Art, the videodisc edition of photographs from the National Air and Space Museum, and the Non-Print Pilot Project which used video-

discs to record photographs and motion picture films from the collections of the Library of Congress. Published descriptions of such applications are provided by Binder (1988), Chen (1985), Kamisher (1986), Lamielle and De Heaulme (1986), and Parker (1985). Photo CD technology, introduced in the early 1990s by Eastman Kodak, provides similar image storage capabilities on compact discs rather than videodiscs. Photo CD images are generated by scanning 35mm photographic films. Image conversion is performed by authorized service bureaus. Like their videodisc counterparts, Photo CD images can be displayed on conventional television sets.

While systems that store images in video formats can address some document storage requirements, the most broadly applicable electronic document imaging systems are computer-based products. The convenient availability of suitable computer hardware components was a necessary precondition for the development and successful commercialization of such systems. Mainframes and minicomputers with adequate processing power have, of course, been available for several decades. Document scanners and appropriate video monitors were available, though not commonplace, in the 1970s; high-resolution displays were utilized, for example, in the microfacsimile installations described above.

Historically, the principal impediment to implementation of computer-based electronic document imaging systems was the lack of reasonably priced direct-access storage devices and media with sufficient capacity to accommodate high-volume applications. As discussed later in this book, electronic document images require formidable amounts of storage space. Magnetic disk drives can satisfy high-speed retrieval requirements, but the devices available in the 1970s were limited to several hundred megabytes of storage capacity. At twenty to thirty letter-size page-images per megabyte, a 200MB hard disk drive can hold less than half a file cabinet's worth of documents. High-capacity read/write optical disk drives—the storage devices currently employed in most electronic document imaging installations—became available in the early 1980s, and the first computer-based electronic document imaging systems were implemented shortly thereafter.

The earliest examples were minicomputer-based turnkey systems developed by Japanese and European manufacturers of optical disk drives. Such products as Philips' MEGADOC system, Hitachi's HITIFILE system, Toshiba's TOSFILE system, and Matsushita's PANAFILE system are described by De Vos (1980), Ishigame et al.. (1984), Ito and Takahashi (1987), Kudo et al. (1988), Mori (1984), and Mori et al.(1983). Advertised as "optical filing" systems, they featured preconfigured combinations of computer hardware and software intended for automated document storage and retrieval in a "paperless" office environment. In addition to a proprietary minicomputer with magnetic disk storage, typical turnkey system components included a document scanner, one or more optical disk drives, a high-resolution video monitor, a laser printer, and database management software for document indexing and retrieval. Initial availability was limited to Japanese and European domestic markets, although some models were eventually exported.

During the early 1980s, several Japanese and European optical filing systems were demonstrated at professional conferences and trade shows in the United States. In some cases, the demonstrations were sponsored by microfilm equipment vendors interested in building awareness and testing customer reactions to an emerging and possibly competing technology. By the mid-1980s, several American companies had begun actively marketing turnkey optical filing systems, some of which were imported from foreign suppliers. Thus, the Tab Laser-Optic 2500 System was manufactured by Hitachi, while the 3M Docutron 2000 was produced by Toshiba. In late 1984, FileNet Corporation became the first U.S. company to introduce a preconfigured optical disk-based document storage and retrieval system that was not based on a foreign product line, although it did incorporate hardware components from Japanese and European manufacturers. The first microcomputer-based optical filing system, the DISCUS 1000, was introduced by Advanced Graphics Applications in 1985. Similar products from other companies soon followed.

The earliest U.S. installations of optical disk-based electronic document imaging systems, however, were implemented by consulting firms and information services companies—a group collectively described as systems integrators—on a customized rather than a preconfigured turnkey basis. Operating as contractors to businesses, government agencies, and other organizations, systems integrators develop the hardware and software interfaces necessary to combine computer and document imaging components (including scanners, optical disk drives, and high-resolution video monitors) from various sources.

Some systems integrators acquired their technical expertise and document management experience in the 1970s by implementing complex microfacsimile installations that incorporated electronic imaging concepts and components; others were formed in the 1980s specifically to develop optical disk-based document imaging systems. Much publicized early examples of such systems were implemented in the early to mid-1980s by Integrated Automation for the Library of Congress, General Electric, and the Internal Revenue Service; by Planning Research Corporation and Falcon Systems for the U.S. Patent and Trademark Office; by RCA Government Systems for the Marshall Space Flight Center and the Rome Air Development Center; by Systems Development Corporation at the U.S. National Archives and Records

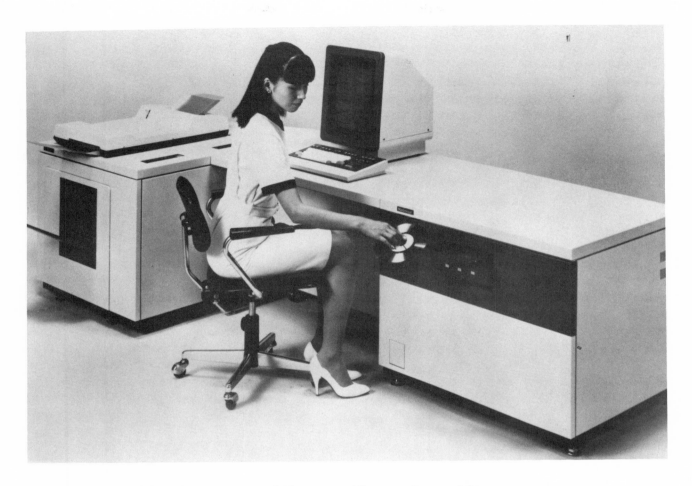

*Figure 1–3. An early Japanese turnkey optical filng system. (Courtesy: Panasonic)*

Administration; and by TRW Financial Services for American Express. Published descriptions of these and similar customized implementations by systems integrators are provided by Ammon (1983), Bovee (1988), Friedan (1989), Hooton (1986, 1988), Jacobson (1990), Kurtenbach (1988), Manns (1988), Price (1984, 1985), Searle and Lechner (1985), and Urrows and Urrows (1985), among others.

Systems integration activity expanded rapidly during the 1980s. By the end of that decade, dozens of companies, ranging from information management consulting firms to software specialists, were actively involved in some aspect of systems integration and customized systems development for electronic document imaging. The number of such systems integrators is increasing

steadily. Examples, in addition to those companies cited above, include Advanced Data Management Incorporated, Advanced Projects International, Advanced Systems Development Incorporated, Alpharel Incorporated, American Management Systems, Amitech Corporation, Andersen Consulting, Applied Computer Technology, Arthur Young and Company, BDM International, CACI, Computer Horizons Corporation, Computer Sciences Corporation, Coopers and Lybrand, CSSI, DataImage Incorporated, Data Management Design Incorporated, Document Imaging Systems Corporation, EDS Corporation, Ernst and Young, FORMTEK, Genesis Imaging Technologies, Grumman InfoConversion, GTX Corporation, Image Business Systems Corporation, Image Conversion Technologies, Image Data Corporation, KMPG Peat Marwick, La-

*Figure 1–4. An early FileNet configuration, one of the first electronic document imaging systems available in the United States. (Courtesy: FileNet Corporation)*

ser Recording Systems, OGDEN/ERC Government Systems, Optical Storage Solutions, Oracle Corporation, Science Applications International Corporation (SAIC), Sigma Imaging Systems, ST Systems Corporation, Systemhouse Incorporated, Trident Systems, TSC, Vision Three, and Xerox Corporation. Some systems integrators specialize in electronic document imaging implementations for specific applications or vertical markets, such as banking, insurance, health care, pharmaceutical research, engineering, local government, and law enforcement. The role of document imaging in such specialized applications is discussed by Brown (1989), Costanzo (1991), MacLeod (1989), Prokupets and Somers (1990), Sypherd (1990), and Vacca (1992).

During the late 1980s, various mainframe and minicomputer manufacturers added electronic document imaging capabilities and services to their product offerings. Some industry analysts contend that IBM's ImagePlus system, which was introduced in mid-1988, legitimized electronic document imaging technology in the minds of many prospective users. The initial implementation, intended for IBM mainframes, was subsequently joined by versions for AS/400 systems and PS/2 microcomputers in standalone or networked configurations. It is described by Plesums and Bartels (1990), Addink and Mullen (1990), Anderson et al. (1990), Avers and Probst (1990), and Dinan et al (1990). Among other computer manufacturers, document imaging systems and services are offered by Bull Worldwide Information Systems, Data General, Digital Equipment Corporation, Hewlett-Packard, Motorola, NCR, Nixdorf, Tandem, Unisys, and Wang Laboratories. The number of companies offering turnkey optical filing systems and other electronic document imaging implementations has likewise increased dramatically since the mid-1980s. Examples, in addition to those already cited, include Adaptive Information Systems, Bell and Howell, Canon, COM Squared, Conversion Dynamics, CPT Corporation, DataPoint, DIT Graphics, Eastern Computers, Eye Communications, Filequest, Genesys Data Technology, Grundig, Image-X International, Integrated Software, IMNET Corporation, LaserData, Micro Dynamics Limited, Minolta, OptiPlex, and Summit Software.

**Motives for Imaging**

As a completely computerized approach to document management, electronic document imaging has attracted the attention of a diverse group of information systems specialists, many of whom had little interest in or involvement with document storage and retrieval based on paper filing methodologies or microfilm technology. Document management conferences, once dominated by records managers and microfilm systems specialists, are increasingly attended by management information systems (MIS) professionals and data processing personnel who are eager to learn about electronic

*Figure 1–5. IBM ImagePlus, an electronic document imaging system for mainframe computer installations. Versions are also available for other computer platforms. (Courtesy: IBM Corporation)*

document imaging technology and products. Electronic document imaging systems are increasingly procured and implemented by, or with the assistance of, MIS personnel; greater MIS involvement can be expected as the scope and complexity of document imaging implementations expands.

When discussing factors that motivate the prospective user's interest in electronic document imaging, industry analysts increasingly emphasize the technology's potential as a strategic component in the re-engineering of business processes. Broadly defined, such re-engineering involves a thorough rethinking and redesign of business operations to make the most effective use of information technology. Enthusiastic advocates of re-engineering contend that computer-based information systems, many of which were initially implemented in the 1960s and 1970s, have unimaginatively automated existing procedures without evaluating the appropriateness of those procedures or considering alternative approaches made possible by innovative technologies, such as electronic document imaging. They suggest that comprehensive, enterprise-wide imaging implementations can radically and beneficially affect the work of corporations, government agencies, and other organizations. For corporations in particular, electronic document imaging is extolled as a valuable resource that can enhance competitiveness by increasing productivity and dramatically improving customer service. For government agencies and not-for-profit organizations, re-engineering of operations to incorporate electronic document imaging can result in faster, more effective delivery of services.

While the role of enterprise-wide imaging systems as components in a pervasive re-engineering of business practices is conceptually interesting, most electronic document imaging implementations are more modest in scope and purpose. Rather than addressing the document management requirements of an entire organization, the typical electronic document imaging system automates one or more information storage and retrieval applications in an office, department, or other business unit within a corporation, government agency, or not-for-profit institution. In most installations, electronic document imaging is designed to minimize or eliminate specific problems associated with conventional paper filing systems and offer one or more advantages that could not be obtained with paper records management methodologies. In such situations, widely cited motives for electronic document imaging implementations include: improved retrieval, rapid document delivery, simplified file maintenance, automated workflow, and compact document storage.

*Improved Retrieval.*

Improved document retrieval capability when compared to paper files or other manual record-keeping methodologies is a widely encountered objective of computer-based information systems in general and an important motivation for electronic document imaging implementations in particular. The retrieval limitations of conventional paper-based document management systems have long been recognized. Effective filing systems for paper documents can prove difficult to design and implement. Appropriate file arrangements can be especially difficult to determine. A widely cited records management aphorism advises the filing system designer to select the arrangement that corresponds to the way in which documents will be requested, but that oversimplified guideline ignores the possibility that documents may be requested in different ways by persons with different information needs. Alphabetic and numeric arrangements, the easiest filing practices to understand, are principally useful for applications with straightforward, predictable retrieval characteristics (a medical records file, for example, where documents are invariably requested by patient name, or a customer order file where documents are invariably requested by order number). Where retrieval requirements vary (physicians may request medical records by patient name, for example, while insurance claims processors request them by social security number) a system of cross-references must be implemented and maintained. Subject-oriented filing systems are particularly challenging and time consuming to construct. Correspondence, reports, and other business documents often treat multiple subjects, necessitating elaborate cross-referencing or the preparation of copies for filing in multiple locations.

Alphabetical arrangements of topical headings cannot address complex subject retrieval requirements. Hierarchical filing schemes based on logically interrelated subject categories offer a more systematic approach to document organization, but the complexity of such schemes often renders them difficult to learn and use. As a complicating factor, filing and retrieval of paper documents is often denigrated as a relatively mindless task that is best relegated to entry-level clerical employees with limited office skills and little work experience.

Addressing these limitations, an electronic document imaging system creates and maintains a database that serves as an index to document images recorded on optical or magnetic media. The index facilitates the identification of documents pertinent to users' retrieval requirements. Retrieval operations begin with a database search to determine the existence and media locations of document images that satisfy particular information needs. While specific retrieval characteristics and capabilities depend on the database management software employed by a given system, database searches will usually prove more convenient and much faster to perform than browsing through paper files. All electronic document imaging systems will quickly retrieve and display database records that contain specified data values in designated fields. Most systems can also perform complex searches involving combinations of fields and truncated search terms. Such searches may be difficult or impossible to perform in conventional filing installations.

*Rapid Document Delivery*

Electronic document imaging systems can further improve retrieval by delivering needed documents quickly and conveniently to requestors. With conventional paper files, physical proximity to documents is a precondition for access and use. In some organizations, document storage and retrieval activities are centralized; a single file room serves all employees in a given department or division, for example. Organization-wide record repositories are also possible, but their scope is typically limited to predefined types of documents. While centralized document storage offers several advantages (including standardization of filing practices, tighter control over document access, greater completeness of information on specific topics, and improved utilization of clerical staff), any distance between documents and users can delay retrieval. In some installations, the centralized repository is located away from its clientele; the distance may be as short as down the hall or as great as across town. The repository may receive telephone requests for documents to be delivered via intracompany mail service or, if great distance is involved, external delivery services. At best, such arrangements typically yield next-day response to retrieval requests. Where documents are needed more quickly, the requestor—or a designee—must come to the centralized filing location. To eliminate this requirement, individual employees may circumvent the centralized repository by maintaining "personal" files in their own work are-

as. While such files are conveniently accessible by their creators, they may be unusable by others. Often they are incomplete or contain earlier, possibly inaccurate versions of documents that have been superceded by replacements.

Electronic document imaging implementations can address these problems by providing online access to centralized repositories of documents and their associated database records. Such implementations offer the advantages of a centralized document repository while eliminating its inconvenience. Assuming the existence of appropriate communications facilities, the physical location of a document repository is irrelevant. In timeshared or local area network computer installations, the database records described above can be searched from any authorized workstation to determine the existence and location of document images that satisfy specific retrieval requirements. Once pertinent database records are identified, their associated document images can be quickly retrieved for display, printing, or other purposes. The images are transmitted electronically to retrieval workstations. Time consuming trips to remote file areas are eliminated. Depending on the system configuration, image retrieval may be preceded by manual mounting of specified optical or magnetic recording media; in most multi-workstation installations, however, the required image storage media are automatically retrieved and mounted without operator intervention. If the hardware and software configuration permits it, retrieved document images can be routed through an electronic messaging system or faxed to designated locations without first printing them out.

*Simplified File Maintenance*

Sorting and filing newly received documents, removing them when requested for reference purposes, and refiling them following retrieval activity are essential but time-consuming operations in paper-based record repositories. They are also error-prone activities; misfiling is a common reason for loss of valuable records, and considerable time and effort may be wasted in searches for misfiled documents. Additional complications are posed by documents that have been removed from a record repository for reference or other purposes; such

*Figure 1–6. The space saving potential of optical disks is illustrated with a CD-ROM, which can store the equivalent of voluminous printed manuals.*

documents must be tracked to determine their locations in the event they are needed and to ensure that they are returned to the repository in a timely manner following use. Even when extensive precautions are taken, documents removed from a paper-based record repository for reference purposes may be misplaced, stolen, or damaged by accident or through malicious intent. Frequently referenced documents are subject to cumulative wear and tear which may impair their utility.

Electronic document imaging systems simplify file maintenance by eliminating filing, refiling, and the potential for misfiling. Scanning and indexing replace filing for newly received documents. In many electronic document imaging implementations, documents are converted to electronic images in the order of their arrival at a scanning station. Time consuming sorting procedures are eliminated. The media locations of specific document images are system assigned with access obtained through database records which serve as an index to the stored images. File integrity is likewise enhanced. Once document images are recorded on optical or magnetic media, their sequence is fixed. Removal or misfiling of individual pages is impossible. Document tracking requirements are eliminated, since images are not removed from storage media for reference purposes; instead, copies of images are transferred electronically to the retrieval workstation. The document images themselves are unaffected by reference activity; unlike paper records, they cannot be damaged by use, stolen, or misplaced. While individual recording media may be damaged, lost, or stolen, backup copies can ensure the continued availability of document images.

*Automated Workflow*

In many applications, documents are routed among designated employees in a formally defined sequence in order to process transactions, obtain approvals, or otherwise perform designated operations or complete specific activities. Each employee adds information to or extracts information from a given document, then passes it on to the next person in the predefined routing path. Depending on employee proximity and the urgency with which particular operations must be completed, documents may be hand-carried from person to person; alternatively, interdepartmental mail or other physical delivery methodologies may be employed. Both approaches are time consuming and subject to delays. Unless routing procedures are closely monitored, documents may be misplaced or allowed to languish in the in-baskets of designated recipients. Downstream operations, which must await the arrival of documents, cannot proceed.

The desire to simplify and expedite transaction processing and other operations by automating the flow of documents is a strong motive for electronic document imaging implementations. Such automated workflow capabilities are among the most widely publicized and dramatically effective characteristics of electronic document imaging systems. Under program control, document images can be routed from one workstation to another over a local area network or other data communications facility. The workflow program defines the routing procedure and monitors each document's progress. Such automated workflow implementations can ensure that documents will be processed in the correct sequence; they also increase the likelihood that specific operations will be performed in a timely, accurate manner.

*Compact Document Storage*

In many corporations, government agencies, and other organizations, office space is an expensive and scarce resource. Few work areas provide sufficient space to comfortably accommodate the personnel and documents essential to office opera-

tions. A typical letter-size, vertical-style file cabinet requires 7 to 8 square feet of installation area, including space for extended drawers. Two cabinets can occupy more than 15 percent of the available space in a 100-square-foot private office. Larger cabinets require proportionally greater amounts of floor space. With typical annual office space costs in U.S. cities ranging from about $15 to more than $30 per square foot, depending on office type and geographic location, the cost of the space occupied by a single file cabinet routinely exceeds $100 per year and may be much higher in newer buildings and/or prestigious addresses in high demand.

Compared to paper files, electronic document images can significantly reduce storage space requirements for a given quantity of documents, thereby freeing a significant percentage of available floor space for other purposes. Depending on media size, recording density, and other system characteristics discussed in subsequent chapters, an optical disk cartridge can store tens of thousands to hundreds of thousands of document images. A relatively low-capacity, 650MB, 5.25-inch optical disk cartridge, for example, can store the contents of two letter-size, vertical-style file cabinets. A collection of thirty such cartridges, containing approximately 600,000 document images, can be stored in a desktop file that occupies less than half of a cubic foot of space. An equivalent number of paper documents would occupy sixty letter-size, vertical file cabinets requiring at least 420 square feet of installation space.

Some electronic document imaging systems are implemented as replacements for micrographic technology rather than paper-based filing systems. The motives delineated above apply in such situations. Compared to micrographic systems, electronic document imaging technology offers improved retrieval, simplified file maintenance, and faster document delivery capabilities. Automated workflow, one of the strongest motivates for electronic document imaging implementations, is not possible in micrographic installations. While micrographics is itself a space-saving technology, some optical disks and high-density magnetic tapes can store the equivalent of dozens of rolls of microfilm or hundreds of microfiche. As an additional advantage, electronic document imaging systems provide online access by multiple users to document images maintained in centralized repositories. Microforms, in contrast, must be duplicated for distribution to multiple-use sites. In high-volume applications, such duplication and distribution can prove time consuming and expensive. As noted above, the elimination of microform duplication was a motivation for microimage transmission implementations during the 1970s. A detailed, point-by-point comparison of the competitive relationship of electronic document imaging and micrographic technology is provided by Saffady (1992).

## Imaging Systems Overview

Electronic document imaging technology and concepts are discussed, in varying levels of detail, in a sizable and rapidly growing number of books, articles, and other publications. Useful overviews are provided by Cinnamon (1988), D'Alleyrand (1989), Fruscione (1988), Kalthoff (1990), Lunin (1990), Morgan (1989), Skelton et al. (1989), Thoma et al. (1985, 1986),

Walker and Thoma (1989, 1990), and Walter (1984, 1990). As described above, electronic document imaging systems provide a completely computer-based approach to document storage and retrieval. They utilize computer hardware and software to record and store digitized document images on computer-processable media for subsequent retrieval, display, printing, and/or distribution. From the hardware standpoint, a basic system configuration includes a central processor, which may be a microcomputer, a Unix-based workstation, a minicomputer, or a mainframe; one or more scanners for conversion of paper documents to electronic form; one or more video monitors for data and image display with keyboards for data entry and retrieval; one or more laser printers for hardcopy output; and an appropriate group of computer storage peripherals. Depending on the volume of documents to be stored and the required retrieval speed, electronic images may be recorded on magnetic disks, magnetic tape, or optical disks.

As previously noted, a computer database, which is typically maintained on magnetic disks, serves as an index to document images. The database

typically contains one record for each indexable document stored by the system. An indexable document consists of one or more pages recorded as one or more electronic images. Each database record contains fields that correspond to index categories specified by an application designer. Index data entry, file maintenance, and retrieval operations are supported by database management software.

Figure 1-7 depicts a typical sequence of input steps in an electronic document imaging installation. It intentionally omits an initial implementation requirement that is common to all computer-based document indexing and retrieval methodologies; as noted above, an application designer must determine index categories appropriate to a given collection of source documents and establish procedures for the selection of index values appropriate to those categories. As explained in Chapter Two, index planning involves a careful analysis of application requirements with particular emphasis on the ways in which document images will be retrieved. For purposes of this conceptual overview, it is assumed that source documents are fully indexed—that is, all indexing decisions have been made and index values for specific documents have been selected and are clearly identified—prior to the documents' arrival at the system's input workstation.

Once the intellectual work of indexing is completed, input to an electronic document imaging system encompasses three interrelated operations: document scanning, image inspection, and index data entry. As noted above, scanners are peripheral devices that convert source documents to digitized images suitable for computer storage. The scanner's role in electronic document imaging implementations is comparable to that of a microfilm camera in a micrographic storage and retrieval system, although scanners more closely resemble photocopiers and fax machines in appearance. Most source documents will require some preparation prior to scanning. Specific preparation worksteps depend on various factors, including the physical characteristics of the documents to be scanned, the type of scanner to be used, and the conditions under which the documents are currently maintained. At a minimum, documents must be removed from file folders, binders, or other containers. Folded pages must be unfolded. Torn pag-

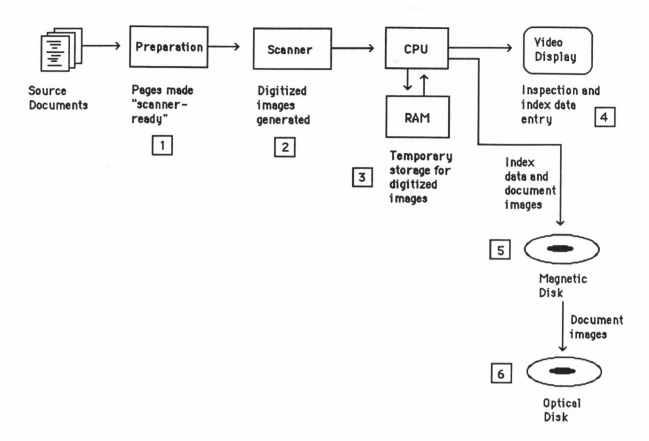

*Figure 1–7. Input work steps in a typical electronic document imaging installation.*

es should be mended or photocopied. Scanners equipped with page feeders require removal of staples, paper clips, and other fasteners.

In many applications, source documents can simply be scanned in order of their arrival at an input station; logical relationships among particular documents are reflected in database records which contain pointers to the media locations of document images associated with specific index values. In some implementations, however, documents are sorted prior to scanning in order to group logically-related images on the same medium or the same directory within a given medium. As its principal advantage, document sorting can minimize media interchange requirements and speed access in applications where related documents are customarily retrieved in a predictable sequence. Documents may also be sorted into batches by size or color to minimize scanner adjustments.

In addition to a document scanner, an electronic document imaging system's input worksta-

tion includes a video monitor with keyboard. It is used for image inspection and index data entry. Depending on software requirements, a mouse, trackball, light pen, or other input device may also be provided. In some installations, particularly those with high volumes of input, documents are scanned in batches for inspection and index data entry at a later time. An offline scanning station may be utilized in such implementations. Often, however, document images are inspected immediately following scanning. In such cases, the document scanner transfers each digitized page image to a host computer where it is stored in random-access memory and displayed on a video monitor for operator examination. Illegible, skewed, or otherwise unacceptable documents can be rescanned at once.

Figure 1-7 depicts the most common method of entering index data: once satisfactory image quality is confirmed, the index values associated with a particular document are typed at the input workstation's keyboard in a manner prescribed by the database management software employed in a particular application. To facilitate this process, most electronic document imaging systems provide specially formatted screens with prelabeled fields accompanied by adjacent blank spaces into which specific index values are to be typed. As alternative data entry methodologies described later in this book, index values may be downloaded from existing computer databases or extracted from document images using optical character recognition or other auto-indexing techniques.

Following data entry, index values are typically transferred to a database that is maintained on a fixed magnetic disk drive (a so-called "hard" drive). Electronic document images may also be stored on a hard drive; more commonly, however, they are recorded on removable media, such as optical disk cartridges, magnetic disk cartridges, or magnetic tapes. With many systems, a hard drive provides temporary buffer storage for images prior to their recording on removable media. This is usually done to make the best use of system resources (to improve throughput during recording, for example) and is typically transparent to the user. In the simplest implementations, the removable media used for image recording are stored offline (on shelves or in cabinets, for instance) until they are needed. At that time, a given medium must be manually retrieved from its storage location and mounted in a designated peripheral device. More complex installations are equipped with autochangers, such as optical disk jukeboxes or magnetic tape library units, that will automatically select and mount a specific medium when so instructed by a host computer.

As depicted in Figure 1-8, retrieval operations begin with a database search to determine the existence and media addresses of electronic document images that satisfy specified retrieval parameters. Potentially relevant index records associated with particular document images are displayed for operator perusal. A field in each index record identifies the particular medium on which its associated image is recorded. If a desired image is stored on an online medium, such as a hard disk, it can be retrieved and displayed on operator command. Removable media must be obtained from their storage locations and mounted in a retrieval device, as

described above. Once a given medium is mounted, the database management program locates the desired image and displays it for operator examination. Often, the retrieved document images are transferred to a hard drive which provides temporary buffer storage. Most systems also permit hardcopy production via laser printers.

**Implementation Options**

As described above, the earliest electronic document imaging systems were implemented either as customized configurations by systems integrators or as preconfigured turnkey combinations of hardware and software. Those two approaches are at opposite poles of a spectrum of implementation options available to organizations interested in electronic document imaging. The advantages and disadvantages of each approach have been widely discussed.

Customized electronic document imaging implementations, by definition, are tailored by contractors to particular applications. Such implementations are typically based on specifications, requirements statements, and expectations delineated in requests for proposals (RFPs) or similar documents. Alternatively, the contractor consults with the customer to determine required document imaging capabilities; requirements analysis and the preparation of system specifications are among the services offered by most systems integrators. Whether specifications are developed independently or with the contractor's assistance, the contractor obtains or develops hardware and software components appropriate to the specifications. In theory, a customized electronic document imaging implementation should satisfy the requirements of a given application completely and without compromise. Hardware components should be appropriate to the tasks they must perform, and software should operate in a manner envisioned at the time the system was planned. In actual practice, however, some compromises are inevitable and may represent a beneficial modification of unrealistic expectations. Too often, the initial system specifications constitute a "wish list" of features suggested by prospective users rather than a true statement of requirements based on a detailed analysis of application characteristics.

As their most obvious disadvantage, customized electronic document systems can be time consuming and prohibitively expensive to develop and implement. As with all projects that involve computer software development, delays and cost overruns are commonplace. The contractor is not invariably at fault; customized system development is characteristically selected for complicated document management problems that do not admit of simple, preformulated solutions. In some cases, the complexity of implementation is initially underestimated. Often, however, the customer increases the implementation time and cost by revising, augmenting, or otherwise modifying the specifications while the system is being developed.

As an alternative to customized development, preconfigured turnkey systems offer faster, less expensive (but not necessarily inexpensive) implementation of electronic document imaging capabilities. Strictly defined, a turnkey electronic document imaging system consists of preselected hardware and prewritten software components that are offered for sale as a bundled package ready for immediate use by non-technical personnel. Such systems may be microcomputer- or minicomputer-based. The computer and its associated peripheral devices are included in the bundled configuration, as is document indexing and retrieval software.

As a group, turnkey electronic document imaging systems offer broadly applicable, plug-and-play solutions to widely encountered document storage and retrieval problems. They are designed for straightforward implementation and operation by non-technical personnel in an office environment. Complicated set-up routines and software modifications are not required. Training is limited to instruction in specific system operations. Ideally, the customer installs the system, powers it up, and begins scanning documents, entering index data, recording document images, and performing retrieval operations. Because they are developed for a general class of document storage and retrieval applications, however, turnkey electronic document imaging systems may not effectively address the requirements of specific installations. The scanner provided with a given system may be too slow, for example; the optical disk drives may be too limited in capacity, or the display resolution may be unsuitable. Prewritten document indexing

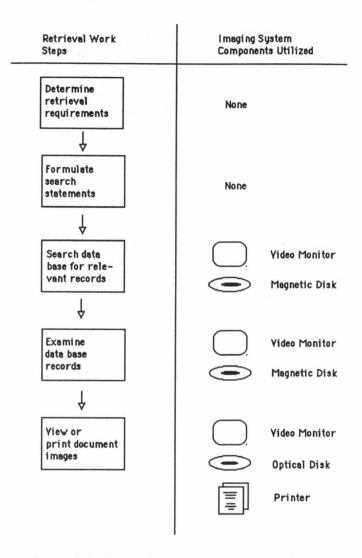

*Figure 1–8. Retrieval operations in a typical electronic document imaging installation.*

and retrieval software may not support a sufficient number of fields to accommodate the desired depth of indexing. Limitations on field lengths may similarly constrain implementation. In many cases, the customer's expectations must be modified to compensate for product limitations. Reexamination of application requirements is frequently necessary.

While they provide a useful framework for categorization of implementation options, the alternatives described above were most clearly delineated in the mid to late 1980s. Today, few electronic document imaging systems can be

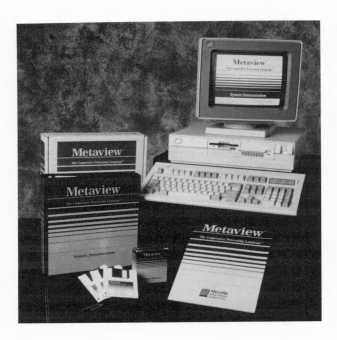

*Figure 1–9. Document imaging software. (Courtesy: Metafile Information Systems)*

conclusively identified as either customized configurations or turnkey systems. While the earliest customized installations incorporated unique combinations of hardware and software, few electronic document imaging implementations are now conceptualized from a blank sheet of paper and developed from the ground up. Systems integrators and other contractors are invariably guided by their favorable or unfavorable experiences with particular hardware and software components; there is an understandable and often desirable tendency to replicate approaches previously utilized in successful installations—assuming, of course, that such replication satisfies the customer's requirements. Similarly, few products advertised as turnkey systems permit the straightforward plug-and-play implementation described above. Nominally turnkey configurations are increasingly marketed by value-added resellers, systems integrators, and others who offer systems analysis, database set-up, software modifications, and other support services and customizations at extra cost. As turnkey electronic document imaging systems are selected for an increasingly diverse range of applications, such extra services are necessary to address the requirements and expectations of individual customers.

True plug-and-play implementations are typically limited to the simplest applications.

Customization aside, turnkey electronic document imaging systems are sold as bundled configurations of computer hardware and software. Often, a prospective customer owns one or more of the hardware components—an IBM-compatible microcomputer or a document scanner, for example—included in a given turnkey package and is understandably reluctant to purchase those components from the turnkey system vendor. In other cases, customers may want to reduce the cost of a given installation by obtaining certain hardware components from sources other than the turnkey system vendor; a government agency or large corporation can often purchase computers and peripheral devices—such as scanners and optical disk drives—at substantial discounts, for example. Some turnkey system vendors prohibit the substitution of components, arguing—with considerable justification—that their bundled configurations consist of hardware and software that are tested for compatibility and interoperability. Seemingly minor differences among allegedly compatible devices can have an adverse impact on system performance; adapter boards that operate properly with a given microcomputer, for example, may not work at all when a substitute device is utilized.

Increasingly, however, customer-supplied hardware components are permitted in turnkey configurations—provided, of course, that they rigidly conform to the turnkey vendor's specifications. An interesting and rapidly growing group of electronic document imaging systems carries this approach to an extreme; they are marketed as prewritten software packages for use with specific hardware components which the customer must furnish. Such packages support document digitization, database creation, document image recording, database searching, document image display, and other imaging operations. As with all purchased software, the computer configuration must meet minimum requirements for random-access memory, disk storage, and system software. The software developer provides a list of compatible document scanners, storage peripherals, video displays, laser printers, and other hardware components. In some cases, the software vendor also sells hardware, but customers are free to purchase designated equipment components at the best price from any source they choose.

Sometimes described as "shrink-wrapped" imaging solutions, such software-based implementations are conceptually appealing. By positioning electronic document imaging as an add-on application for a customer-owned computer system, they take the mystery out of the technology and treat it, in effect, like word processing, electronic mail, and other applications that are designed to automate widely encountered business tasks. Most document imaging software packages are intended for IBM-compatible microcomputer installations running under the MS-DOS operating system—often in conjunction with Microsoft Windows—in standalone or networked configurations. Examples of such products include Target from AIM Systems, the Desktop Document Manager from Alacrity Systems, Liberty Image Management System from Alliance Infonet, AlosView from Alos Micrographics Corporation, ImageFast from Benson Computer Research Corporation, ByteQuest from PATI, Coastal for Windows from Coastal Software, LaserFiche from Compulink, UltraPlus from the Courtland group, DeltaImaging for Windows from DeltaTech Corporation, Visage from Document Image Development Corporation, SearchExpress Document Imaging System from Executive Technologies, Feith Document Database from Feith Systems and Software, PaperTamer from Flagstaff Engineering, File Plus from Greengage Development Corporation, PaperGate from Image Tech Incorporated, Keyfile from Keyfile Corporation, Power Plus from Microseal Corporation, Fileflo from Newport Canyon Associates, NeoView from NeoTech Systems, PaperLess Filer from Paperless Corporation; ImageFiler from Optika Imaging Systems, Target from Software Alliance, FastCab from TMS Incorporated, and Imagic from Westbrook Technologies. Imara Research Corporation and Cirrus Technology offer document imaging programs for IBM-compatible microcomputers running under the OS/2 operating system. Examples of document imaging software packages for Macintosh computers include MARS from Micro Dynamics Limited, CD*STAR from Conversion Dynamics Limited, and Optix from Blueridge Technologies. Document imaging software is also available for IBM mainframes and other full-size

*Figure 1–10. An image-enabled application in which photographs are added to a personnel data base. (Courtesy: Image Data Corporation)*

computers; for minicomputer systems, such as mid-range VAX configurations, Wang VS systems, and the IBM AS/400; and for Unix-based minicomputers and workstations. Such products are available from the computer manufacturers themselves or from third-party software developers such as Metafile Information Systems, Plexus Software, Image Network Technology (INT), and JTS Computer Systems Limited.

In an alternative approach to software-based system implementations, electronic document imaging capabilities can be added to existing database management systems, electronic mail systems, workgroup programs, or other software products. When such programs and applications are augmented by the incorporation of document images, they are said to be "image-enabled". This approach to electronic document imaging can yield significant functional enhancements in certain situations. It is particularly useful in applications involving compound documents that contain graphic information, such as signatures or illustrations, which cannot be represented in character-coded form. In a customer service department, for example, a database of order information may provide online access to most of the information needed to respond to customer inquiries about deliveries and payments, but some inquiries may require examination of purchase orders, invoices, or other source documents. In such cases, the required documents must be obtained from paper files or other storage locations—procedures that can prove time consuming and labor intensive. To facilitate responses to customer inquiries in such circumstances, images of the required documents can be added to the database. Depending on the implementation, a database record might incorporate a document image as a field type, the image being treated as a binary large object (BLOB). Alternatively, database records may be linked to document images stored in separate files. In either case, database searches are followed by the rapid, online retrieval of document images pertaining to specific database records. Similarly, document image files may be appended to or incorporated into messages for routing to participants in an electronic mail installation. In some implementations, database records and their associated document images are stored on separate computers; software links the database records and images at retrieval time in a manner that is transparent to the user.

Specific implementation methods aside, electronic document imaging systems include input, output, and storage components. Those components, and procedures associated with their implementation and operation, are described and discussed in the following chapters.

## References

Addink, M. and Mullen, J. (1990). AS/400 Image-Plus system view. IBM Systems Journal 29: 451-66.

Ammon, G. (1983). An optical disk jukebox mass memory system. In Proceedings of the SPIE, vol. 412. Bellingham, WA: Society of Photo-Optical Instrumentation Engineers, pp. 2-9.

Anderson, G. et al (1990). ImagePlus workstation program. IBM Systems Journal 29: 398-407.

Avers, C. and Probst, R. (1990). ImagePlus as a model for application solution development. IBM Systems Journal 29: 356-70.

Barrett, R. (1974). Remote Access to Original Text for Information Handling. Hatfield, England: National Reprographic Centre for Documentation.

Barrett, R. and Farbrother, B. (1977). Automatic Retrieval, Remote Transmission and Display of Text Held in Microform Stores. Hatfield, England: National Reprographic Centre for Documentation.

Binder, R. (1988). Videodiscs in Museums: A Project and Resource Directory. Falls Church, VA: Future Systems.

Bovee, D. (1988). The Alpharel experience: optical solutions for today and tomorrow. Optical Information Systems 8: 70-75.

Brown, S. (1989) Managing a retirement system's records using optical disk technology. Government Finance Review 7: 7-10.

Bush, V. (1945). As we may think. Atlantic Monthly 176/7: 101-18.

Chen, C. (1985). Micro-based optical videodisc applications. Microcomputers for Information Management 2/4: 217-40.

Cinnamon, B. (1988) Optical Disk Document Storage and Retrieval Systems. Silver Spring, MD: Association for Information and Image Management.

Clemens, J. (1982). Video disks: three choices. IEEE Spectrum 19/3: 38-42.

Costanzo, C. (1991). Image processing: imaging's cost/benefit tug of war considerations. Bankers Monthly 108/5: 13-16.

Costigan, D. (1971) Microfacsimile: a status report. Journal of Micrographics 4/4: 189-99.

_____. (1978). Electronic Delivery of Documents and Graphics. New York: Van Nostrand.

Costigan, D. and Burger, R. (1982). Videomicrographics: a positive new trend in online information retrieval. Journal of Micrographics 15/4: 16-24.

D'Alleyrand, M. (1989). Image Storage and Retrieval Systems. New York: McGraw-Hill.

De Vos, J. (1980). Megadoc: a modular system for electronic document handling. Philips Technical Review 39: 329-43.

Dinan, R. et al (1990). ImagePlus high performance transaction system. IBM Systems Journal 29: 421-34.

Fain, D. and Gruener, G. (1979). Automated records management system. Journal of Micrographics 12/5: 305-309.

Felton, R. (1979). Implementing records management systems in large, multiple user environments. Journal of Micrographics 12/4: 331-35.

French, M. (1981). Future applications of the Navy's Microfiche Image Transmission System (MITS). Journal of Micrographics 14/6: 25-31.

Friedan, P. (1989). Large document image systems: experiences and opportunities. In OIS International 1989: Proceedings of the Sixth Annual Conference on Optical Information Systems. London: Meckler Corporation, pp. 110-24.

Fruscione, J. (1988). Conceptual Design Guidelines for Optical Disk Document Management Systems. Silver Spring, MD: Association for Information and Image Management.

Hooton, W. (1986). An update on the optical digital image storage system (ODISS) at the National Archives and Records Administration. In Optical Information Systems 86: Conference Proceedings. Westport, CT: Meckler Corporation, pp. 153-57.

_____. (1988). Status report on the optical digital image storage systems at the National Archives and Records Administration. In Optical Information Systems 88: Conference Proceedings. Westport, CT: Meckler Corporation, pp. 128-31.

Hopkins, W. (1977). Microfiche Image Transmission System (MITS). Journal of Micrographics 11/3: 83-90.

_____. (1982). The Navy's Microfiche Image Transmission System (MITS). Journal of Micrographics 15/10: 17-24.

Horder, A. (1980). Developments in systems providing remote access to graphic information stores. Reprographics Quarterly 13: 51-54.

_____. (1981). Videodiscs—Their Application to Information Storage and Retrieval. Hatfield, England: National Reprographic Centre for Documentation.

Isailovic, J. (1985). Videodisc and Optical Memory Systems. Englewood Cliffs, NJ: Prentice-Hall.

Ishigame, M. et al. (1984). Advanced system for optical document file system: Panafile 1000. National Technical Report 30: 574-81.

Ito, S. and Takahashi, N. (1987). Hitfile 650 optical disk filing system. Hitachi Review 36: 213-20.

Jacobson, S. (1990). The use of optical storage for patent image retrieval: the U.S. Patent and Trademark Office's Automated Patent System. In Proceedings of the SPIE, vol. 1248. Bellingham, WA: International Society for Optical Engineering, pp. 18-25.

Kalthoff, R. (1990). Buying Electronic Image Management Systems. Cincinnati: Strategy Incorporated.

Kamisher, L. (1986). The images system: videodisc and database integration for architecture. Optical Information Systems 6/6: 501-503.

Kloosterboer, J. and Lippits, G. (1986). Replication of video discs using photopolymerization: process design and study of network formation. Journal of Imaging Science 30: 177-83.

Knudson, D. and Marcus, R. (1972). The design of a microimage storage and transmission capability into an integrated transfer system. Journal of Micrographics 6/2: 15-20.

Kudo, T. et al. (1988). Workstation for an automated office. Sanyo Technical Review 20: 56-67.

Kurtenbach, G. (1988). The retrieval and display of patent images from optical storage. In National Online Meeting Proceedings 1988. Medford, NJ: Learned Information, pp. 191-98.

Lamielle, J. and De Heaulme, M. (1986). A general bank of referential images using Laservision disk in biomedicine. In Optical Information Systems 86. Westport, CT: Meckler Corporation, pp. 184-91.

Lippits, G. and Melis, G. (1986). High precision replication of Laservision video discs using UV-curable coatings. In Integration of Fundamental Polymer Science and Technology. London: Elsevier Applied Science Publishers, pp. 663-68.

Lunin, L. (1990). An overview of electronic image information. Optical Information Systems 10: 114-30.

MacLeod, D. (1989). Adding document imaging of office systems at British Airways. In OIS International 1989: Proceedings of the Sixth Annual Conference on Optical Information Systems. London: Meckler Corporation, pp. 235-37.

Manns, B. (1988). Status of the Library of Congress document storage and retrieval system. In Optical Information Systems 88: Conference Proceedings. Westport, CT: Meckler Corporation, pp. 132-35.

Meyers, W. (1970). Remote viewing and printing of graphic materials. Journal of Micrographics 3: 173-78.

Mole, D. (1981). The videodisc as a pilot project of the National Archives of Canada. Videodisc/Videotex 1: 154-61.

Morgan, R. (1989). The growing requirement for electronic document management systems. In OIS International 1989: Proceedings of the Sixth Annual Conference on Optical Information Systems. London: Meckler Corporation, pp. 202-26.

Mori, H. (1984). Hitachi optical disk file system Hitfile 60. Hitachi Review 33: 115-18.

Mori, M. et al. (1983). The application of optical discs to memory systems. Journal of the Institute of Television Engineers of Japan 37: 381-88.

Overhage, C. and Reintjes, J. (1974). Project Intrex: a general review. Information Storage and Retrieval 10: 157-88.

Parker, E. (1985). The Library of Congress nonprint optical disk pilot program. Information Technology and Libraries 4: 288-99.

Peck, R. (1983). Digital imaging technology at the Federal Energy Regulatory Commission. Journal of Micrographics 16/3: 48-56.

Penniman, W. and Tressel, G. (1975). The effect of transmission techniques on the future of microforms. Drexel Library Quarterly 11: 75-82.

Plesums, C. and Bartels, R. (1990). Large-scale image systems: USAA case study. IBM Systems Journal 29: 343-55.

Price, J. (1984). The optical disk pilot program at the Library of Congress. Videodisc and Optical Disk 4: 424-32.

_____. (1985). Library of Congress use of microcomputers in the Optical Disk Pilot Program. Microcomputers in Information Management 2: 241-50.

Prokupets, R. and Somers, D. (1990). Implementing WORM storage in a law enforcement environment. Optical Information Systems, vol. 10, no. 4, pp. 183-87.

Saffady, W. (1992). Optical Disks vs. Micrographics, 2nd Edition. Westport, CT: Meckler Corporation.

Schipma, P. (1981). Videodisc for storage of text. Videodisc/Videotex 1: 168-71.

Schwerin, J. (1984). The reality of information storage, retrieval and display using videodiscs. Videodisc and Optical Disk 4: 113-22.

Searle, D. and Lechner, B. (1985). Optical disks speed retrieval of engineering drawings. CIME 4/1: 12-19.

Skelton, J. et al. (1989). Document image processing: the new image processing frontier. In Proceedings of the SPIE, vol. 1153. Bellingham, WA: International Society for Optical Engineering, pp. 442-55.

Sypherd, A. (1990). Optical disk uses in criminal identification systems. In *Proceedings of the SPIE*, vol. 1248. Bellingham, WA: International Society for Optical Engineering, 1990, pp. 176-83.

Thoma, G. et al. (1985). A prototype system for the electronic storage and retrieval of document images. ACM Transactions on Office Information Systems, 3: 279-91.

_____. (1986). Integration of an optical disk subsystem into an electronic document storage and retrieval system. Optical Information Systems 6: 128-29.

Urrows, H. and Urrows, E. (1985). FAISR, DIAG, and Federal Vistas. Videodisc and Optical Disk 5: 196-210.

Vacca, J. (1992). Metaview's cooperative processing in the medical and pharmaceutical industries. Document Image Automation 12/2: 8-15.

Van Rijsewijk, H. et al. (1982). Manufacture of Laservision video discs by a photopolymerization process. Philips Technical Review 40: 287-97.

Walker, F. and Thoma, G. (1989). Techniques for creating and accessing a document image archive. In National Online Meeting Proceedings. Medford, NJ: Learned Information, pp. 453-62.

_____. (1990). Access techniques for document image data bases. Library Trends 38: 751-68.

Walter, G. (1979). Digital conversion of microforms. IMC Journal 1/6: 38-41.

_____. (1982). Redundancy reduction and data compaction technology in microform image transmission systems. Journal of Micrographics 15: 25-35.

_____. (1982a). Video Disks in the Automated Office? Silver Spring, MD: National Micrographics Association.

_____. (1984). Optical digital storage of office and engineering documents. Journal of Information and Image Management 17/4: 27-35.

_____. (1990). Trends in systems architectures of optical disk based document management systems (OD/DMS). International Journal of Micrographics and Optical Technology 8/1: 1-14.

Wilkins, K. (1982). U.S. Army Advanced Micrographic Access and Retrieval System (AMARS). Journal of Micrographics 15/3: 22-25.

# Chapter Two
# Input

As in all computer applications, the task of input in electronic document imaging implementations is to convert information to a form suitable for computer storage and processing. The information to be converted consists of source documents and index data. As outlined in Chapter One, input work-steps include the selection of index values; document scanning, including document preparation; inspection of digitized images; and entry of index data. This chapter provides a detailed explanation and discussion of these work steps. It begins with a survey of document indexing concepts and methodologies, emphasizing the determination of indexing parameters, subject term selection, and other aspects of indexing that influence the design and implementation of electronic document imaging systems. The discussion of indexing is followed by an explanation of document digitization and descriptions of typical scanner characteristics. The chapter closes with a review of data entry methodologies, including alternatives to keyboarding.

## Document Indexing Concepts

When electronic document imaging systems are demonstrated at information management conferences, vendors appropriately emphasize the distinctive performance characteristics and capabilities of specific hardware and software components. Hardware demonstrations often highlight the most impressive features of specific devices, such as the operating speed of document scanners, the convenience of optical disk autochangers, or the quality of displayed images. Software demonstrations typically emphasize interface characteristics that promote learning and use; electronic document imaging systems increasingly incorporate graphical user interfaces that simplify training requirements and facilitate human/computer interaction. Document indexing is usual-

ly demonstrated in the context of hypothetical, rudimentary business applications that can be readily understood with a minimum of explanation by a broad spectrum of prospective customers. Documents utilized in such demonstrations are usually preindexed, and application development is presented as a *fait accompli*. Indexing concepts and the rationale for utilizing particular indexing methodologies are rarely discussed.

While hardware and software components are undeniably important, the successful implementation and distinctive retrieval capabilities of electronic document imaging systems ultimately depend on the characteristics and effectiveness of indexing concepts and methodologies employed in particular applications. If document indexing is not carefully planned and properly executed, retrieval failures can be expected. Frequently cited studies by Lancaster (1969, 1969a) emphasize that indexing errors, particularly the omission of subject terms to describe topics and the assignment of inappropriate subject terms, contribute to a significant percentage of retrieval failures. The relationship between document indexing characteristics and retrieval effectiveness is also discussed by Penn (1962), Artandi (1969), Clarke (1970), Cooper (1978), Robertson (1978), Gerrie (1983), Kesselman and Perry (1984), Deschatelets (1986), White and Griffith (1987), and Barber et al. (1988).

Most electronic document imaging systems include data base management software that can accommodate a broad range of application requirements, but the implementation of document indexing capabilities is typically the customer's responsibility. Some systems integrators and other vendors will assist customers in the identification of indexing parameters and the establishment of indexing procedures, but—apart from a general familiarity with information management and systems analysis concepts—vendors' account representatives and application specialists receive little, if any, formal training in document indexing. While many publications have described the capabilities of electronic document imaging systems, there is little published discussion of the systems analysis principles associated with document indexing itself. Similarly, the large published literature on indexing in general emphasizes content analysis of journal articles and other publications. It rarely deals specifically with the indexing and retrieval of general business documents. Pennix (1984) and Thiel et al. (1991) are notable exceptions.

The following discussion surveys document indexing concepts and procedures, emphasizing analytical and application development principles that are most significant for electronic document imaging implementations. The discussion reviews basic indexing concepts, the identification of indexing parameters, the selection of index values, the establishment of indexing procedures, and the calculation of indexing costs. Published studies are cited where pertinent.

*Indexing Parameters*

The phrase "indexing parameters" denotes one or more of the categories of information by which documents will be indexed for subsequent retrieval. The identification of appropriate indexing parameters or categories is an essential first step in the planning and implementation of an electronic document imaging system. If a document is not indexed by a given parameter, it cannot be conveniently retrieved by that parameter; with some electronic document indexing systems, it may not be retrievable at all. The identification of indexing parameters often precedes hardware and software selection. This may occur at an early stage in systems analysis when application requirements are initially delineated. Thus, when preparing a proposal to replace paper filing methodologies with an electronic document imaging system, an information specialist, systems analyst, records manager, or consultant will usually include a suggested list of indexing parameters or an equivalent discussion of the proposed system's indexing characteristics. In most cases, such preliminary indexing decisions will be modified or refined in later stages of system planning and implementation.

As described in Chapter One, an electronic document imaging system maintains a computer-processable data base that serves as an index to document images. The data base, which is usually stored on fixed magnetic disk drives, contains one record for each indexable document encountered in a given application. Multi-page documents are typically treated as a unit for indexing purposes. Individual data base records are organized into fields that correspond to indexing parameters and descriptive data elements identified by application planners. While the characteristics and capabilities of specific implementations may vary considerably, fields are customarily divided into two broad types: key fields and non-key fields.

Key fields, the most important type in electronic document imaging implementations, correspond to the indexing parameters identified for a particular application. They contain names, subject terms, quantitative values, or other information that will be used to identify documents meeting specific retrieval requirements. The data base management programs furnished with most electronic document imaging systems create inverted files that permit the rapid retrieval of documents by specified key field values. This is done automatically, usually in a manner that is transparent to the user. The inverted files are essentially alphabetical lists of field values with pointers to the data base records that contain them. The data base records typically include fields that indicate the storage locations, on optical disks or other media, of the electronic document images to which the key field values pertain.

Non-key fields, in contrast, contain descriptive information that is important but will not be used to retrieve specific documents. Inverted files are not created for non-key fields. The information contained in non-key fields can be displayed, however, when data base records are retrieved through searches involving key fields. Non-key fields can prove especially useful where electronic document imaging capabilities are incorporated into broader data base management applications. In such situations, the information contained in the non-key fields within data base records may satisfy many retrieval requirements. In the case of employee resumes, for example, data base records may include non-key fields for employee addresses and telephone numbers, thereby eliminating the need to consult document images to obtain such information. As an additional advantage, information contained in non-key fields can facilitate relevance judgements where many data base records are retrieved by a given search, thereby minimizing the number of document images that must be examined. For that purpose, some electronic document imaging implementations include an abstract, annotation, or other document summary as a non-key field within data base records.

Key fields are typically identified by studying existing work methodologies and by interviewing users to determine their retrieval requirements. To identify appropriate non-key fields, the application planner must determine the additional descriptive information that should be displayed once data base records are retrieved. While the selection of key and non-key fields will necessarily vary from one application to another, the following discussion gives examples of record structures and field specifications associated with some commonly encountered types of documents. The examples identify typical key and non-key fields, including field types and lengths.

Difficulties associated with the organization and retrieval of office correspondence and memoranda—a group of documents encountered in almost every work environment—make correspondence control and tracking excellent candidates for electronic document imaging implementations. Table 2-1 identifies and characterizes key and non-key fields for a correspondence control system in the office of an elected government official where staff members must be able to quickly and reliably locate letters and responses to and from constituents. In this example, incoming correspondence is indexed by the author's name and geographic location (city, county, state, or other designation, depending on the nature of the political constituency). For outgoing correspondence, the author field will contain the names of staff members who prepare responses to constituents; the geographic location field is left blank in such cases. The date field, a key field, stores the date on which a given item of correspondence was written, assuming that the document is dated. The date received, a non-key field, is used for incoming correspondence that will be stamped on arrival in the office. Key

fields are provided for up to five subject descriptors, the nature of which will be discussed later in this chapter. The notes field, a non-key field, may contain remarks, special instructions, or a brief annotation or other document summary.

Assuming that index values are accurately selected, the key fields presented in Table 2-1 will permit the retrieval of correspondence written by or to a given constituent or staff member about a particular subject on a specified date. As discussed in Chapter Four, most electronic document imaging systems include retrieval software that will permit searches by such combinations of indexing parameters. Key fields will also permit searches for previous responses dealing with a specific topic, thereby promoting a consistent viewpoint in outgoing communications. The indexing parameters employed in this example will likewise facilitate research into and analyses of constituent opinions on particular subjects as expressed in their correspondence.

As a more broadly applicable variation of the indexing parameters outlined above, Table 2-2 provides a generalized list of key and non-key fields for the control of office correspondence in a wide range of business settings. It is assumed that indexable items will be limited to letters (documents written to or received from persons outside of the organization) and memoranda (documents written to or received from persons within the organization). The field for document type utilizes a single-character code to differentiate these two types of correspondence. Indexing parameters such as date, author name, and addressee name are self-explanatory. In many cases, however, the authors and recipients of correspondence are more meaningfully identified by their internal departments or the external corporations, government agencies, or other organizations with which they are affiliated. A manager evaluating the procurement of some equipment, for example, may need to retrieve all correspondence to and from the vendor of that equipment, regardless of the author of the correspondence. As in the preceding example, a key field is provided for up to five subject descriptors.

Scientific and technical reports created by engineering organizations, pharmaceutical companies, product development facilities, government laboratories, and other research and development

**Table 2-1. Indexing Parameters for Constituent Correspondence**

| Field Name | Key Field | Field Length* | Field Type |
|---|---|---|---|
| Date | yes | 6 | numeric |
| Date Received | no | 6 | numeric |
| Author | yes | 20 | alpha |
| Geographic Location | yes | 15 | alpha |
| Addressee | yes | 20 | alpha |
| Subjects (5) | yes | 10 | alpha |
| Notes | no | 120 | alpha |

\* In characters, maximum length

organizations have attracted the attention of document storage and retrieval specialists since the 1950s. Computer-based retrieval systems for technical reports have been widely implemented in libraries and information centers, and their characteristics and indexing requirements are well understood. Table 2-3 lists typical key and non-key fields appropriate to electronic document imaging implementations involving such documents. As with the previous examples, most of the field designations are self-explanatory. The list provides fields for up to three authors, although only the first author is designated a key field in this example. The title, page length, and abstract fields likewise provide descriptive information that will be displayed with retrieved records. In some applications, however, the title and abstract may be designated as key fields, in which case searches could be performed for specific words contained in them. Again assuming that index values are accurately selected, the key fields presented in this example will permit searches for scientific and technical reports written by a given person, produced by a particular division or department, associated with a given project, or dealing with a specific subject.

Addressing a common document retrieval application in architectural firms, engineering organizations, and construction companies, Table 2-4 lists key and non-key fields for electronic images of engineering drawings associated with completed construction projects. Assuming that appropri-

ate retrieval capabilities are provided, the indicated key fields will permit the retrieval of drawings by various combinations of date, project number, building name, drawing number, contractor, drawing type (such as a design drawing, a bid drawing, or an as-built drawing), and revision number. Title information, taken from the drawing's title block, is stored in a non-key field. Other non-key fields contain information about the original drawing's size (represented by code letters or international paper-size designations) and medium (such as paper, vellum, or mylar).

Table 2-5 lists key and non-key fields for an electronic document imaging implementation to replace order files maintained by a customer service department. In paper form, such files may be arranged by customer name or order number. They may contain purchase orders, invoices, correspondence, or other documents necessary to answer customers' questions and resolve problems pertaining to particular orders. With the key fields outlined in this example, customer service representatives will be able to locate document images by various combinations of document type, date, purchase order number, and invoice number.

*Index Values*

As an information management activity, indexing assumes that the content of documents can be adequately represented by descriptive labels that serve

**Table 2-2. Indexing Parameters for General Business Correspondence**

| Field Name | Key Field | Field Length* | Field Type |
|---|---|---|---|
| Date | yes | 6 | numeric |
| Date Received | no | 6 | numeric |
| Document Type | no | 1 | alpha |
| Author | yes | 20 | alpha |
| Author Affiliation | yes | 15 | alpha |
| Recipient | yes | 20 | alpha |
| Recipient Affiliation | yes | 15 | alpha |
| Subjects (5) | yes | 10 | alpha |
| Notes | no | 120 | alpha |

* In characters, maximum length

as document surrogates. Indexing involves an analysis of the content or other characteristics of documents and the determination of appropriate labels for designated indexing parameters. For purposes of this discussion, the descriptive labels associated with specific indexing parameters are termed index values. Indexing parameters, as discussed above, are delineated for an application as a whole; index values describe specific documents in a manner determined by those parameters.

Often, the values appropriate to specific indexing parameters can be determined by a cursory examination of documents. This is the case, for example, with the dates, author names, and recipient names used to index office correspondence and memoranda. Such documents are usually formatted in a manner that highlights the indicated information. Interdepartmental memoranda, for example, are often created on special stationery that includes labelled heading areas for dates and names. Similarly, purchase orders and other standardized business forms contain labelled sections for dates, purchase order numbers, vendor names, and other information. The title block of a construction drawing will likewise contain the drawing number, date, building name, project number, producer, and revision number. The drawing's size, material, and number of pages can usually be determined by physical examination.

In such straightforward situations, appropriate index values may be quickly and easily extracted from documents by data entry clerks or other clerical personnel. This is not the case with subject indexing. Broadly described, the indexing of documents by subject requires content analysis—that is, a determination of "aboutness"—and the expression of that determination in words or phrases that are variously called subject headings, subject descriptors, subject identifiers, or subject keywords. Subject indexing concepts and processes have been discussed in many publications; examples include Vickery (1955, 1958), Bigelow (1965), George (1964), Sharp (1965), Baxendale (1966), Fairthorne (1965, 1969), Oliver et al. (1966), Ullmann (1966), Coates (1966), Harvey (1976), Hickey (1976), Liston and Howder (1977), Hutchins (1977, 1978), Maron (1977), Svenonius and Schmierer (1977), Jones (1981), Foskett (1982), Travis and Fidel (1982), Milstead (1984), and Williamson (1984).

Most authorities agree that subject indexing is an intellectually demanding and potentially time-consuming task. Recognizing the problems inherent in subject interpretation, some information specialists, including Gould et al. (1969) and Maron and Shoffner (1969), have suggested the use of simpler indexing parameters, such as author names, organizational affiliations, and trade names

**Table 2-3. Indexing Parameters for Technical Reports**

| Field Name | Key Field | Field Length* | Field Type |
|---|---|---|---|
| Report Number | yes | 10 | numeric |
| Project Number | yes | 10 | numeric |
| Principal Author | yes | 20 | alpha |
| Second Author | no | 20 | alpha |
| Third Author | no | 20 | alpha |
| Title | yes | 75 | alpha |
| Originating Department | yes | 20 | alpha |
| Date | yes | 6 | numeric |
| Page Length | no | 5 | numeric |
| Subjects (5) | yes | 10 | alpha |
| Abstract | no | 500 | alpha |

* In characters, maximum length

as an alternative to subject indexing where practical. In many electronic document imaging applications, however, subject indexing is unavoidable. This is the case, for example, with most correspondence, technical reports, and management reports. In such situations, application planners must develop and implement indexing procedures that will facilitate document analysis and promote effective retrieval. The following discussion outlines major issues in subject analysis of documents and reviews the distinctive characteristics and limitations of particular subject indexing methodologies.

*Subject Term Selection*

Subject indexing can be based on assigned or derived terms. In the former approach, indexers select descriptive words or phrases based on a reading and analysis of all or part of a document. The selected words or phrases may or may not appear in the document itself. In either case, the assigned subject terms represent the indexer's understanding of concepts treated in the document. As a result, subject indexing by term assignment is sometimes called concept indexing.

Alternatively, subject terms may be extracted, or derived, from all or specified portions of a

document. In manual indexing systems, some analysis of document content is required, but the selected index terms must appear in the document itself. The derived term approach to document indexing is also compatible with computer programs that automatically extract words from titles, abstracts, or other document segments—assuming, of course, that the indicated segments have been converted to character-coded form. A widely encountered form of automated indexing—described by Luhn (1960), Fischer (1966), Feinberg (1973), and others—is based on words derived from titles of technical reports, journal articles, or other documents. Carrying the derived term approach to its extreme, full-text retrieval programs create subject indexes that are based on every word in the body of a document. They will be described later in this chapter.

Automated methodologies aside, proponents of the derived term approach to subject indexing contend that it can be performed quickly, often with little more than a cursory examination of document content. An experiment by Shaw and Rothman (1968), for example, suggests that the time required for subject indexing can be significantly reduced by having indexers underline terms that appear in documents rather than assigning terms

**Table 2-4. Indexing Parameters for Construction Drawings**

| Field Name | Key Field | Field Length | Field Type |
|---|---|---|---|
| Date Created | yes | 6 | numeric |
| Project Number | yes | 6 | numeric |
| Building Name | yes | 20 | alpha |
| Drawing Number | yes | 10 | numeric |
| Drawing Title | no | 60 | alpha |
| Revision Number | yes | 2 | numeric |
| Drawing Type | yes | 10 | alpha |
| Contractor/Producer | yes | 20 | alpha |
| Original Size | no | 2 | alpha |
| Original material | no | 6 | alpha |
| Number of Sheets | no | 2 | numeric |
| Notes | no | 120 | alpha |

* In characters, maximum length

reflective of concepts treated in the documents. Such claims argue for the use of derived term indexing in high-volume electronic document imaging applications where rapid work throughput and timely availability of index data are important considerations.

Several researchers suggest that the derived term approach offers retrieval advantages. Moss (1970) found that the replacement of assigned index terms by trade names, chemical terms, and other words and phrases derived from documents yielded significant retrieval improvements in an application involving technical reports dealing with plastics. Schumacher et al. (1973) found that 81 percent of relevant items in a collection of technical documents could be identified on the basis of subject terms derived from titles, abstracts, tables of contents, and author-assigned keywords, yet the time required to derive those terms accounted for only 53 percent of total indexing time. They concluded that content analysis of the body of documents can be effectively excluded as a source of index terms. In a study of the COMPENDEX data base, Byrne (1975) found that indexer-assigned subject terms offered no retrieval advantage when compared to words derived from titles and abstracts.

Other investigators, however, have reached different conclusions or obtained inconclusive results. Hersey et al. (1971), for example, found that indexer-assigned subject terms yielded significantly better retrieval results when compared to words derived from the text of documents. Difondi et al. (1973) found no significant difference in retrieval performance when comparing indexer-assigned terms with derived subject words. Olive et al. (1973) concluded that assigned index terms offered a slight retrieval advantage over words derived from titles of scientific documents, but both indexing approaches left many relevant documents unretrievable. In a study of articles dealing with petroleum engineering, Graves and Helander (1970) found that many useful index terms were not contained in titles or abstracts, making assigned index terms based on analysis of document content essential for comprehensive retrieval.

*Vocabulary Control*

The phrase "indexing vocabulary" denotes the subject terms utilized to index documents. As discussed by Pickford (1971), Sharp (1971, 1975), Townley (1971), Bhattacharyya (1974), Svenonius

**Table 2-5. Indexing Parameters for Customer Service Documents**

| Field Name | Key Field | Field Length | Field Type |
|---|---|---|---|
| Document Date | yes | 6 | numeric |
| Document Type | yes | 2 | alpha |
| Customer Name | yes | 30 | alpha |
| Order Date | yes | 6 | numeric |
| Internal Order Number | yes | 10 | numeric |
| Customer Order Number | yes | 10 | numeric |
| Invoice Number | yes | 10 | numeric |
| Order Amount | yes | 10 | numeric |
| Description of Order | no | 200 | alpha |
| Notes | no | 120 | alpha |

* In characters, maximum length

(1976), and Laursen (1980), among others, derived term indexing utilizes the vocabulary of the document to represent subject concepts. It is variously described as an unstructured, natural, or free language indexing methodology. Except for the requirement that subject words and phrases be contained in the document itself, no attempt is made to limit the number or type of subject terms. The indexing vocabulary is consequently uncontrolled. Synonomous terms, related words, and singular or plural forms of nouns can be used without restrictions, although Bloomfield (1966) recommends the consistent use of singular noun forms—a practice employed by most dictionaries—as a rudimentary form of vocabulary control.

The principles and advantages of comprehensive vocabulary control are outlined in various publications, including Hyslop (1965), Moss (1967), Wall (1969), Coblans (1971), Lancaster (1972, 1977), Auld (1982), Sievert and Boyce (1983), and Batty (1982, 1989). In assigned-term indexing, a list of authorized words and phrases is sometimes utilized to facilitate the selection of subject terms. Such an indexing aid is variously called a thesaurus (plural form: thesauri) or a subject authority list. The general characteristics and utility of thesauri as indexing aids have been discussed by Herner (1963), Korotkin et al. (1965),

Gull (1966), Tinker (1968), Mandersloot et al. (1970), Jones (1972), Bottle (1974), Soergel (1974), Seetharama (1976), Booth (1987), among others. An effectively designed thesaurus presents a structured view of a particular activity or field of knowledge as reflected in subject words or phrases. In addition to providing a codified, standardized list of authorized index terms, a thesaurus typically includes cross references from unauthorized synonyms to approved terms and from authorized terms to broader, narrower, or otherwise related terms. It may also contain scope notes that define the ways in which authorized terms can be used for indexing purposes. Kochen and Tagliacozzo (1968), Kochen (1971), and Willetts (1975) discuss cross reference structures employed by thesauri and other indexing aids. Thesauri for specific subject disciplines or types of documents are described by Booth (1979), Norris (1981), Petersen (1981), and Sanders (1986).

As discussed below, some research studies suggest that the use of a thesaurus for subject term selection promotes consistency in indexing. A thesaurus can also guide users of an electronic document imaging system in the identification of appropriate search terms and the formulation of retrieval strategies. The time and cost associated with thesaurus creation and maintenance, however, are major impediments to their use in electronic document imaging implementations. The thesaurus developer must collect potential subject terms from various sources, including other thesauri, where available; consolidate the terms into a single listing; review the terms for suitability; prepare scope notes for authorized terms; eliminate synonyms and plural noun forms; and construct cross references to link related terms and to direct indexers from unauthorized terms to approved entries. These thesaurus construction procedures are described by Weinstein (1966), Rostron (1968), Eichhorn and Reinecke (1969), Wolff-Terroine et al. (1969), Rolling (1970), Kim (1973), Wall (1975), Ghose and Dhawle (1977), Batty (1989), and Crouch (1990). Milstead (1990, 1991) describes computer software for thesaurus construction and maintenance. Once the initial edition of a thesaurus is prepared, a formal maintenance procedure must be established to deal with new terms and the modifications of existing entries.

Requiring months or even years to complete, thesaurus construction can significantly delay the implementation of an electronic document imaging system. Despite their attractive features, thesauri must consequently be judged impractical in business-oriented document imaging applications where rapid implementation is a paramount consideration. As a notable exception, electronic document imaging installations in specialized subject areas, such as aeronautics, medicine, petroleum engineering, or pharmaceuticals, may be able to adapt existing thesauri or lists of subject headings created for use with published indexes or online data bases.

While discussions of vocabulary control most often deal with the selection of subject terms, personal and corporate names can pose problems for both indexers and searchers. As noted in examples provided earlier in this chapter, author and recipient names and affiliations are commonly encountered indexing parameters in electronic document imaging installations. As a variant form of thesaurus, a name authority list specifies standardized forms of personal and corporate names to be used as index values. It also includes cross references from unauthorized forms of names to approved forms. In the absence of standardized forms, index values for personal name fields may variously, inconsistently, and unpredictably contain complete forenames and middle names, complete forenames and middle initials, or simply one or more initials. These name components may be entered in conventional or inverted sequence. Unless standardized forms are specified, corporate names may likewise be entered in different ways. In the absence of a name authority list, an electronic document imaging system's data base may variously contain entries for International Business Machines, International Business Machines Corporation, IBM, or IBM Corporation.

*Indexing Consistency*

As explained by Hurwitz (1969), indexing consistency is customarily measured by the agreement, or lack thereof, in the type and number of terms selected by indexers to represent particular documents. Consistency is principally an issue in subject indexing; there is relatively little scope for inconsistency in the selection of field values for author names, dates, project names, or other indexing parameters listed in previous examples.

For any given document or group of documents, inter-indexer consistency denotes agreement in the selection of subject terms by different indexers. Intra-indexer consistency denotes agreement in the selection of subject terms when a document is indexed by the same person at different times. Although Cooper (1969) questions the impact of consistency on indexing quality, King and Dailey (1964) reflect the traditional view that indexing consistency and quality are closely related and that consistent selection of subject terms promotes effective retrieval. The desirability of indexing consistency is similarly emphasized by Bryant (1965), Slamecka and Jacoby (1965), Zunde and Dexter (1969a), Leonard (1975), Rolling (1981), and Markey (1984).

However important it may be, a number of studies suggest that indexing consistency is more often the exception than the rule. Zunde and Dexter (1969) and Borko and Tarr (1974), for example, contend that indexing consistency is influenced by many factors, including the readability and other semantic characteristics of documents, the ability to recognize indexable concepts, the verbal paraphrasing of concepts, and even the temperature of the work area. Reflecting the complex relationship between document analysis and subject term selection, Preschel (1971, 1972) found that the degree of consistency in indexers' perception of indexable matter was invariably higher than their consistency in choice of index terms.

Among published analyses of indexer consistency, Macmillan and Welt (1961) describe a cardiovascular literature project in which 171 documents were accidentally indexed twice, mostly by different persons. One-third of the documents were indexed so differently that no comparisons were possible. Others varied in the number of index terms assigned or in the use of synonymous terms. The study further indicated that subject specialists with different backgrounds tended to approach indexing tasks in different ways. Medical and chemical specialists preferred terms from their own fields. Psychologists tended to omit terms describing widely recognized psychological concepts while chemists indexed them. In one of the few published studies of intra-indexer consistency, Rodgers (1961) reported a 59-percent agreement in assigned subject terms for sixty documents indexed by one person and subsequently reindexed by the same person.

While inconsistency is apparently characteristic of many document indexing applications, several studies suggest procedures and techniques that may improve consistency in electronic document imaging implementations:

1. Various studies confirm the value of indexing aids in improving consistency. Slamecka and Jacoby (1963) found that an alphabetical list of subject headings and a hierarchically arranged classification list significantly improved consistency in the indexing of chemical patents. A study by Korotkin and Oliver (1964) likewise concluded that a list of suggested descriptors improved inter-indexer consistency. As an interesting point, familiarity with the subject matter in the documents being indexed had no impact on consistency. Fried and Prevel (1966) found that indexers using structured worksheets and lists of approved subject terms had higher consistency than those working without indexing aids. In a study of Information Science Abstracts, Sievert and Andrews (1991) found that indexing consistency was highest for subject terms taken from a small controlled vocabulary and lowest where the subject vocabulary was uncontrolled. Several innovative indexing aids have proven effective in demonstration projects but are not readily supported by the data base management programs associated with electronic document imaging systems. Berns (1969), for example, describes a list of index term candidates consisting of all words from documents ranked by frequency of use. Herr (1970) likewise notes the value of previously used index terms as an aid to subject analysis.

2. Jacoby and Slamecka (1962) found that experienced indexers working without mutual consultation or other assistance showed less variation and an overall higher level of consistency than inexperienced indexers. Fried and Prevel (1966) confirmed that experienced indexers were more consistent in their selection of subject terms than inexperienced indexers.

3. Experiments described by Slamecka and Jacoby (1965) indicated that indexing based on titles or abstracts yielded higher inter-indexer consistency than indexing from complete documents. Tell (1969) reported similar results in a study at the Royal Institute of Technology in Stockholm.

## Indexing Depth

Application planners must address the issue of indexing depth—that is, the number of indexing parameters to be applied to individual document images. As the examples cited earlier in this chapter indicate, document images are commonly indexed by multiple parameters, thereby permitting flexible retrieval approaches. Where subject indexing is involved, multiple subject terms are customarily allowed. Indexing depth may also denote the specificity of terms employed in subject indexing. Svenonius (1972), for example, contends that narrow subject terms are more effective than broad ones in improving retrieval precision, while broad subject terms can prove useful in searches where high recall is desired. As used in this context, precision denotes the number of relevant documents retrieved by a given search as a percentage of the total documents retrieved; recall refers to the number of relevant documents retrieved by a given search as a percentage of the relevant documents in a given collection. The data base management software employed in electronic document imaging installations imposes few restrictions on the number or specificity of subject terms that can be assigned to documents. If desired in a given application, documents can be indexed with dozens of subject terms at varying levels of specificity, but—considering the time and cost associated with extended document analysis—such exhaustive indexing may be neither practical nor justifiable.

Reflecting the traditional view, Lancaster and Mills (1964) cite exhaustivity of indexing, with subject terms of varying levels of specificity, as a critical parameter in retrieval effectiveness, but Svenonius (1971), Sparck-Jones (1973), and Maron (1979) question exhaustivity's impact on retrieval results. Describing a much publicized series of retrieval experiments, Cleverdon (1963, 1965) reports that recall improves but precision is degraded as the number of subject terms assigned to documents increases. Aitchison and Cleverdon (1963) found that exhaustive indexing was partly responsible for low precision in an index to metallurgical literature, although the test results were questioned by Rees (1965). Studies summarized by Seely (1972) indicate that, up to a certain point, retrieval effectiveness increases with the depth of indexing. Experiments by Burgin (1991) confirmed that the best retrieval results are obtained with exhaustive indexing; retrieval performance decreased as index terms were eliminated. An interesting study of microfiche-based retrieval systems by Levine (1974, 1975) concluded that users may be willing to trade off some precision for higher recall if they can view documents and make immediate relevance judgements. He further suggests that the ability to quickly browse through documents, a capability offered by electronic document imaging systems, may make relatively shallow indexing, with its associated cost savings, acceptable.

*Indexing Personnel*

As discussed by Platau (1960), Brenner and Smyth (1961), McKinney and Rees (1963), Resnick (1963), Norris (1972), Brenner (1987), Young (1987), and Dickman (1988), among others, professional associations, publishing companies, and other organizations that produce printed indexes or online data bases typically hire subject specialists and/or persons with previous indexing training or experience. In many electronic document imaging implementations, index terms are selected by the creators or recipients of documents who will then route them to a data entry station. In such situations, indexers receive little or no training, and their subject knowledge, experience, and motivation will vary considerably.

Cleverdon (1962) describes one of the first experiments to scientifically assess performance differences associated with document indexing performed by persons of varied knowledge, training, and experience. In the much publicized Cranfield Project, one-hundred technical reports and articles on aeronautics were indexed by three different persons using four different indexing systems in different time periods. One of the indexers had both indexing experience and subject knowledge of aeronautics. Of the other two, one had indexing experience but not subject knowledge, while the other lacked both experience and subject knowledge. From the standpoint of retrieval effectiveness, the study found no significant differences between documents indexed by the three persons. Scheffler (1967, 1968) describes the successful use of undergraduate students to index technical documents at the Aerospace Materials Information Center. In an indexer training experiment at Massachusetts Institute of Technology, Lufkin (1968) reported that the learning period was shorter for undergraduate students than for professional librarians. Given the varied indexing arrangements encountered in electronic document imaging installations, these findings are encouraging.

Based largely on experience with published journal articles, several studies suggest that authors can effectively index their own documents. Diodata (1985) notes that approximately 25 percent of scientific journals include author-supplied index terms with articles, and that most professional indexing services consider such author-supplied terms a useful adjunct to their own subject analysis. Falk and Tompkins (1970) report that at the Institute of Electrical and Electronics Engineers (IEEE), where authors routinely suggest index terms for their papers from a hierarchically-arranged list of 450 categories, such selections are often more appropriate than those made by professional indexers. An analysis of biomedical journal articles by Orr et al. (1965) concluded that author-assigned index terms were substantially better than index terms derived from titles. In a study of journal articles published by the American Mathematical Society, Diodata (1981, 1981a) reported no significant difference, measured by retrieval effectiveness, for index terms supplied by authors and by professional indexers. Diodata and Gandt (1991) draw similar conclusions for back-of-book indexes prepared by authors and non-authors.

## Document Scanning

As described in Chapter One, document scanners (sometimes described as document digitizers) are the principal image capture devices in electronic document imaging installations. Broadly defined, a document scanner is a computer peripheral that converts source documents to digitally-coded, electronic images suitable for computer processing and storage. In most cases, the source documents are in paper form, although film scanners, as describe below, are also available. The source documents may be handwritten, typed, or printed. They may contain textual or graphic information in black and white or color. In either case, the scanners utilized in electronic document imaging systems produce images that are variously described as digitized or bit-mapped. Scanning technology and devices are discussed by Mori et al. (1983), Painter (1988), and Terry (1988).

The scanning process, which is properly termed document digitization, divides a page into a series of horizontal lines called scan lines. Each line is subdivided into small, scannable units called picture elements, pixels, pels, or, in some cases, dots. The pattern of scan lines and pixels employed by a given document scanner is termed a raster and the resulting electronic images are often described as raster images. Using photosensitive components, a scanner measures the amount of light reflected by successively encountered pixels and transmits a corresponding electrical signal to an image processing unit. Depending on equipment design, individual scan lines and pixels are successively illuminated by a fluorescent lamp, an incandescent lamp, a light-emitting diode, or some other light source. Light reflected from the scanned pixels passes through a lens and onto a photosensor, which typically consists of a charge-coupled device (CCD) array. While equipment designs vary, the CCD array usually contains one photoelectric element for each pixel in a scan line; an entire line can thus be scanned at one time. The width of the CCD array defines the maximum width of input documents.

Regardless of array size, each CCD element generates an electrical voltage that is proportional to the intensity of the light that strikes it. Light areas of a scanned line, which reflect light, will generate the strongest voltages; dark areas, which absorb light, will generate relatively weak voltages. The scanner's image processing unit converts the resulting electrical output into digital bit patterns that represent the tonal values of successively encountered pixels.

In electronic document imaging implementations, the simplest and most widely encountered digitization requirement involves black-and-white textual documents and line drawings. In such cases, one bit is used to encode each pixel. Pixels that reflect light in excess of a predetermined threshold amount are considered white and are each encoded as zero bits. Typically, such white pixels constitute the background areas of a page. Where light reflectance values and their associated voltages are lower than the predetermined threshold value, the corresponding pixels are considered black and are each encoded as a one bit. Such pixels typically represent the information-bearing areas of a page. In most cases, the voltage threshold is set midway between black and white. Gray or colored pixels are treated as either black or white, depending on their relative lightness or darkness. As discussed below, grayscale and color scanners are available; such devices employ multiple bits to encode individual pixels.

### Equipment Design

In terms of size and appearance, document scanners can be divided into desktop, floor-standing, and handheld varieties. Of these, desktop devices are most widely available and most often encountered in electronic document imaging installations. They are also employed in desktop publishing, computer-based facsimile transmission, optical character recognition, and similar image processing applications. As their name indicates, desktop scanners are designed for installation on a desk, table, or other flat surface in an office or similar work environment. As input workstation components, desktop scanners are usually installed next to or near the display devices utilized for image inspection and index data entry. Typical space requirements range from 150 to 600 square inches. One of the most widely installed models measures 27 inches wide by 20 inches deep by 6.5 inches high.

Physical dimensions aside, desktop scanners can be subdivided by mode of operation into flatbed and sheetfed varieties. Flatbed models, as their name suggests, feature a flat exposure surface on which pages are individually positioned for scanning. Most flatbed desktop scanners, like the photocopiers which they closely resemble, feature a glass platen on which pages are positioned face down for digitization by optical and photosensitive components located beneath the glass. During scanning, a CCD array and lens system are transported by a mechanical assembly across an illuminated page. Less commonly, some flatbed scanners feature an overhead design in which individual pages are positioned face up on a flat surface for scanning by optical and photosensitive components positioned at the top of a vertical column. Such devices resemble planetary micro filmers in both appearance and operation. Several models are equipped with special CCD arrays which employ ambient illumination, thereby eliminating the need for a separate light source.

Sheetfed document scanners, sometimes described as pass-through or pull-through scanners, resemble facsimile transceivers in appearance and operation. Each page to be scanned is inserted into a narrow opening where it is grabbed by rollers that transport it across a stationary optical head assembly and light source. Individual pages can be inserted manually. Alternatively, most models can be support a multi-page stacker as a standard feature or optional accessory; fifty pages is a common capacity. Depending on equipment design, the scanned page will be ejected at the back or bottom

of the machine. As a potentially significant disadvantage, some sheetfed scanners cannot accommodate bound materials. Such documents must either be unbound or the individual pages photocopied for scanning. Addressing this limitation, some scanners combine sheetfed and flatbed operation; the sheet-feeding mechanism can be lifted or removed, revealing a glass platen on which bound volumes can be positioned.

Floor-standing scanners are intended for high-speed operation in high-volume, production-intensive document conversions. They are often utilized in applications where large numbers of documents will be scanned in batches for subsequent indexing. Some floor-standing models are designed to accommodate large documents, such as engineering drawings, for which desktop devices are inappropriate. Most floor-standing scanners are sheetfed devices.

As their name implies, handheld scanners must be manually moved, slowly and in a straight line, across a document that is positioned face up on flat surface. They incorporate a light source and photosensitive components in a relatively compact housing. With most models, the scanning array is approximately four inches wide. Letter-size and larger pages must consequently be scanned in sections or strips that are linked together through software. Given this limitation and the slowness inherent in manual operation, handheld scanners are rarely suitable for electronic document imaging implementations. They are principally intended for occasional digitization requirements in desktop publishing and other applications.

*Input Characteristics*

As noted above, flatbed scanners can accommodate bound volumes as well as individual sheets of paper, while sheetfed scanners are limited to unbound sheets. All scanners impose restrictions on the sizes of input documents. With flatbed devices, input is constrained by the dimensions of the glass platen or other surface on which pages are positioned for scanning. With the lowest priced devices, the glass platen measures approximately 9 by 12 inches. Input is consequently limited to U.S. letter-size (8.5-by-11-inch) pages or international A4-size (210-by-297mm) pages. Other flatbed models feature 8.75-by-14-inch imaging surfaces that are suitable for B5-size (legal-size) pages. Flatbed scanners capable of accommodating large documents are available for special applications. Some devices can accept engineering drawings, charts, and other documents measuring up to A2-size (420 by 594mm, approximately 18 by 24 inches).

Sheetfed scanners can usually accommodate larger pages than their flatbed counterparts. While B5 is the maximum input size for the least expensive models, more versatile devices can accept U.S. computer printout (11-by-14-inch) pages, international B4-size (297-by-364mm) pages, U.S. ledger-size (11-by-17-inch) pages, and international A3-size (297-by-420mm) pages. Desktop and floor-standing scanners for engineering drawings and other large documents typically employ sheetfed designs. Such devices can accommodate drawings that measure up to A0 size (841 by 1,189mm), the international counterpart of U.S. E-size. At the opposite extreme, some sheetfed scanners specify a minimum page size for reliable document pass-through. While 4 inches by 4 inches is typical, pages smaller than the minimum size can be inserted into transparent carriers for scanning. Through software, most flatbed scanners allow an operator to restrict scanning to a designated portion of a page.

Most document scanners digitize one side of a page at a time. Double-sided pages must be turned over and repositioned for scanning. Some electronic document imaging systems employ software-based techniques to minimize the resulting inconvenience. As an example, the top sides in a stack of double-sided pages may be scanned in sequence. The stack is then turned over and the opposite sides scanned in reverse sequence. Software automatically links the related sides. Such single-sided scanners are generally acceptable in applications where the job stream includes occassional double-sided pages. Double-sided scanners are preferred, however, for high-speed document conversions involving large quantities of double-sided pages. Such devices can digitize both sides of a page simultaneously. They typically feature two sets of optical and photosensitive components located on opposite sides of the paper path. As might be expected, double-sided scanners are more expensive than their single-sided counterparts.

## Digitization Modes

The digitization mode refers to the number of bits that a scanner uses to encode the tonal values of individual picture elements in a source document. The digitization mode determines the type of information that a given scanner can convert to computer-processible form. Depending on the model, a scanner may operate in one or more of the following modes: binary, halftone, grayscale, or color.

Binary-mode digitization is supported by all document scanners employed in electronic document imaging installations. It is suitable for black-and-white documents containing text or line art. The binary mode is sometimes called the one-bit mode because it uses a single bit to represent each pixel. As described above, a threshold reflectance value differentiates light and dark pixels. Where reflectivity values exceed the predetermined threshold, pixels are considered white and are encoded as zero bits. Pixels with reflectivity values below the threshold are considered black and are encoded as one bits. Gray pixels are encoded as either one or zero bits depending on their relative lightness or darkness. Gray shades are not preserved in binary images.

To accommodate photographs and other documents that contain grayscale information, some binary-mode scanners can also operate in a halftone mode. They employ a technique called dithering to simulate shades of gray by combining adjacent black and white pixels into blocks called dither matrices. Within each dither matrix, individual pixels are rendered in various combinations of black and white to give the appearance of gray areas. A four-by-four block, for example, can be used to simulate fifteen shades of gray plus black and white. Larger blocks permit more combinations. With a dither matrix that measures eight by eight pixels, sixty-three gray shades plus black and white are possible. If the pixels in a given dither matrix are evenly divided between black and white, a medium shade of gray is simulated. Lighter or darker gray tones can be represented by adjusting the percentages of black and white pixels. The appearance of dithered images is also affected by the arrangement of black and white pixels within a given matrix.

*Figure 2–1. A grid of picture elements. In this example, dark (text) areas of the document will be encoded as "1" bits, while the light (backround) areas are encoded as "0" bits.*

Dithering may yield satisfactory images in document imaging applications that include occasional grayscale documents. Where more faithful reproduction of gray tones is required, true grayscale scanners, once very expensive and in limited supply, are now widely available at reasonable prices. Such devices utilize multiple bits to represent gray pixels. The number of gray shades that a given scanner can reproduce depends on the number of bits used to encode each pixel. A 4-bit scanner, for example, can differentiate sixteen shades of gray. In most applications, an 8-bit scanner, which can differentiate 256 shades of gray, will prove more versatile. Compared to dithering, multi-bit coding of pixels provides a more accurate representation of gray tones, an advantage in desktop publishing applications where grayscale images may be edited, resized, or otherwise manipulated. Such image editing capabilities are rarely required or desired, however, in the electronic document imaging applications discussed in this book. As a further constraint, electronic document imaging systems seldom include video monitors or printers appropriate to grayscale display or reproduction. In addition, grayscale images based on multi-bit coding require much greater storage

space than dithered images. An 8-bit grayscale image of a photographic document, for example, will require eight times more storage space than its dithered counterpart. For maximum flexibility, most grayscale scanners can also operate in the binary-mode. Some models also support dithering.

Binary-mode and grayscale scanners can digitize colored documents, but they necessarily encode specific colors as black, white, or gray, depending on their tonality. Information conveyed by color will consequently be lost. As a further complication, most binary and grayscale scanners have one color, termed the dropout color, to which they are blind. In certain applications, such as optical character recognition, the dropout color can be used for information that the scanner should ignore. In other situations, however, binary-mode and grayscale scanners may fail to capture important information printed in dropout colors. To minimize such problems, colored filters can be inserted into the scanner or over particular documents, but such special preparation can significantly increase the time required for document input.

True color scanners, in contrast, are specifically designed to recognize and encode colors. They utilize multiple bits to represent each of the three primary colors: red, blue, and green. Most devices employ 8 bits per primary color for a total of 24 bits per pixel. Such scanners can theoretically recognize almost 16.8 million different colors. Some devices require three passes to capture all color information in a document. To simulate the eye's color sensitivity, red, green, and blue filters are used in the various passes. As an alternative design, some color scanners incorporate differently colored lamps to detect red, blue, and green in a single pass. In either case, color scanners are typically much slower than their binary-mode and grayscale counterparts. As with grayscale operation, images digitized in the color mode will require significantly more storage space than images digitized in the binary mode. Most color scanners can also operate in binary and grayscale modes.

*Resolution*

As previously described, scanners divide source documents into scan lines that are, in turn, subdivided into pixels which are sampled for their light reflectance characteristics. <u>Res</u>-olution denotes the specific pattern and number of pixels sampled by a scanner in a given document. It is typically expressed as the number of pixels or dots per inch or millimeter of a scanned page. While the scanning resolution is measured both horizontally and vertically, it is often identical in both directions. Where such is the case, one resolution measurement is stated, and it is assumed to apply to both the horizontal and vertical dimensions of the scanned page.

As the scanning resolution is increased for a given document, the number of pixels per square inch or millimeter is correspondingly increased, while the size of each pixel is decreased. A scanning pattern with small pixels can capture finer details than a scanning pattern with large pixels. Scanning resolution is consequently an important determinant of image quality—to the extent, of course, that quality is equated with the amount of detail in or sharpness of digitized images. Resolutions supported by available document scanners range from less than 50 pixels per inch to more than 1,000 pixels per inch, although that broad range is not supported by every device or appropriate for every application. Commonly encountered choices include 100, 150, 200, 240, 300, 400, and 600 pixels per inch. In many cases, the desired resolution is operator-selectable by switches mounted on the scanner or through software controls.

The choice of scanning resolution is affected by various factors, including the characteristics of

*Figure 2–2. Two varieties of flatbed desktop scanner: above, the inverted type with a glass platen (Courtesy: Epson America), and below, the overhead type (Courtesy: Chinon America).*

the documents to be scanned, the applications in which the resulting digitized images will be used, and the computer components on which the images will be processed, stored, displayed, and/or printed. To determine an appropriate resolution, a

*Figure 2–3. A sheetfed desktop scanner. (Courtesy: Microtek)*

representative selection of the documents encountered in a given application should be scanned at various resolutions, and displayed or printed representations of the resulting images evaluated for their intended purposes.

For the electronic document imaging applications discussed in this book, 200 pixels per inch is generally considered the minimum scanning resolution compatible with consistently legible digitization of typewritten business documents and much printed material. Lower resolutions are most suitable for digitization of pictorial images in applications such as desktop publishing. At 200 pixels per inch, a letter-size page will be divided into 2,200 horizontal scan lines with 1,700 pixels per line. The quality of the resulting images is comparable to that of copies produced by facsimile transceivers that conform to the CCITT Group III standard protocol, which supports a nominal resolution of 200 pixels per inch when operating in the fine mode. Most facsimile transmission is based on the

CCITT Group III protocol's normal mode which employs a nominal resolution of 200 by 100 pixels per inch.

Where greater image quality is desired or required, some document scanners can optionally operate at user-selectable resolutions of 300 or 400 pixels per inch. The quality of document images digitized at 300 pixels per inch is comparable to that of popular laser printers, most of which generate output at 300 dots per inch. It approaches office copier quality. Images digitized at 400 pixels per inch closely resemble original documents. While they will unquestionably enhance the appearance and readability of digitized images produced from any documents, such higher resolutions are particularly advantageous in records management and library applications involving journal articles, contracts, preprinted business forms, and other typewritten or typeset materials that contain footnotes or other text segments printed in very small type sizes. Higher scanning reso-

*Figure 2–4. A floor-standing high-speed document scanner. (Courtesy: Eastman Kodak)*

lutions are likewise advantageous where optical character recognition (OCR) technology will be utilized to extract index values from designated portions of digitized images. This technique, sometimes described as auto-indexing, is discussed later in this chapter. For accurate recognition, most OCR algorithms require a minimum scanning resolution of 300 pixels per inch.

As a potentially significant disadvantage, higher scanning resolutions generate a greater number of pixels which, as discussed later in this book, will significantly increase storage requirements for digitized document images. At 200 pixels per inch, for example, digitized images contain 40,000 pixels per square inch; at 300 pixels per inch, the number

of pixels per square inch increases to 90,000, and, all other things being equal, storage space requirements increase by a factor of 2.25.

As an additional constraint, the display resolutions of video monitors employed in electronic document imaging systems are usually limited to 200 pixels per inch or less, and display resolutions of 100 or 150 pixels per inch are increasingly common. Resolutions supported by microcomputer displays are even lower. Images scanned at higher resolutions must be adjusted for display at lower resolutions, in which case the greater detail provided by high scanning resolutions is effectively lost for display purposes. Alternatively, partial-page images can be displayed at full resolution, but that approach can require considerable panning and scrolling to view required information. In some electronic document imaging configurations, however, laser printers can produce hardcopy output at resolutions up to 400 pixels per inch. Scanning resolutions in excess of 200 pixels per inch should consequently be limited to applications where high-quality paper prints must be produced from digitized document images. This emphasis on high-quality printing defeats one of the principal purposes of electronic document imaging implementations, many of which are designed to streamline workflow by replacing paper records with "softcopy" displays.

*Speed*

Scanning speed is an obvious and important determinant of labor requirements and costs in electronic document imaging installations. Rated equipment speed is perhaps the most widely cited and potentially misleading measure of scanning speed. It denotes the time required to convert one page to a digitized image from the moment the page is positioned for digitization until it can be removed from scanner. As its principal limitation, this method of measuring scanning speed ignores the impact of equipment design on work throughput; that is, on the amount of work that can be realistically completed with a given scanner in a specified amount of time. Because of significant differences in document positioning times, sheetfed scanners usually support faster throughput rates than flatbed models. Once a document is positioned, the speed attainable with specific equipment in a particular application will vary with the digitization mode, the scanning resolution, and the dimensions of pages being scanned. Binary-mode operation is usually faster than multi-bit grayscale or color scanning. Because more pixels must be sampled, scanning time typically increases with resolution, although the increase may be measured in fractions of a second with some devices. Because they have greater surface areas, large pages will take longer to scan than small ones.

Ignoring variations associated with these parameters, technical specification sheets for scanners employed in electronic document imaging installations customarily indicate rated speeds in

*Figure 2–5. A handheld scanner. (Photo by Carolyn Saffady)*

seconds per page or pages per minute. Such specifications typically assume a letter-size page digitized in the binary mode at a horizontal and vertical resolution of 200 pixels per inch, although that assumption may be unstated. Typical operating speeds for desktop scanners range from less than three seconds to more than twenty seconds per letter-size page. As might be expected, the slowest devices are encountered in the lowest-cost, entry-level, microcomputer-based equipment configurations. Desktop scanners employed by more sophisticated systems typically operate at three to six seconds per letter-size page. Some high-speed floor-standing scanners can digitize one or more letter-size pages per second. As previously noted, such devices are intended for high-volume document conversions.

To facilitate the calculation of scanning times for larger and smaller documents, scanner speeds are more usefully measured in inches or centimeters per second. A device that can digitize a letter-size page in four seconds operates at 2.75 inches per second. It will require 5.1 second to digitize a legal-size page and 6.2 seconds to digitize an A3-size page. Longer scanning times are required for larger pages. A typical scanner designed for engineering applications, for example, may operate at just 0.3 inches per second and will require two minutes to digitize an A0-size drawing. These operating speeds represent the time required for document digitization only; they do not include document positioning time or the time associated with image compression, image enhancement, or other image processing routines which may be performed following digitization.

*Prices*

Prices for document scanners range from less than $200 for handheld devices of limited utility to more than $100,000 for high-speed, floor-standing models intended for high-volume document conversions. Typical prices for the desktop models encountered in most electronic document imaging installations range from $1,500 to $10,000. These prices apply to the scanner only; they do not include interface cards, cables, software, and other components required for installation and operation of a scanner in a given document imaging application.

To address the broadest range of customer requirements, vendors of electronic document imaging systems increasingly offer a choice of scanners with different price/performance characteristics. There is relatively little variation in the resolution capabilities of differently priced scanners; most devices can operate at 200 or 300 pixels per inch, the two most appropriate and widely utilized resolutions in electronic document imaging applications. The principal price-dependent characteristics of available models are scanning speed and the maximum acceptable document size.

*Microfilm Scanning*

In some installations, electronic document imaging technology replaces previously installed micrographic systems which convert source documents to miniaturized photographic images for recording on 16mm or 35mm microfilm reels, 16mm self-threading microfilm cartridges, 105mm microfiche, 16mm or 35mm microfilm jackets, or 35mm aperture cards. In such microfilm replacement applications, conventional scanners are used to digitize newly acquired documents, but many users want to incorporate older documents into their electronic document imaging implementations, thereby eliminating the requirement for parallel operation of electronic document imaging and micrographic systems. Often, however, the original source documents were discarded following microfilming. Consequently, digitized images of backfile documents must be produced from microforms using a microfilm scanner.

A microfilm scanner combines the capabilities of an image digitizer and a microdensitometer. Like the document scanners described above, it divides individual microimages into a grid of picture elements, each of which is analyzed for its relative lightness or darkness and encoded as a zero or one bit. Microfilm scanners have been developed for various types of microforms. Predating the commercial availability of electronic document imaging systems discussed in this book, such devices have been utilized for microimage transmission (so-called microfacsimile) since the 1960s. Implementations of that type are described in Chapter One.

In many electronic document imaging installations, microfilm scanning is a single occurrence or an occasional requirement that is most effectively and economically performed by an imaging service bureau. In other cases, however, source documents may be routinely recorded on microfilm prior to scanning, necessitating an in-house scanning operation. In such situations, microforms play two roles: they offer stable recording media for long-term storage, and they serve as input to an electronic document imaging system. Whether one-time conversions or ongoing digitization requirements are involved, the successful implementation of a microfilm scanning system depends on the characteristics of microimages encountered in a particular application. Most microform backfiles were created for display or printing; because digitization was not anticipated, the microimages may lack attributes appropriate to that purpose. Photometric parameters critical to microfilm scanning are outlined by Westcott (1992). High-quality microimages are essential. Whenever possible, scanning should be performed on first generation, camera original microforms rather than duplicates. Image density should conform to specifications outlined in ANSI/AIIM MS23, *Practice for Operational Procedures/Inspection and Quality Control of First Generation, Silver Microfilm of Documents*. Density variations from frame to frame should be kept within as narrow a range as possible. To minimize the need for operator intervention in the scanning process, image size, placement, and alignment should be consistent within a given set of microforms. Software can be used to correct misaligned images, but that approach will degrade throughput. Microfiche that rigidly conform to ANSI/AIIM specifications, aperture cards, and blip-encoded 16mm microfilm will pose the fewest alignment problems. Microfilm jackets, which contain unaligned film strips, can prove difficult to scan.

## Index Data Entry

As described above, an electronic document imaging system maintains a computer-processible data base that serves as an index to digitized document images. The data base typically contains one record for each indexable item in a given document collection. The records are divided into fields that correspond to index parameters or categories determined at the time the implementation was planned. Index data entry involves the entry of values associated with specific fields. Index data entry should not be confused with document indexing; that is, the determination of values appropriate to particular indexing parameters.

Depending on application characteristics and the capabilities of hardware and software employed in a given installation, field values may be key-entered or extracted from documents via optical recognition methodologies. In some cases, data entry requirements are minimized or eliminated by downloading index values from existing computer data bases or by linking electronic document images to data bases that contain appropriate field values.

### Key-Entry

As in computer applications generally, key-entry of index values is the most common data entry methodology in electronic document imaging installations. Index values that correspond to designated fields within data base records are typed at a keyboard attached to a video display device. Key-entry is often integrated with image inspection; digitized document images are individually displayed for operator examination. Once satisfactory image quality is confirmed, the index values are typed in a manner prescribed by the data base management software employed by a particular system. Most programs support specially formatted screens with prelabeled fields accompanied by adjacent blank spaces, to facilitate the key-entry of field values. In many cases, index values are entered and displayed in a separate window that is adjacent to or overlaps the digitized document image to which they pertain.

As with conventional typing, key-entry of data is an error-prone activity; as much as 5 percent of characters may be incorrectly typed. Since many retrieval operations depend on exact matches of specified character strings, even a small quantity of keystroking errors can have a negative impact on retrieval performance. It is consequently important that keystroking errors be detected and corrected. This can be accomplished in several ways. Displayed field values, for example, can be inspected following key entry; alternatively, a list of entered field values can be printed for proofreading. Unfortunately, such visual verification techniques often leave incorrect characters undetected. Furthermore, proofreading is generally an ineffective method of detecting errors in numeric field values. The preferred alternative is variously called keystroke verification or double-keying. Each field value is typed twice. The second keying may occur immediately after initial entry of a given field value or at some later time; it may be performed by the same data entry operator or by a different person. Data verification software compares the two sets of keystrokes and alerts the operator when a discrepancy is detected. The entered values are then examined for correctness. Since it is unlikely that the same errors will be made during both initial data entry and retyping, keystroke verification is a highly effective method of error detection. As an obvious disadvantage, however, it doubles the effort and time required for data entry.

### Auto-Indexing

In some electronic document imaging applications, barcode or optical character recognition technologies are utilized to minimze or eliminate the key-entry of index data. Such data entry methodologies are collectively described as auto-indexing or keyless data entry because they involve the automatic extraction of index values from specified portions of input documents. Depending on the hardware and software components employed in a given system, auto-indexing may be performed during the scanning process simultaneous with document digitization or following scanning from digitized document images.

In barcode recognition, one or more field values are encoded by predetermined patterns of closely spaced vertical lines of varying widths. The barcodes may be printed directly on source documents or on labels that are affixed to documents. The meanings of specific line patterns are defined by the coding scheme utilized in a particular system. Examples of coding schemes in current use include Code 128, Code 39, Codabar 3, and Interleaved 3 of 5. Barcodes are an accurate, fast, reliable, and easily implemented alternative to key-entry for certain types of information. While alphabetic coding is possible, most barcodes represent numeric field values, such as sequentially assigned document numbers, case numbers, or project numbers. As a result, barcode recognition cannot fully replace key-entry in most electronic document imaging applications. It will, however, eliminate typing of selected field values, thereby minimizing the data entry workload.

Barcode recognition is most widely encountered in point-of-sale and other retailing applications. As discussed by Lacharite (1991), Noirjean (1989, 1989a), Payne (1988), and Stevens (1991), barcode technology has been successfully utilized in various records management and document control applications, including computer-assisted microfilm retrieval systems as well as electronic document imaging installations. In auto-indexing implementations, barcodes may be read and interpreted by the scanner that is used to digitize document images or by a separate, handheld scanning device called a light pen. Alternatively, software operating on the computer to which the document scanner is attached may recognize barcodes within digitized images. In either case, the interpreted information is assigned as the value of designated fields within data base records associated with particular document images. While barcode recognition is a straightforward technology with proven performance characteristics, accuracy is affected by several factors, including the clarity of vertical line patterns and the contrast between lines and spaces. In some applications, the time and effort required to affix barcode labels to source documents may negate savings associated with the elimination of key-entry.

Designed to address a broader range of data entry and auto-indexing requirements than barcode technology, optical character recognition (OCR) is a computer input methodology that combines scanning with image analysis to recognize or "read" characters contained in source documents. The recognized characters are converted to machine-readable, character-coded form, just as if they had been key-entered. In auto-indexing for electronic document imaging, recognized characters from designated areas within source documents can be assigned as the values of specific fields within data base records. This auto-indexing technique is intended for specially formatted documents, such as purchase orders, invoices, insurance claims, and other business forms. In such cases, the application designer specifies the locations within forms where the indicated field values are to be recognized and extracted. OCR also permits full-text indexing of correspondence, memoranda, reports, and other unformatted documents. Such applications do not employ conventional field-oriented data bases; instead, index entries are crated for every word in the text of input documents. A stoplist may be used to suppress the indexing of certain adverbs, conjunctions, prepositions, interjections, and other meaningless words.

In most OCR implementations, the recognizable repertoire includes letters of the alphabet, numeric digits, punctuation marks, and other symbols encountered in correspondence, reports, business forms, publications, and similar textual documents. Character-coding is usually based on the American Standard Code for Information Interchange (ASCII), which is supported by computers of all types and sizes. In IBM computer installations, the Extended Binary Coded Decimal Interchange Code (EBCDIC) may be utilized. Character recognition research and OCR product capabilities are discussed, in varying levels of technical detail, by Fruchterman (1988), Gonzalez (1987), Govindan and Shivaprasad (1990), Greenblatt (1988), Impedovo et al. (1990), Mantas (1986), Pritchard (1989), Scheinberg (1988), and Schurmann (1987).

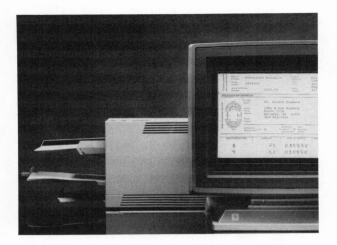

*Figure 2–6. An OCR reader (Courtesy: Recognition Equipment Incorporated)*

As noted above, optical character recognition combines document digitization with image analysis. Because document scanning is an essential preliminary to optical character recognition, the terms "OCR" and "scanning" are often used interchangeably, but that usage is imprecise and misleading. Document scanning is merely one workstep in an OCR system; digitized images must be analyzed and the recognized characters converted to computer-processable codes. OCR implementations may be hardware- or software-based. In the former case, document digitization and character recognition are performed by the same device in a single scanning operation. Recognition programs reside in processing circuitry that is built into a document scanner, which is usually described as an "OCR reader" to distinguish it from a conventional scanner. In a variant approach, recognition may be performed by a coprocessor board to which a conventional scanner is attached. In either case, OCR readers that recognize text contained in business forms are sometimes categorized as "document readers." Such devices, which date from the 1960s, are principally intended for data processing applications where the layout and typographic characteristics of input documents can be tightly controlled. Widely utilized in transaction processing applications involving payroll forms, airline and railway tickets, response cards employed in direct mail solicitations, and remittance forms, their recognition capabilities may be limited to specially

designed type fonts, such as OCR-A and OCR-B. This typically constrains their utility for auto-indexing in electronic document imaging implementations.

OCR readers that can recognize text contained in office documents, book pages, and other unformatted materials are termed "page readers." Such machines must be able to recognize a variety of typeset, typewritten, and computer-printed fonts in different sizes and styles. They are typically described as multifont or, in the case of OCR readers that impose no significant restrictions on type fonts, omnifont devices. In addition to identifying text, the most sophisticated page readers can recognize and preserve character and page formatting attributes, such as underlining, italics, indentations, centering, tabular presentations, and columnar printing. They can also detect areas within pages that contain charts, illustrations, or other graphic information and will automatically exclude those areas from the recognition process.

The document and page readers described above are currently being utilized in a variety of information management applications, including auto-indexing for electronic document imaging. While progressive improvements in recognition methodologies have broadened the range of acceptable input and significantly improved accuracy, the relatively high cost of OCR readers has stimulated interest in potentially less expensive software-based approaches. Software-based implementations divide OCR into two worksteps: document digitization, which is performed by a peripheral device, and character recognition, which is performed by an OCR program executed by the computer to which the document scanner is attached. OCR programs are increasingly available for computers of all types and sizes, including IBM-compatible microcomputers and Macintosh systems. They are designed to operate with customer-supplied scanners. Depending on the implementation, character recognition may be performed immediately after scanning. Alternatively, digitized images may be stored for subsequent processing. Such deferred recognition may be performed during evening hours when there is little contention for computer resources. As a potential limitation in high-volume applications, software-based implementations are typically slower than hardware-based OCR readers. Recognition speed is influenced by the computer system on which the OCR program operates. With microcomputer software in particular, a fast central processor is recommended.

Implementation methods aside, OCR's suitability for auto-indexing in electronic document imaging installations depends on its ability to accurately recognize characters contained in source documents. Accuracy is determined by recognition algorithms. The most broadly useful OCR products offer omnifont recognition capabilities based on feature extraction algorithms. Such algorithms identify characters on the basis of their distinctive features. As an example, the uppercase letter "A" is recognized as a character with two diagonal lines that are joined at the top and bisected by a horizontal crossbar, while an uppercase "D" is recognized as having one vertical line joined at the ends by a loop. As their most important advantage, feature extraction algorithms transcend ornamental differences associated with particular type fonts, sizes and styles. Presumably, the letter "O" will be recognizable as a continuous loop whether it is printed in the Courier or Times Roman font, boldface or italicized, large or small. The most powerful omnifont OCR products supplement feature extraction with contextual analysis, dictionary searches, frequency counts, or other techniques that increase the likelihood of accurate character identification. Such products are sometimes described as Intelligent Character Recognition (ICR) systems.

As an alternative or supplement to feature extraction, some OCR products employ matrix matching techniques. In matrix matching, the light and dark pixel patterns contained in digitized images are compared to character reference sets or templates that define pixel patterns for specific letters of the alphabet, numeric digits, punctuation marks, and other symbols. Character identification is based on the closest match between a given pattern of light and dark pixels and a character definition contained in a template. As an obvious limitation, accurate matrix matching depends on the availability of an appropriate font file. While matrix matching methodologies may prove acceptable for documents that are created under controlled conditions by a limited number of output devices, no OCR product can provide templates for all possible combinations of type fonts, sizes, and styles. As a result, matrix matching is typically associated with multifont rather than omnifont OCR products.

Whether character recognition is based on feature extraction or matrix matching algorithms, OCR readers and programs can be categorized as trainable or nontrainable. Trainable OCR products must be taught to recognize a specific type font prior to analyzing documents printed in that font. In most cases, the OCR product displays successive characters from a digitized document image printed in the font to be learned. The operator identifies each displayed character by typing it. The OCR product stores the learned characters in a font file or feature classification list. To allow for typographic variations, trainable OCR products must be introduced to multiple examples of individual characters.

Because training procedures are laborious and time consuming, trainable OCR products are best suited to large collections of documents with identical typographic characteristics. The ideal training document will contain all characters associated with a particular type font printed several times by the same device that will be used to print subsequent documents to be recognized. In most cases, separate training sessions are required for different sizes and styles of a given font. Although the adjective "nontrainable" implies a functional deficit, the most versatile and accurate OCR products do not require training. They incorporate feature extraction algorithms and offer immediately usable omnifont recognition capabilities. For maximum versatility some OCR products combine built-in, omnifont recognition with trainability for unusual fonts or special characters.

In their advertisements and technical specification sheets, OCR vendors typically claim very high accuracy but warn that recognition performance is necessarily limited by such factors as the typographic characteristics of particular documents. The best results will be obtained with high-contrast documents that contain sharply defined, dark characters on a white background. Accuracy will be compromised by faded printer ribbons and speckled photocopies. Some OCR devices and programs cannot recognize characters printed in very small or very large sizes or in certain styles, such as italics or underlined. Some OCR products allow the operator to adjust recognition parameters for monospaced or proportionally-spaced text. An increasing number of OCR devices and programs can recognize documents produced by nine-pin, draft-quality, dot-matrix printers.

Unfortunately, application planners have little control over the quality or typographic characteristics of source documents encountered in electronic document imaging installations. Among those factors that application planners can control, however, scanning resolution selected for document digitization will have the greatest impact on recognition accuracy. All other things being equal, the higher the scanning resolution, the greater the amount of detail that will be captured in digitized images and the higher the image quality will be. For accurate recognition, most OCR products recommend or require a scanning resolution of 300 pixels per inch. Lower resolutions rarely produce acceptable results. Some OCR devices and programs can accommodate document images scanned at 400 pixels per inch. While such high resolutions may improve recognition accuracy for contract clauses, footnotes, and other information printed in very small type sizes, they can significantly degrade recognition speed.

OCR readers and software packages convert the contents of document images to character-coded text that may be assigned to specified fields within a data base or saved in an operator-designated file. As with key-entered data, the recognized characters must be proofread to detect and correct errors. Some OCR products incorporate an editing module to facilitate such error correction; alternatively, word processing software can be utilized. With some OCR readers and software packages, unrecognizable characters are marked with a specified symbol, such as a circumflex or tilde, that is unlikely to be contained in the text itself. OCR accuracy levels must be very high to avoid unacceptable error correction workloads. A 2,000-character page recognized with 90-percent accuracy, for example, will contain 200 errors. At five seconds per error, correction will require approximately seventeen minutes. At thirty words per minute, however, the entire page could be typed in less than twelve minutes.

## References

Aitchison, J. and Clevedon, C. (1963). A Report on a Test of the Index of Metallurgical Literature of Western Reserve University: Report to the National Science Foundation on the Aslib-Cranfield Research Project. Cranfield, England: College of Aeronautics.

Artandi, S. (1966). The searchers: links between inquirers and indexes. Special Libraries 57: 571-74.

Auld, L. (1982). Authority control: an eighty-year review. Library Resources and Technical Services 26: 319-30.

Barber, J. et al. (1988). Case studies of the indexing and retrieval of pharmacology papers. Information Processing and Management 24: 141-50.

Batty, D. (1982). Microcomputers in index language design and development. Microcomputers for Information Management 1: 303-12.

_____. (1989). Thesaurus construction and maintenance: a survival kit. Database 12/1: 13-20.

Baxendale, P. (1966). Content analysis, specification and control. In Annual Review of Information Science and Technology, vol. 1. New York: Interscience, pp. 71-106.

Berns, G. (1969). Description of FORMAT, a text processing program. Communications of the Association for Computing Machinery 12: 141-46.

Bhattacharyya, K. (1974). The effectiveness of natural language in science indexing and retrieval. Journal of Documentation 30: 235-54.

Bigelow, J. (1965). Rational and irrational requirements upon information retrieval systems. In Information System Sciences: Proceedings of the Second Congress. Washington, DC: Spartan Books, pp. 85-94.

Bloomfield, M. (1966). A study of singular and plural words as index terms. In American Documentation Institute: Proceedings of the Annual Meeting. Washington, DC: American Documentation Institute, pp. 201-205.

Booth, B. (1979). A new ERIC thesaurus, fine-tuned for searching. Online 3/1: 20-29.

Booth, P. (1987). Thesauri: their uses for indexers. Indexer 15: 141-50.

Borko, H. and Tarr, D. (1974). Factors influencing inter-indexer consistency. In Proceedings of the American Society for Information Science: 37th Annual Meeting. Washington, DC: American Society for Information Science, pp. 50-55.

Bottle, R. (1974). Thesaurus controlled indexing and the incidence of synonyms and related terms. In Informatics 1: Proceedings of a Conference Held by the Aslib Coordinate Indexing Group. London: Aslib, pp. 145-53.

Brenner, E. (1987). API patent abstracting and indexing: cooperative efforts in historical perspective. World Patent Information 9: 27-33.

Brenner, E. and Smyth, V. (1961). The evolution of petroleum abstracts. Special Libraries 52: 558-60.

Bryant, E. (1965). Control of Indexing Errors. Bethesda, MD: Westat Corporation.

Burgin, R. (1991). The effect of indexing exhaustivity on retrieval performance. Information Processing and Management 27: 623-28.

Byrne, J. (1975). Relative effectiveness of titles, abstracts, and subject headings for machine retrieval from the COMPENDEX services. Journal of the American Society for Information Science 26: 223-39.

Clarke, D. (1970). Query formulation for on-line reference retrieval: design considerations from the indexer/searcher viewpoint. In Proceedings of the American Society for Information Science: 33rd Annual Meeting. Washington, DC: American Society for Information Science, pp. 83-86.

Cleverdon, C. (1962). Report on the Testing and Analysis of an Investigation into the Comparative Efficiency of Indexing Systems. Cranfield, England: College of Aeronautics.

_____. (1963). The Cranfield WRU experiment: conclusions. In Information Retrieval in Action. Cleveland: Western Reserve University Press, pp. 101-107.

_____. (1965). The Cranfield hypotheses. Library Quarterly 35: 121-24.

Coates, E. (1966). Scientific and technical indexing. Indexer 5/1: 27-34.

Coblans, H. (1971). Words and documents: the fifth Aslib annual lecture. Aslib Proceedings 23: 337-50.

Cooper, W. (1969). Is interindexer consistency a hobgoblin? American Documentation 20: 268-78.

_____. (1978). Indexing theory and retrieval effectiveness. Drexel Library Quarterly 14: 40-46.

Crouch, C. (1990). An approach to the automatic construction of global thesauri. Information Processing and Management 26: 629-40.

Deschatelets, G. (1986). The three languages in information retrieval. International Classification 13: 126-33.

Dickman, J. (1988). The recruiting of chemists for a chemical abstracting and information service. Journal of Documentation 44: 42-52.

Difondi, N. et al. (1973). Benefits and costs of free-text searching on the FTD CIRC reference retrieval system. In Proceedings of the American Society for Information Science: 36th Annual Meeting. Westport, CT: Greenwood Press, pp. 47-48.

Diodata, V. (1981). Author indexing. Special Libraries 72: 361-69.

_____. (1981a). "Author Indexing in Mathematics." Ph.D. Dissertation. Urbana-Champaign: University of Illinois.

_____. (1985). Source indexing in science journals and indexing services: a survey of current practices. Science and Technology Libraries 6: 103-18.

Diodata, V. and Gandt, G. (1991). Back of book indexes and the characteristics of author and non-author indexing—report of an exploratory study. Journal of the American Society for Information Science. 42(5): 341–350.

Eichhorn, M. and Reinecke, R. (1969). Development and implementation of a thesaurus for the visual sciences. Journal of Chemical Documentation 9: 114-17.

Fairthorne, R. (1965). "Use" and "mention" in the information sciences. In Proceedings of the Symposium on Education for Information Science. Washington, DC: Spartan Books, pp. 9-12.

_____. (1969). Content analysis, specification, and control. In Annual Review of Information Science and Technology, vol. 4. Chicago: Encyclopedia Brittanica, pp. 71-109.

Falk, H. and Tompkins, H. (1970). Author-assisted indexing. In Proceedings of the American Society for Information Science: 33rd Annual Meeting. Washington, DC: American Society for Information Science, pp. 283-90.

Feinberg, H. (1973). Title Derivative Indexing Techniques: a Comparative Study. Metuchen, NJ: Scarecrow Press.

Fischer, M. (1966). The KWIC index concept: a retrospective view. American Documentation 17: 57-70.

Foskett, A. (1982). The Subject Approach to Information. London: Bingley.

Fried, C. and Prevel, J. (1966). Effects of Indexing Aids on Indexing Performance. Bethesda, MD: General Electric Company.

Fruchterman, J. (1988). Ominfont text recognition: linking paper, electronic, and optical output. Inform 2/5: 16-19.

George, A. (1964). Qualitative and Quantitative Procedures in Content Analysis. Santa Monica, CA: Rand Corporation.

Gerrie, B. (1983). Online Information Systems: Use and Operating Characteristics, Limitations, and Design Alternatives. Arlington, VA: Information Resources Press.

Ghose, A. and Dhawle, A. (1977). Problems of thesaurus construction. Journal of the American Society for Information Science 28: 211-17.

Gonzalez, R. (1987). Designing balance into an OCR system. Photonics Spectra 21/9: 113-16.

Gould, L. et al. (1969). An Experimental Inquiry into Context Information Processing. Los Angeles: University of California, Institute of Library Research.

Govindan, V. and Shivaprasad, A. (1990). Character recognition: a review. Pattern Recognition 23: 671-83.

Graves, R. and Helander, D. (1970). A feasibility study of automatic indexing and information retrieval. IEEE Transactions on Engineering Writing and Speech 13: 58-59.

Greenblatt, J. (1988). Information technology: industry update on optical character recognition and image scanners. Information Management Review 3/3: 71-74.

Gull, C. (1966). Structure of indexing authority lists. Library Resources and Technical Services 10: 507-11.

Harvey, J. (1976). Analysis of documents. In Specialized Information Centers. Hamden, CT: Shoe String Press, pp. 35-40.

Herner, S. (1963). The role of thesauri in the convergence of word and concept indexing. In Automation and Scientific Communication: Short Papers. Washington, DC: American Documentation Institute, pp. 183-84.

Herr, J. (1970). Use of data-base access for interindexer communication and for indexer training. In Proceedings of the American Society for Information Science: 33rd Annual Meeting. Washington, DC: American Society for Information Science, pp. 163-66.

Hersey, D. et al. (1971). Free text word retrieval and scientist indexing: performance profiles and costs. Journal of Documentation 27: 167-83.

Hickey, D. (1976). Subject analysis: an interpretative survey. Library Trends 25: 273-91.

Hurwitz, F. (1969). A study of indexer consistency. American Documentation 20: 92-94.

Hutchins, W. (1977). On the problem of "aboutness" in document analysis. Journal of Informatics 1: 17-35.

_____. (1978). The concept of "aboutness" in subject indexing. Aslib Proceedings 30: 172-81.

Hyslop, M. (1965). Sharing vocabulary control. Special Libraries 56: 708-14.

Impedovo, S. et al. (1990). Recent developments of the optical character reading systems. In Proceedings of the Fifth International Conference on Image Analysis and Processing: Progress in Image Analysis and Processing. Singapore: World Scientific, pp. 615-22.

Jacoby, J. and Slamecka, V. (1962). Indexer Consistency under Minimal Conditions. Bethesda, MD: Documentation Incorporated.

Jones, K. (1972). Some thesauric history. Aslib Proceedings 24: 408-11.

_____. (1981). How do we index: a report on some Aslib informatics group activity. Journal of Chemical Education 39: 1-23.

Kesselman, M. and Perry, I. (1984). What online searchrs should know about indexing and what indexers should know about online searching. In Proceedings of the Fifth National Online Meeting. Medford, NJ: Learned Information, pp. 141-48.

Kim, C. (1973). Theoretical foundations of thesaurus construction and some methodological considerations for thesaurus updating. Journal of the American Society for Information Science 24: 148-56.

King, D. and Daley, J. (1964). Quality control of coordinate indexing. In Proceedings of the American Documentation Institute. Washington, DC: American Documentation Institute, pp. 389-92.

Kochen, M. (1971). A cost-effectiveness analysis of see-reference structures in directories. In Proceedings of the Israel Society of Special Libraries and Information Centres International Conference on Information Science. Tel Aviv: Israel Society of Special Libraries and Information Centers, pp. 289-98.

Kochen, M. and Tagliacozzo, R. (1968). A study of cross-referencing. Journal of Documentation 24: 173-91.

Korotkin, A. and Oliver, L. (1964). The Effect of Subject Matter Familiarity and the Use of an Indexing Aid upon Inter-Indexer Consistency. Bethesda, MD: General Electric Company.

Korotkin, A. et al. (1965). Indexing Aids, Procedures, and Devices. Bethesda, MD: General Electric Company.

Lacharite, R. (1991). Rethinking bar coding: turning preconceptions into system tools. ARMA Records Management Quarterly 25/2: 3-11.

Lancaster, F. (1969). Evaluating the performance of a large computerized information system. Journal of the American Medical Association 207: 114-20.

_____. (1969a). MEDLARS: report on the evaluation of its operating efficiency. American Documentation 20: 119-42.

_____. (1972). Vocabulary Control for Information Retrieval. Washington, DC: Information Resources Press.

_____. (1977). Vocabulary control in information retrieval systems. Advances in Librarianship 7: 1-40.

Lancaster, F. and Mills, J. (1964). Testing indexes and index language devices: the Aslib-Cranfield project. American Documentation 15: 4-13.

Laursen, J. (1980). Effectiveness of using natural language in searching volcanic stratigraphy titles. In Proceedings of the American Society for Information Science: 43rd Annual Meeting. White Plains, NY: Knowledge Industry Publications, pp. 191-93.

Leonard, L. (1975). "Inter-Indexer Consistency and Retrieval Effectiveness: Measurement of Relationships." Ph.D dissertation. Champaign-Urbana: University of Illinois.

_____. (1977). Inter-Indexer Consistency Studies, 1954-1975: a Review of the Literature and a Summary of Study Results. Occasional Papers no. 31. Champaign-Urbana: Graduate School of Library Science, University of Illinois.

Levine, E. (1974). Effect of instantaneous retrieval on indexing criteria. Journal of the American Society for Information Science 25: 199-200.

_____. (1975). Potential savings in indexing costs through the use of high speed, random access microfiche. In Information Roundup: Proceedings of the 4th ASIS Mid-Year Meeting. Washington, DC: American Society for Information Science, pp. 105-10.

Liston, D. and Howder, M. (1977). Subject analysis. In Annual Review of Information Science and Technology, vol. 12. White Plains, NY: Knowledge Industry Publications, pp. 81-118.

Lufkin, R. (1968). Determination and Analysis of Some Parameters Affecting the Subject Indexing Process. Cambridge: Massachusetts Institute of Technology, Electronic Systems Laboratory.

Luhn, H. (1960). Keyword-in-context index for technical literature. American Documentation 9: 288-95.

Macmillan, J. and Welt, I. (1961). A study of indexing procedures in a limited area of the medical sciences. American Documentation 12: 27-31.

Mandersloot, W. et al. (1970). Thesaurus control: the selection, grouping and cross-referencing of terms for inclusion in a coordinate index word list. Journal of the American Society for Information Science 21: 49-57.

Mantas, J. (1986). An overview of character recognition methodologies. Pattern Recognition 19: 425-30.

Markey, K. (1984). Interindexer consistency tests: a literature review and report of a test of consistency in indexing visual materials. Library and Information Science Research 6: 155-77.

Maron, M. (1977). On indexing, retrieval, and the meaning of about. Journal of the American Society for Information Science 28: 38-43.

_____. (1979). Depth of indexing. Journal of the American Society for Information Science 30: 224-28.

Maron, M. and Shoffner, R. (1969). The Study of Context: An Overview. Los Angeles: University of California, Institute of Library Research.

McKinney, A. and Rees, A. (1963). Selecting and training abstractors and indexers. In Information Retrieval in Action. Cleveland: School of Library Science, Case Western Reserve University, pp. 231-40.

Milstead, J. (1984). Subject Access Systems: Alternatives in Design. Orlando, FL: Academic Press.

_____. (1990). Thesaurus software packages for personal computers. Database 13/6: 61-65.

_____. (1991). Specifications for thesaurus software. Information Processing and Management 27: 165-75.

Mori, M. et al. (1983). High speed document scanner using charge coupled device (CCD) image sensors. In Proceedings of the SPIE, vol. 350. Bellingham, WA: Society of Photo-Optical Instrumentation Engineers, pp. 66-72.

Moss, R. (1967). Minimum vocabularies in information indexing. Journal of Documentation 23: 179-96.

_____. (1970). Analysis of indexing terms for plastics. Journal of the American Society for Information Science 21: 164-66.

Noirjean, R. (1989). Bar code indexing—clearing the inputting bottleneck for improved document management. International Journal of Micrographics and Video Technology 7/3: 103-5.

_____. (1989a). Bar code indexing: clearing the input bottleneck. IMC Journal 25/3: 19-21.

Norris, C. (1972). MEDLARS indexing. NLL Review 2: 56-60.

_____. (1981). MeSH: the subject heading approach. Aslib Proceedings 33: 153-59.

Olive, G. et al. (1973). Studies to compare retrieval using titles with that using index terms. Journal of Documentation 29: 169-91.

Oliver, L. et al. (1966). An Investigation of the Basic Processes Involved in the Manual Indexing of Scientific Documents. Bethesda, MD: General Electric Company, Information Systems Operation.

Orr, R. et al. (1965). Comparative indexing: terms supplied by biomedical authors and by document titles. American Documentation 16(4): 299–312.

Painter, D. (1988). Scanners for document storage and retrieval: the state of the art. In OIS International 1988: Proceedings of the Fifth Annual Conference on Optical Information Systems. London: Meckler Corporation, pp. 196-206.

Payne, N. (1988). Bar code indexing: automating document flow. Inform 2/4: 12-14.

Penn, C. (1962). How an indexer thinks in describing information, in framing search questions, and in conducting searches. Journal of Chemical Documentation 2: 220-24.

Pennix, G. (1984). Indexing concepts: an overview for records managers. ARMA Records Management Quarterly 18/2: 5-9.

Petersen, T. (1981). Computer-aided indexing in the arts: the case for a thesaurus of art terms. Art Libraries Journal 6: 6-11.

Pickford, A. (1971). Some problems of using an unstructured information retrieval language in a co-ordinate indexing system. Aslib Proceedings 23: 133-38.

Platau, G. (1960). Training of patent abstractors for Chemical Abstracts. American Documentation 11: 40-43.

Preschel, B. (1971). Improved communication between information centers through a new approach to indexer consistency. In Proceedings of the American Society for Information Science: 34th Annual Meeting. Westport, CT: Greenwood Press, ppp. 363-69.

_____. (1972). Indexer Consistency in Perception of Concepts and in Choice of Terminology. New York: Columbia University, School of Library Service.

Pritchard, J. (1989). Optical character recognition (OCR) and intelligent character recognition (ICR). Information Media and Technology 22/12: 21-24.

Rees, A. (1965). The Aslib-Cranfield test of the Western Reserve University indexing system for metallurgical literature: a review of the final report. American Documentation 16: 73-76.

Resnick, A. (1963). Educational requirements for indexers in a selective dissemination system. In Automation and Scientific Communication: Short Papers. Washington, DC: American Documentation Institute, pp. 163-64.

Robertson, S. (1978). Indexing theory and retrieval effectiveness. Drexel Library Quarterly 14: 40-56.

Rodgers, D. (1961). A Study of Intra-Indexer Consistency. Washington, DC: General Electric Company.

Rolling, L. (1970). Compilation of thesauri for use in computer systems. Information Storage and Retrieval 6: 341-50.

_____. (1981). Indexing consistency, quality, and efficiency. Information Processing and Management 17: 69-76.

Rostron, R. (1968). The construction of a thesaurus. Aslib Proceedings 20: 181-87.

Sanders, R. (1986). The company index: information retrieval thesauri for organizations and institutions. ARMA Records Management Quarterly 20/2: 3-14.

Scheffler, F. (1967). Indexer Performance Analysis and Operation of a Document Retrieval System. Dayton, OH: Dayton Research Institute.

_____. (1968). Student Indexer Training Program and the Improved Operation of a Document Retrieval System. Dayton, OH: Dayton Research Institute.

Scheinberg, I. (1988). Image/OCR data capture for high speed document processing: an update. In Electronic Imaging 88: International Electronic Imaging Exposition and Conference, vol. 2. Boston: Institute for Graphic Communication, pp. 892-94.

Schumacher, H. et al. (1973). The Use of Selected Portions of Technical Documents as Sources of Index Terms and Effect on Input Costs and Retrieval Effectiveness. Dayton, OH: University of Dayton Research Institute.

Schurmann, J. (1987). Status and development of optical character recognition. In Systems 87: Proceedings of the Symposium. Munich: Munchener Messe und Ausstellungsgesellschaft, pp. 97-113.

Seely, B. (1972). Indexing depth and retrieval effectiveness. Drexel Library Quarterly 8: 201-208.

Seetharama, S. (1976). Term-concept relationship in an information retrieval thesaurus. Library Science with a Slant to Documentation 13: 67-73.

Sharp, J. (1965). Some Fundamentals of Information Retrieval. New York: London House.

_____. (1971). Where do we go from here? Aslib Proceedings 23: 33-46.

_____. (1975). Natural language. Journal of Documentation 31: 191-95.

Shaw, T. and Rothman, H. (1968). An experiment in indexing by word-choosing. Journal of Documentation 24: 159-72.

Sievert, M. and Andrews, M. (1991). Indexing consistency in Information Science Abstracts. Journal of the American Society for Information Science 42: 1-6.

Sievert, M. and Boyce, B. (1983). Hedge trimming and the resurrection of the controlled vocabulary in online searching. Online Review 7: 489-94.

Slamecka, V. and Jacoby, J. (1963). Effect of Indexing Aids on the Reliability of Indexers. Bethesda, MD: Documentation Incorporated.

_____. (1965). The consistency of human indexing. In The Coming Age of Information Technology. Bethesda, MD: Documentation Incorporated, pp. 32-56.

Soergel, D. (1974). Indexing Languages and Thesauri: Construction and Maintenance. Los Angeles: Melville Publishing.

Sparck-Jones, K. (1973). Does indexing exhaustivity matter? Journal of the American Society for Information Science 24: 313-16.

Stevens, J. (1991). Combining bar coding and image processing for document processing. Chief Information Officer Journal 4/2: 23-31.

Svenonius, E. (1971). "The Effect of Indexing Specificity on Retrieval Performance." Ph.D. Dissertation. Chicago: University of Chicago.

_____. (1972). An experiment in index term frequency. Journal of the American Society for Information Science 23: 109-21.

_____. (1976). Natural language vs. controlled vocabulary. In Proceedings of the Fourth Canadian Conference on Information Science. Ottawa: Canadian Association for Information Science, pp. 141-50.

Svenonius, E. and Schmierer, H. (1977). Current issues in the subject control of information. Library Quarterly 47: 326-46.

Tell, B. (1969). Document representation and indexer consistency. In Proceedings of the American Society for Information Science: 32nd Annual Meeting. Westport, CT: Greenwood Publishing, pp. 285-92.

Terry, D. (1988). Scanners and image processing on a personal computer. In Electronic Imaging '88: International Electronic Imaging Exposition and Conference, vol. 1. Waltham, MA: Institute for Graphic Communication, pp. 539-40.

Thiel, T. et al. (1991). Document indexing for image-based optical information systems. Document Image Automation 11/2: 82-88.

Tinker, J. (1968). Imprecision in indexing. American Documentation 19: 322-30.

Townley, H. (1971). A look at natural language retrieval systems. Information Scientist 5: 3-15.

Travis, I. and Fidel, R. (1982). Subject analysis. In Annual Review of Information Science and Technology, vol. 17. White Plains, NY: Knowledge Industry Publications, pp. 123-57.

Ullmann, H. (1966). Indexing Techniques. Santa Monica, CA: System Development Corporation.

Vickery, B. (1955). Developments in subject indexing. Journal of Documentation 11: 1-11.

_____. (1958). Subject analysis for information retrieval. In Proceedings of the International Conference on Scientific Information. Washington, DC: National Academy of Sciences, pp. 855-65.

Wall, E. (1969). Vocabulary building and control techniques. American Documentation 20: 161-64.

_____. (1975). Symbiotic development of thesauri and information systems: a case history. Journal of the American Society for Information Science 26: 71-79.

Weinstein, S. (1966). Biological dictionary preparation, control, and maintenance. American Documentation 17: 190-98.

Westcott, D. (1992). New images from an old master. Inform 6/5: 36-40, 51.

White, H. and Griffith, B. (1987). Quality of indexing in online data bases. Information Processing and Management 23: 211-24.

Willetts, M. (1975). An investigation of the nature of the relation between terms in thesauri. Journal of Documentation 31: 158-84.

Williamson, N. (1984). Subject access in the online environment. Advances in Librarianship 13: 49-97.

Wolff-Terroine, M. et al. (1969). Use of a computer for compiling and holding a medical thesaurus. Methods of Information in Medicine 8: 34-40.

Young, E. (1987). Abstractor and indexer: careers in scientific and technical information. Science and Technology Libraries 7: 47-62.

Zunde, P. and Dexter, M. (1969). Factors affecting indexing performance. In Proceedings of the American Society for Information Science: 32nd Annual Meeting. Westport, CT: Greenwood Press, pp. 313-22.

Zunde, P. and Dexter, M. (1969a). Indexing consistency and quality. American Documentation 20: 259-67.

# Chapter Three
# Storage

An electronic document imaging system includes storage peripherals and recording media for digitized document images and the data bases that serve as indexes to them. Chapter One briefly noted the formidable storage requirements associated with electronic document imaging implementations. This chapter opens with a detailed explanation of those requirements. It delineates factors which influence page storage characteristics and examines the role of compression in document image storage. Subsequent sections describe the characteristics of particular optical and magnetic storage devices and media and discuss their suitability for image and data recording in electronic document imaging installations.

## Image Storage Requirements

While electronic document images offer a compact alternative to paper files, they occupy considerable amounts of computer storage space—far more, for example, than is required to store a given page as character-coded text. Storage requirements associated with specific applications depend on several factors, including the linear dimensions of documents being recorded, the scanning resolution and digitization mode employed, and the effectiveness of compression algorithms used to reduce the amount of information to be stored about each image. The following formula calculates the number of bytes required to store a single page of a given size digitized at a specified scanning resolution:

$$S = \frac{(H \times R \times B) \times (W \times R \times B)}{8} \times \frac{1}{C}$$

where:

S = the storage requirement per page in bytes;

H = the height of a typical subject document in inches or millimeters;

W = the width of a typical subject document in inches or millimeters;

R = the scanning resolution in, pixels per inch or millimeter, along the document's horizontal and vertical dimensions;

B = the number of bits utilized to encode each pixel; and

C = an image compression factor.

The calculation $((H \times R \times B) \times (W \times R \times B))$ yields the uncompressed page storage requirement in bits. The value of B is determined by the digitization mode. With binary-mode digitization of black-and-white documents, the most common scenario in electronic document imaging implementations, the value of B is one; other possible values are eight for grayscale scanning of photographs and twenty-four for color-mode scanning. The most common scanning resolutions, as previously discussed, are 200 and 300 pixels per inch, but lower or higher values are possible. Scanning resolution is usually, but not necessarily, identical for the horizontal and vertical dimensions of a page. The impact of increased scanning resolution on image storage requirements was briefly noted in Chapter Two. At 200 pixels per horizontal and vertical inch, each square inch of a page contains 40,000 pixels; at 300 pixels per horizontal and vertical inch, the number of pixels per square inch increases to 90,000. All other things being equal, the higher resolution image will require 2.25 times more storage space.

Storage requirements are similarly affected by page size. Larger documents require additional pixel coding and occupy more storage space at all scanning resolutions. All other things being equal, for example, a legal-size page will contain 27 percent more pixels than a legal-size page and will re-

**Table 3-1. Approximate Storage Requirement (Uncompressed) in Bytes for Documents of Various Sizes**

| Page Size (in inches) | Scanning Resolution | | |
| --- | --- | --- | --- |
| | 200 pixels per inch | 300 pixels per inch | 400 pixels per inch |
| 8.5 x 11 | 467,500 | 1,051,900 | 1,870,000 |
| 8.5 x 14 | 595,000 | 1,338,750 | 2,380,000 |
| 11 x 14 | 770,000 | 1,732,500 | 3,080,000 |
| 11 x 17 | 935,000 | 2,103,750 | 3,740,000 |
| 18 x 24 | 2,160,000 | 4,860,000 | 8,640,000 |
| 24 x 36 | 4,320,000 | 9,720,000 | 17,280,000 |
| 34 x 44 | 7,480,000 | 16,830,000 | 29,920,000 |

quire 27 percent more storage space. Space requirements for engineering drawings are significantly greater than those for office documents.

Applying the above formula to letter-size pages scanned in the binary mode at 200 pixels per horizontal and vertical inch, the calculation (11 x 200 x 1) x (8.5 x 200 x 1) yields an uncompressed storage requirement of 3.74 million bits per page. Division by eight converts the uncompressed page storage requirement to bytes, the most common measure of computer media capacity. In this example, the uncompressed page storage requirement is 467,500 bytes. That amount is then multiplied by the reciprocal of the compression factor, that is, a fraction with the anticipated compression as the denominator and the value one as the numerator.

*Image Compression*

Most electronic document imaging systems employ computer-based compression algorithms to reduce the amount of disk space required to store digitized document images, thereby conserving media capacity and minimizing the number of media required to store a given quantity of pages. Compression algorithms are applied before digitized document images are recorded on computer storage media. In some electronic document imaging implementations, compression is performed in hardware, that is, by a specially-designed circuit board installed in the computer to which a document scanner is attached. The circuit board incor-

porates a co-processor that compresses digitized images generated by the scanner. In most cases, the circuit board also includes decompression components that reconstruct images for display, printing, or other operations. Alternatively, image compression may be performed by software that operates on the computer to which the scanner is attached. Generally, software-based compression will prove slower than hardware-based approaches. The software-based approach is usually less expensive, however, since compression boards are not required.

Whether hardware- or software-based methodologies are utilized, the most widely encountered image compression algorithms employ run-length encoding methodologies (so-called because they produce coded messages which indicate the number of successively encountered pixels of a given tonality within a digitized image). Many typewritten and printed pages contain relatively long, uninterrupted stretches of light or dark areas. Margins are an obvious example; if a letter-size page with a 1-inch top margin is digitized in the binary mode at 200 pixels per horizontal and vertical inch, the first 340,000 pixels will be white and each will be encoded by a zero bit. Stored in uncompressed form, those 340,000 pixels would occupy 42,500 bytes. Instead of generating a string of bits representing the tonal values of successively encountered pixels, run-length encoding records the line positions of alternating tonal values—indicating, in effect, how many pixels of a given tonality occur in sequence. Rather than storing 340,000 zero bits associated with a 1-inch margin, the compression algorithm substitutes a much shorter code indicating that the digitized image begins with 340,000 white pixels in a row. The resulting reduction in storage requirements will vary with document characteristics. Pages with large amounts of contiguous light or dark space, such as typewritten pages with wide margins or other large blank areas, are well-suited to run-length encoding and will yield high compression factors. On the other hand, densely printed documents with more frequent light-to-dark transitions offer much less compression potential. Business forms with vertical lines can prove particularly troublesome.

Some electronic document imaging implementations utilize proprietary compression algorithms that yield dramatic reductions in storage requirements for digitized images. Increasingly, however, the image compression methodologies employed by electronic document imaging systems are based on standard algorithms. The two most widely encountered examples are the CCITT Group III and CCITT Group IV algorithms developed for facsimile transmission by the Consultative Committee on International Telephony and Telegraphy. The CCITT Group III algorithm employs the Modified Huffman (MH) compression technique which applies run-length encoding to a single horizontal line at a time. Described as a one-dimensional compression algorithm, it yields typical compression ratios of 10:1 for office documents and 15:1 for engineering drawings. The CCITT Group IV algorithm recognizes that black or white pixels on a given line are often surrounded by pixels of identical tonality on adjacent lines. It consequently employs the two-dimensional Modified Modified READ (MMR) technique which compresses digitized images both horizontally and vertically. It yields typical compression ratios of 15:1 for office documents and 20:1 for engineering drawings. Since most newer compression circuit boards and software packages support both Group III and Group IV compression, they are equally available to electronic document imaging system applications on an operator-selectable basis. Unless there is some product-specific reason to utilize Group III algorithms, Group IV is preferred for its higher compression ratios.

Applying the formula given above, Table 3-2 calculates the storage requirement per page, in bytes, for widely encountered sizes of office documents and engineering drawings digitized at scanning resolutions of 200, 300, and 400 pixels per horizontal and vertical inch. The calculations assume binary-mode digitization of black-and-white documents with CCITT Group III compression of 10:1 for A3-size and smaller pages. A compression factor of 15:1 is assumed for engineering drawings. Table 3-3 presents similar calculations for binary-mode digitization at various resolutions with CCITT Group IV algorithms. The calculations assume a compression factor of 15:1 for A3-size and smaller pages and 20:1 for engineering drawings. Both tables clearly indicate the previously discussed relationship between document size, scanning resolution, compression algorithms, and storage requirements. A letter-size page digitized at 400 pixels per inch with a compression factor of 10:1 requires four times as much storage space space as the same page digitized at 200 pixels per inch. Even with their higher compression potential, large engineering drawings require more storage space than smaller office records.

Repeating a point made above, it must be emphasized that the compression ratios employed in the foregoing examples are not guaranteed. The specific compression ratios attainable in a given application depend on the tonal characteristics of documents being scanned and may be higher or lower than those stated here. Pages with large amounts of contiguous light and dark space will yield higher compression ratios than densely printed documents with frequent light-to-dark transitions. Partial-page business memoranda, for example, may be compressed by a factor of 20:1 or higher, while densely printed journal articles, technical reports, or business forms may offer little compression potential. Although it is a relatively rare occurence, images of certain densely printed documents can actually require more storage space when compression algorithms are applied. *how?*

While CCITT Group III and Group IV algorithms currently dominate electronic document imaging implementations, other methodologies are being explored. One of the most widely publicized examples, the JPEG compression methodology developed by the Joint Photographic Experts Group, is

**Table 3-2.  Approximate Storage Requirements in Bytes for Pages of Various Sizes with CCITT Group III Compression**

| Page Size (in inches) | Scanning Resolution | | |
| --- | --- | --- | --- |
| | 200 pixels per inch | 300 pixels per inch | 400 pixels per inch |
| 8.5 x 11 | 46,750 | 105,200 | 187,000 |
| 8.5 x 14 | 59,500 | 133,900 | 238,000 |
| 11 x 14 | 77,000 | 173,250 | 308,000 |
| 11 x 17 | 93,500 | 210,400 | 374,000 |
| 18 x 24 | 216,000 | 486,000 | 864,000 |
| 24 x 36 | 432,000 | 972,000 | 1,728,000 |
| 34 x 44 | 748,000 | 1,683,000 | 2,992,000 |

intended for continuous-tone images generated by grayscale or color scanners. JPEG is actually an interrelated group of algorithms that supports various combinations of image quality and compression. The possibilities range from merely recognizable images that are compressed by as much as 160:1 to compressed images at 11:1 that are virtually indistinguishable from the original. Most JPEG implementations are based on "lossy" compression techniques; compression is achieved by omitting some information from the original image. In contrast, the CCITT Group III and Group IV algorithms are lossless compression techniques; compressed images produced by those algorithms that incorporate all information from the original.

*Image Enhancement*

As previously described, document scanners analyze the reflectivity characteristics of individual pixels. Each pixel is compared to a predetermined threshold value. In binary mode digitization, pixels that exceed the threshold value are considered black; the others are considered white. The threshold should be set low enough to detect light pencil marks, but high enough to exclude specks of dust and stained areas of documents. As a standard or optional feature, some electronic document imaging systems employ image enhancement algo-

rithms to adjust scanning thresholds, thereby improving the appearance of digitized document images prior to recording. Typical forms of image enhancement include the suppression of isolated, randomly occurring black spots that may result from inappropriately low threshold settings; image sharpening, which emphasizes edges and small image details; and adaptive thesholding, which automatically adjusts the scanning threshold to accommodate local variations in contrast within a page.

Forms removal is a potentially useful feature that combines image enhancement and compression capabilities. As its name suggests, forms removal is intended for standardized business forms. Forms removal software separates the static (preprinted) and dynamic (user-supplied) information within a business form. The static information is stored one time as an image of a blank business form, leaving only the dynamic information to be stored for each page. Because the static information is removed, the storage requirement per page is greatly reduced. As an additional advantage, forms removal software usually eliminates vertical lines that can interfere with the image compression algorithms described above. At retrieval time, the static image of the business form is superimposed on the dynamic information, thereby reconstructing the document for display, printing, or other purposes.

**Table 3-3. Approximate Storage Requirements in Bytes for Pages of Various Sizes with CCITT Group IV Compression**

| Page Size (in inches) | Scanning Resolution | | |
| --- | --- | --- | --- |
| | 200 pixels per inch | 300 pixels per inch | 400 pixels per inch |
| 8.5 x 11 | 31,200 | 70,150 | 124,700 |
| 8.5 x 14 | 39,700 | 89,250 | 158,700 |
| 11 x 14 | 51,350 | 115,500 | 205,350 |
| 11 x 17 | 62,350 | 140,250 | 249,350 |
| 18 x 24 | 144,000 | 324,000 | 576,000 |
| 24 x 36 | 288,000 | 648,000 | 1,152,000 |
| 34 x 44 | 498,700 | 1,122,000 | 1,994,700 |

## Optical Storage

Optical storage products use light—specifically, the light from lasers—to record and retrieve electronic document images and other computer-processable information by selectively altering the light reflectance characteristics of specially designed storage media. The alterations may take any of several physical forms, including light-scattering holes, bumps, or bubbles. The recorded information is read by a laser and pickup mechanism that senses variations in reflected light, much as magnetic read/write heads sense variations in the alignment of metallic particles within magnetic disks and tapes. The playback laser operates at lower power or a different wavelength than the laser used for recording.

As described in the preceding sections, digitized document images occupy many bytes of computer storage, even when compression algorithms are applied. The prominence of optical storage products in electronic document imaging installations is principally attributible to their high areal recording densities and correspondingly high capacities when compared to other computer storage technologies. While areal recording densities of magnetic storage media seldom exceed sixty million bits per square inch, those supported by optical media routinely exceed 200 million bits per square inch, and some products support recording

densities which are several times that amount. While the capacities of specific products vary considerably, optical storage technology can accommodate very large quantities of digitized document images.

Optical storage products include platter-shaped media (optical disks), coated ribbons of film (optical tape), and rectangular media (optical cards). Of these, optical disks are most widely encountered and best suited to electronic document imaging. Optical disk systems include recording/playback equipment (so-called optical disk drives) and recording/storage media (the optical disks themselves). With the exception of devices intended for audio and video applications, optical disk drives are computer peripheral devices; models are available for computers of all types and sizes. Optical disks and their associated drives are typically divided into two broad groups: read/write and read-only. Read/write optical disks, are the most widely utilized storage media in electronic document imaging installations. As removable media, they are purchased blank in the manner of floppy disks, although they are often pregrooved and may contain some prerecorded control signals. They can accept digitally coded information generated by various input peripherals, including document scanners, as well as document images and data transferred from magnetic disks, magnetic tapes, or other optical media.

Read-only optical disks, in contrast, are purchased with prerecorded contents. Such disks are, in effect, electronic publishing media. They are created by a mastering process, the individual copies being stamped or molded out of plastic. The copies, which are distributed to end-users, have no recordable properties and are read by devices that have no recording capabilities. As discussed later in this chapter, CD-ROM is the most important type of read-only optical disk for electronic document imaging applications.

Read/write optical disks and the drives that utilize them are commonly divided into write-once and rewritable varieties. Write-once optical disks are often described as WORM disks. The acronym variously stands for Write Once Read Many (times) or Write Once Read Mostly. Such disks are not erasable. The write-once designation is potentially misleading, however; WORM disks can be used for repeated recording as long as space remains available, but once information is recorded in a given sector of a write-once optical disk that area cannot be reused. Unlike erasable media, write-once optical disks can become irrevocably full. If previously recorded information is accidently or intentionally over written, it is obliterated rather than replaced. With rewritable optical disks, in contrast, the contents of previously recorded media segments can be erased and/or overwritten with new information. Like their magnetic counterparts, rewritable optical disks are reusable.

The following discussion outlines the most important characteristics of write-once and rewritable optical recording technologies and products, emphasizing factors that influence their suitability as storage media in electronic document imaging implementations. Later subsections will examine the potential of CD-ROM, optical cards, and optical tape for document imaging.

## WORM Technology

While they are often described as recent innovations, WORM products are hardly new. Write-once optical disk drives and media were introduced in the early 1980s and have been readily available for electronic document imaging and general-purpose computer storage since the middle of that decade. Characteristics of write-once optical recording technologies and materials are described, in varying levels of technical detail, in numerous monographs, journal articles, technical reports, and conference papers. Examples include Bracker (1987), Cornet (1983), Croucher and Hopper (1987), Emmelius et al. (1989), Freese et al. (1982), Gravesteijn and Van Der Veen (1984), Gravesteijn (1988, 1989), Harvey and Reinhardt (1990), Hecht (1987), Lee (1989), Nakane et al. (1985), Suh (1985), and Thomas (1987). Comprehensive bibliographies are provided by Saffady (1989, 1992).

At the time this chapter was written, five different technologies (ablative recording of tellurium thin films, dye-based recording, dual alloy recording, phase-change recording, and thermal bubble recording) were being used in write-once optical disk systems offered by various vendors. All five technologies utilize lasers to record information by irreversibly altering the reflectivity characteristics of a thermally-sensitive material coated on a platter-shaped aluminum, glass, or plastic substrate. The technologies differ in their specific recording processes, media attributes, and performance characteristics.

1. In the most extensively researched, widely implemented, and frequently cited approach to write-once optical recording, a highly focused laser beam irradiates a disk that is coated with a thin film of tellurium. The tellurium is usually covered with a protective layer and alloyed with other materials, such as selenium or lead, to enhance stability. During recording, the laser's energy is converted to heat which creates microscopic holes or pits in the thermally sensitive thin film. The pit formation process is termed ablation, and this type of write-once technology is often described as ablative recording. In most implementations, the microscopic pits represent the one bits in digitally-coded information; to represent the zero bits, spaces are left in areas where pits might otherwise have been formed. The pits and spaces are recorded serially in tracks that radiate outward from the center of an optical disk. The recorded data is read by a laser and an optical pickup mechanism that detects differences in the reflectivity characteristics of pits and spaces. To avoid accidental obliteration of information, the recording and playback

lasers typically operate at different wavelengths. Tellurium thin films and ablative recording techniques are employed in write-once optical disk systems manufactured by Fujitsu, Hitachi, Laser Magnetic Storage International, Literal Corporation, Mitsubishi, Toshiba, and other companies.

2. Dye-based optical recording materials (also described as dye-polymer, dye-in-polymer (DIP), and organic dye binder media) feature a transparent polymer layer which contains an infrared absorbing dye. This recording layer is coated on a plastic or glass substrate. In some cases, a reflective metal layer is deposited between the substrate and the recording material. Information is recorded by a laser which operates at the dye's absorption wavelength. The laser's energy is converted to heat, forming pits or bumps with detectable reflectivity characteristics. As with the tellurium thin films described above, the pits or bumps typically represent the one bits in digitally coded data, while the spaces represent the zero bits. Alternatively, a laser may induce the diffusion of a dye into an absorption layer, producing detectable differences in the reflectivity of diffused and pure dye areas. Dye-based recording is utilized in write-once optical disk drives manufactured by Eastman Kodak, Pioneer, and Ricoh. Ricoh's dye-based WORM products are sold in the United States by Maxtor.

3. Dual alloy optical media, sometimes described as bimetallic alloy media, consist of two metal alloys coated as thin films on a platter-shaped polycarbonate substrate. One of the alloys is composed of tellurium and bismuth, the other of selenium and antimony. The recording material is layered, the tellurium-bismuth alloy being surrounded by two selenium-antimony layers. All layers are covered by a protective seal; the media are consequently described as "direct seal" disks. To record the one bits in digitally coded information, a laser fuses the three alloy layers, creating a four-element alloy with reflectivity characteristics that are distinguishable from those of the unfused alloys. Unfused areas of a disk represent the zero bits in digitally coded information. At the time this chapter was written, dual alloy recording was em-

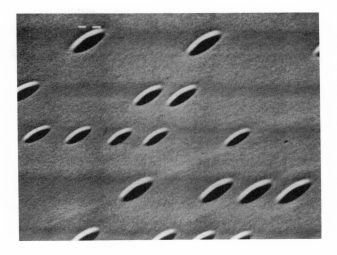

*Figure 3–1. In ablative recording, information is represented by microscopic pits and spaces. (Courtesy: Drexler Technology Corporation)*

ployed exclusively in write-once optical drives and media manufactured by Sony Corporation.

4. As with the ablative recording technology described above, phase-change optical disks consist of tellurium and/or selenium compounds which are typically alloyed with small quantities of other metals. Initially, these compounds exist in either a crystalline or an amorphous state. A laser records information by heating selected areas of the sensitive layer until its glass-transition temperature is reached. A crystalline-to-amorphous or amorphous-to-crystalline transition occurs in the heated areas, accompanied by a detectable change in their reflectivity characteristics. The amorphous areas typically represent the one bits in digitally-coded data, while the crystalline areas represent the zero bits. Phase-change technology is utilized in write-once optical media and drives manufactured by Eastman Kodak and Matsushita. The latter's products are widely marketed under the Panasonic brand name.

5. In the thermal bubble approach to write-once optical recording, heat from a laser evaporates a polymer layer to selectively form bubbles in a thin film composed of precious metals, such as gold or platinum. The bubbles open to form pits

*Figure 3–2. A read/write optical disk drive with recording medium and cartridge. (Courtesy: Pioneer)*

which reveal a reflective underlayer. Areas with the exposed underlayer typically represent the one bits in digitally coded data, while unexposed areas represent the zero bits. Thermal bubble technology is utilized in write-once optical disk drives manufactured by ATG Gigadisc.

*Rewritable Technology*

For purposes of this discussion, rewritability is defined as the ability to delete previously recorded information, typically by overwriting it with new information. Because they can accommodate changing data and text files, rewritable optical disk systems significantly broaden the scope of optical storage applications and offer an alternative, complement, or supplement to conventional magnetic recording technology in a variety of information processing operations. Rewritable optical disk drives and media have been commercially available since 1988. Various publications delineate the char-

acteristics of rewritable optical recording technologies and describe its progress toward commercialization at specific points in time. Examples include Bartholomeusz (1989), Bate (1987), Chen and Rubin (1989), Connell (1986), Crasemann and Hansen (1989), Freese (1988), Funkenbusch (1991), Gravesteijn (1989), Greidanus (1990), Greidanus and Zeper (1990), Hansen (1990), Kawabata and Yamamoto (1988), Kryder (1990), Mansuripur et al. (1985), Meikeljohn (1986), Ojima and Ohta (1988), Rubin and Chen (1989), Ryan (1990), Sponheimer (1990), and Urrows and Urrows (1990).

Measured by the number of available products and their market penetration, magneto-optical (MO) recording, sometimes termed thermo-magneto-optical (TMO) recordings, the dominant technology for rewritable optical storage. Magneto-optical disk systems are manufactured by many companies, including Canon, Hewlett-Packard, Hitachi, IBM, Laser Magnetic Storage International, Literal Corporation, Matsushita, Maxoptix,

Mitsubishi, Nakamichi, Pioneer, Ricoh, Sharp, Sony, Teac, and Toshiba. As its name suggests, magneto-optical recording is a hybrid technology; magneto-optical media store information magnetically, but the information is recorded and read by a laser and optical assembly. Magneto-optical disks are actually multilayered magnetic disks which employ vertical recording techniques instead of the horizontal (sometimes described as longitudinal) recording methodologies associated with conventional magnetic media. In vertical recording, magnetic domains are oriented perpendicular to a disk's surface; with longitudinal media, in contrast, the domains are oriented parallel to the recording surface. As its principal advantage, perpendicular recording permits much closer spacing of magnetic domains with a consequent increase in recording density.

With unrecorded magneto-optical media, all magnetic domains are initially oriented in a direction (north-pole down, for example) which represents the zero bits in digitally-coded information. The one bits are recorded by reversing the orientation of selected magnetic domains. To accomplish this, a highly focused laser beam heats a spot on the disk to its Curie temperature, the point at which the medium's magnetic orientation is lost. With most magneto-optical recording materials, the Curie temperature ranges between 150 and 200 degrees Celsius. When the required temperature is reached, an electromagnet generates a magnetic field which reorients the domains. The magnetic particles assume the desired orientation as the recording material cools. Data is erased by applying a less powerful laser beam which reverses the magnetization in recorded areas, returning them to the orientation which represents zero bits. Those areas can then be overwritten with new information in a subsequent disk rotation.

Retrieval of information recorded on magneto-optical media depends on a phenomenon known as the Kerr effect. A magnetic surface rotates the polarization of reflected light in either a clockwise or a counterclockwise direction, depending on the orientation of magnetic particles. When read by a laser and an optical pickup mechanism, light reflected from a spot on a magneto-optical disk's surface will be detected as either a one or a zero bit.

At the time this chapter was written, one other rewritable optical disk technology—phase-change recording—was commercially available. As described above, a non-rewritable variant of phase-change technology is utilized in write-once optical disk systems. Portions of an optical recording material are selectively converted from a crystalline to an amorphous state, or vice versa. The two states have detectable reflectivity differences which represent the one and zero bits in digitally coded information. With rewritable phase-change recording, the transition between amorphous and crystalline states is reversible, thus permitting the erasure and overwriting of previously recorded information. A highly focused laser beam heats small areas in a thin layer of crystalline or amorphous material to just above the melting point. Rapid cooling of the heated material transforms the affected areas from the crystalline form to an amorphous state. Because the crystalline form is more stable than the amorphous state, the recording material naturally tends to change back to it when reheated to just below its melting point.

Matsushita commercialized the first rewritable phase-change optical disk system in 1990. As its principal operational advantage over magneto-optical recording, phase-change technology supports direct overwriting, that is, phase-change drives can perform erasure and recording in a single pass. The current generation of magneto-optical disk drives requires separate passes for erasure and overwriting. In theory at least, this advantage should result in faster read/write rates for phase-change drives, but phase-change recording materials themselves have traditionally suffered from slow amorphous-to-crystalline transition times which can limit their practicality in applications where information must be recorded and erased quickly.

*Drives and Media*

Available write-once optical disk drives and media are subdivided by size into three groups: 14 inches, 12 inches, and 5.25 inches. The measurements are based on the diameters of the optical disk platters which the WORM cartridges contain. The 8-inch WORM cartridges were briefly available dur-

**Table 3-4. Approximate A4-page Image Capacities of Selected Optical Disk Cartridges at Various Scanning Resolutions with Group III Compression**

| Disk Size (in inches) | Disk Capacity | Scanning Resolution | | |
| --- | --- | --- | --- | --- |
| | | 200 pixels per inch | 300 pixels per inch | 400 pixels per inch |
| 3.5 | 128 MB | 2,750 | 1,200 | 700 |
| 5.25 | 600 MB | 12,800 | 5,700 | 3,200 |
| 5.25 | 650 MB | 13,900 | 6,200 | 3,500 |
| 5.25 | 800 MB | 17,100 | 7,600 | 4,300 |
| 5.25 | 940 MB | 20,100 | 8,900 | 5,000 |
| 5.25 | 1.2 GB | 25,700 | 11,400 | 6,400 |
| 12 | 2 GB | 42,800 | 19,000 | 10,700 |
| 12 | 2.6 GB | 55,600 | 24,700 | 13,900 |
| 12 | 5 GB | 107,000 | 47,500 | 26,700 |
| 12 | 6.6 GB | 141,200 | 62,700 | 35,300 |
| 12 | 7 GB | 149,700 | 66,500 | 37,400 |
| 12 | 9 GB | 192,500 | 85,500 | 48,100 |
| 14 | 10.2 GB | 218,200 | 100,000 | 54,500 |

ing the 1980s and were employed in several document imaging systems marketed in Japan, but they attracted very little attention elsewhere. Rewritable optical disks are available in 5.25-inch and 3.5-inch sizes. The latter are single-sided media.

Data and document image storage capacities of representative products are summarized in the accompanying tables. Some of the listed devices are marketed under different model names by value-added resellers and systems integrators; as with many peripheral devices, optical disk drive manufacturers typically sell their products to OEM clients who repackage them with interface kits, cables, software, and other components appropriate to specific computer configurations. With the exception of 3.5-inch rewritable drives, the indicated recording capacities are based on double-sided media. As previously noted, optical disks are removable media that are encapsulated in protective plastic cartridges to facilitate loading and other handling. While most optical recording media are double-sided, most optical disk drives are single-headed; a given cartridge must be ejected from its drive, turned over, and reinserted to read from or record onto its opposite side. In such situations,

online availability is one-half the indicated cartridge capacity. Image storage calculations assume binary-mode scanning at 200 pixels per horizontal and vertical inch with Group IV compression. Different image capacities will be obtained with other combinations of scanning modes, resolutions, and compression algorithms.

All other things being equal, media capacity varies directly with disk diameter; with their larger surface areas, 12- and 14-inch optical disks can store more information than smaller media. Given their formidable capacities, 14-inch WORM drives and media are well suited to very high-volume, minicomputer- and mainframe-based electronic document imaging installations. Double-sided capacities of 14-inch WORM cartridges are 6.8 or 10.2 gigabytes, depending on the model selected. At the time this chapter was written, Eastman Kodak was the only manufacturer of 14-inch write-once optical disk drives. The 14-inch WORM cartridges utilized by Kodak drives conform to standards for such media published by the International Standardization Organization (ISO).

The standardization of optical disk products is a much discussed and widely misunderstood

**Table 3-5. Approximate A4-page Image Capacities of Selected Optical Disk Cartridges at Various Scanning Resolutions with Group IV Compression**

| Disk Size (in inches) | Disk Capacity | Scanning Resolution | | |
| --- | --- | --- | --- | --- |
| | | 200 pixels per inch | 300 pixels per inch | 400 pixels per inch |
| 3.5 | 128 MB | 4,100 | 1,800 | 1,000 |
| 5.25 | 600 MB | 19,200 | 8,600 | 4,800 |
| 5.25 | 650 MB | 20,800 | 9,300 | 5,200 |
| 5.25 | 800 MB | 25,600 | 11,400 | 6,400 |
| 5.25 | 940 MB | 30,100 | 13,400 | 7,500 |
| 5.25 | 1.2 GB | 38,500 | 17,100 | 9,600 |
| 12 | 2 GB | 64,100 | 28,500 | 16,000 |
| 12 | 2.6 GB | 83,300 | 37,100 | 20,900 |
| 12 | 5 GB | 160,300 | 71,300 | 40,100 |
| 12 | 6.6 GB | 211,500 | 94,100 | 52,900 |
| 12 | 7 GB | 224,400 | 99,800 | 56,100 |
| 12 | 9 GB | 288,500 | 128,300 | 72,200 |
| 14 | 10.2 GB | 326,900 | 145,400 | 81,200 |

topic. As used in this context, standards are published specifications for the design, production, and use of particular products, including optical recording media, disk drives, and related hardware and software components. The standardization of optical storage products presumably benefits both manufacturers and users by shortening development cycles, reducing manufacturing costs, and promoting the compatibility and interchangeability of equipment and media. Of particular significance for electronic document imaging installations, standardization encourages competitive purchasing through the availability of alternative procurement sources. It facilitates the selection and integration of products appropriate to specific applications, simplifies implementation and training, and generally enhances customers' confidence in and acceptance of optical storage and electronic document imaging technologies.

As with other information processing products, the International Standardization Organization (ISO) and the American National Standards Institute (ANSI) are the principal organizations responsible for the development of standards for write-once and rewritable optical storage equip-

ment and media. Their work is accomplished through technical committees and subcommittees which prepare draft standards for review, approval, and eventual publication. Standardization activities to date have emphasized the interchange of optical recording media. Such standards are designed to enable the optical disk drives of one manufacturer to be used with conforming media produced by other manufacturers. Since only one vendor currently manufactures 14-inch WORM drives, proposed standards for 14-inch write-once optical disk cartridges generated no controversy.

The 12-inch WORM drives and media, the first read/write optical storage products to be successfully commercialized, have been utilized in electronic document imaging installations of all types and sizes. Available from various manufacturers, their substantial storage capacities make them an excellent choice for high-volume document imaging applications. Double-sided capacities of 12-inch WORM cartridges have expanded steadily and significantly since the early 1980s. Available capacities range from 2 gigabytes to more than 9 gigabytes, with most newer products offering at least 5 gigabytes. All 12-inch write-once optical disk systems employ proprietary equipment and media. Standards for 12-inch WORM cartridges are being developed, but they are not expected to impact product availability before the mid-1990s.

The 5.25-inch optical disk drives and cartridges—the only size that is available in both write-once and rewritable varieties—are obviously suitable for microcomputer-based electronic document imaging installations where the 5.25-inch form factor is widely employed by rigid and flexible magnetic disk drives. As an important advantage for entry-level electronic document imaging systems, 5.25-inch optical disk drives are much less expensive than their larger counterparts; equipment cost is an important consideration when a second drive must be purchased for media backup or other purposes. As potentially significant disadvantages, however, 5.25-inch media are more expensive on a cost-per-byte basis than 12- and 14-inch optical disks, and their recording capacities are much lower.

With 5.25-inch WORM drives, recording capacities range from 230 megabytes to 1.28 gigabytes per double-sided cartridge. An ISO standard for 5.25-inch write-once optical disk cartridges specifies media with double-sided capacities of 600 or 650 megabytes, depending on the recording format selected. Many electronic document imaging systems, however, utilize higher-capacity 5.25-inch WORM cartridges of proprietary design; models with 800 megabytes, 940 megabytes, and 1.28 gigabytes have proven popular. As a source of potential confusion, the ISO standard recognizes two different recording formats: continuous composite servo (CCS), sometimes described as Format A, and sampled servo (SS), also known as Format B. The two formats employ incompatible methods of handling the control or servo signals which permit accurate tracking and focus of a drive's optical head during recording and playback. Each method requires its own media; continuous servo and sampled servo cartridges are not interchangeable, even though both are advertised as ISO-compliant. When evaluating standard 5.25-inch WORM drives, prospective purchasers must consequently determine the particular format supported by a given product.

Rewritable optical disk drives and media for computer installations are available in two sizes: 3.5 inches and 5.25 inches. Rewritable optical disks are available in other sizes, but they are not intended for electronic document imaging; 12- and 14-inch magneto-optical disks and drives have been developed for video applications, while Sony offers a 2-inch magneto-optical disk (the so-called MiniDisc) for audio recording. With 5.25-inch rewritable drives, storage capacities range from 512 megabytes to one gigabyte per double-sided cartridge. Magneto-optical media employed by the most widely utilized rewritable drives conform to the ISO standard for 5.25-inch rewritable optical disk cartridges. Their double-sided recording capacities are 600 megabytes for disks formatted with 512 bytes per sector and 650 megabytes for disks formatted with 1,024 bytes per sector. Unrecorded media are purchased in versions which support one or the other format. Avoiding the multi-format confusion associated with standards for 5.25-inch WORM disks, ISO-compliant rewritable media employ the continuous composite servo (CCS) format only. As with the 5.25-inch WORM drives discussed above, some non-standard rewritable drives support higher media capacities than their ISO-compliant counterparts.

The 3.5-inch rewritable systems are the first optical storage products to post-date their associated ISO standards for interchangeability of optical disk cartridges. All available products are consequently affected by and conform to the ISO standard, which specifies a nominal recording capacity of 130 megabytes per single-sided magneto-optical disk cartridge. The actual capacity is 128 megabytes for media formatted with 512 bytes per sector and 132 megabytes for media formatted with 1,024 bytes per sector. As an obvious disadvantage for electronic document imaging, these relatively low capacities limit the number of pages that can be recorded on a given cartridge, with a resulting increase in the number of cartridges required in a given application.

Low storage capacity relative to write-once media likewise limits the potential of 5.25-inch rewritable optical disks for high-volume imaging applications. The capacities of rewritable media are necessarily constrained by platter size; as noted above, 12- and 14-inch rewritable optical disks are

**Table 3-6. Comparison of Write-Once and Rewritable Optical Disks**

|  | Write-Once | Rewritable |
|---|---|---|
| Year introduced in North America | 1983 | 1988 |
| Number of recording technologies in use | 5 | 2 |
| Media sizes (disk diameter in inches) | 14, 12, 5.25 | 5.25, 3.5 |
| Media capacities (range for all sizes)* | 230MB–10.2GB | 128MB–1GB |
| Media capacities (range for 5.25-inch disks) | 230MB–1.28GB | 512MB–1GB |
| Media standardization (sizes affected, in inches) | 14, 5.25 | 5.25, 3.5 |

* Single-sided for 3.5-inch rewritables, double-sided for others; includes some discontinued products

not available for document imaging purposes. The added functionality of erasability offers unquestioned advantages for general data processing applications but does not favorably offset the capacity limitations for document imaging. Erasability is seldom expected or required, and may not be desired in electronic document imaging installations. Many electronic document imaging systems are installed as replacements for micrographics products that do not employ erasable media. In document management applications, the nonerasable character of write-once optical disks is considered an advantage that facilitates the legal authentication of document images as unaltered copies of the paper records from which they were produced.

As previously discussed, five write-once and two rewritable recording technologies are in current use. Optical disk drives require media appropriate to the technology employed by a given product. WORM drives require write-once media, while rewritable drives employ erasable media. A special group of rewritable drives, however, can operate in either the rewritable or write-once mode. Designed for 5.25-inch recording media, the only size that is available in both write-once and rewritable varieties, such devices are termed multifunctional optical disk drives. Most combine a specific write-once recording technology with a specific rewritable recording technology (ablative recording of tellurium thin films with magneto-

optical technology, for example). The drive detects the type of optical disk cartridge inserted into it and automatically activates the write-once or rewritable recording mode. In the write-once mode, the multifunctional drive's command set does not support file deletions, media reformatting, or other destructive operations.

Taking a completely different approach, Hewlett-Packard offers a multifunctional optical disk drive which employs magneto-optical media for both write-once and rewritable recording, although different disks are required for each operating mode. Write-once and rewritable media are identified by factory-inscribed codes which are detected by the multifunctional drive when a given optical disk cartridge is loaded. The drive automatically invokes the recording mode appropriate to the loaded cartridge. As noted above, the multifunctional drive's write-once command set does not support deletion or overwriting. Accidental erasure is consequently impossible. Additional coding prevents recording in data blocks which have already been utilized. Write-once and rewritable media are also color-coded and labelled for visual identification.

Whether write-once, rewritable, or multifunctional optical disk drives are employed, document imaging applications with heavy reference activity can require frequent interchanges of optical disk cartridges in order to bring desired data online. In the simplest optical storage equipment configurations, such interchanges are performed manually; specific cartridges are removed from drives and replaced with different ones as required. When not in use, optical disk cartridges are maintained offline on shelves, on storage racks, or in cabinets in the manner of magnetic tapes and floppy disks.

Where warranted by the volume of reference activity, multi-drive equipment configurations can minimize cartridge handling. Most WORM and rewritable drives are equipped with a Small Computer Systems Interface (SCSI) that can support up to eight peripheral devices. Depending on the storage capacity of the optical media employed, multi-drive configurations can provide convenient online access to dozens of gigabytes of data, albeit at the relatively high cost of purchasing two or more optical disk drives. Available in rack-mounted configurations, multiple optical disk drives may be intermixed with hard disk drives, magnetic tape units, and other storage devices for use in file server installations. Alternatively, several optical storage equipment manufacturers offer preconfigured models with twin drives housed in a single chassis.

Multi-drive configurations are particularly useful, and may be required, to produce copies of optical disk cartridges for backup or other purposes, such as distribution to multiple locations. The need for backup copies is frequently overlooked in electronic document imaging installations, and some systems have been implemented without appropriate backup capabilities. To make their products appear more affordable, vendors may omit the second optical disk drive from their proposals. Faced with problematic cost justifications, customers often ignore or accept the omission, but the resulting economy is a false one. Electronic document images recorded on optical disk cartridges may be damaged by hardware malfunctions, software failures, natural or human-induced disasters, environmental contaminants, careless media handling, or other events. Properly implemented backup procedures will facilitate restoration of system operations should such damage occur. Without backup copies, system recovery may require rescanning of source documents, assuming that they were retained. In some cases, recovery of document images may be impossible.

Where the equipment configuration includes dual optical disk drives, backup procedures can be implemented in several ways. Some electronic document imaging systems permit the simultaneous recording of digitized images onto two optical disk cartridges. In most cases, simultaneous recording is the most convenient and effective backup methodology. It is usually performed quickly and transparently. Alternatively, backup operations can be implemented in the batch mode with all or part of the contents of a given optical disk cartridge being copied onto a second cartridge at predetermined intervals. Application designers should be aware that, given the high capacity of optical disk cartridges, batch mode replication of complete disks can require several hours to complete. As a further disadvantage, batch copying of document images from one cartridge to another leaves an application vulnerable to the loss of document images captured in the interval between copying operations.

### Autochangers

Broadly defined, an optical disk autochanger is a mass storage peripheral which provides unattended access to electronic document images or other information recorded on multiple optical disk cartridges. The product group encompasses devices of varying complexity and capacity. Operating on instructions received from a host computer, the most sophisticated examples—variously described as an optical disk jukebox or an optical disk library—feature a robotic picking mechanism that extracts a designated optical disk cartridge from a stack, rack, or bin and mounts it into an optical disk drive. The picker is activated by a microprocessor-based controller. It also removes previously mounted cartridges and returns them to their storage locations. Employing a simpler design, several desktop autochangers accept multiple optical disk cartridges loaded into a specially designed magazine that is inserted into an optical disk drives. As with jukebox-type devices, a host computer instructs the autochanger to select and mount the cartridge required for a particular retrieval operation. Compared to jukeboxes, such magazine-type autochangers store fewer media and less storage capacity. They are less expensive, however, and—

because optical disk cartridges travel a relatively short distance—they offer fast interchange times.

The first optical disk autochangers were custom-engineered for specific installations. Off-the-shelf models were introduced in the mid-1980s; product variety and availability have increased

steadily since that time. Once considered exotic peripheral devices, optical disk autochangers are now commonplace in electronic document imaging installations. An autochanger is virtually required in network implementations where multiple workstations must access document images re-

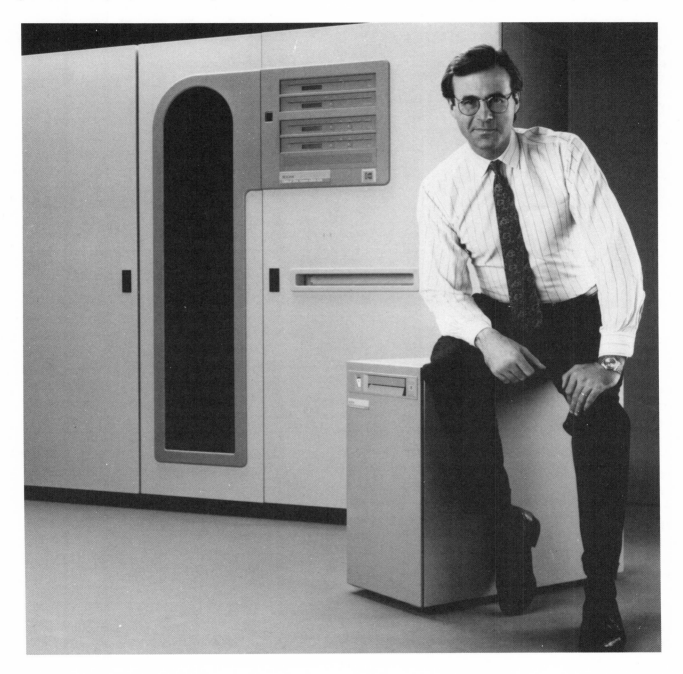

*Figure 3–3. Optical disk jukeboxes for 5.25-inch media (foreground) and 14-inch media. (Courtesy: Eastman Kodak)*

*Figure 3–4. A magazine-type optical disk autochanger. (Courtesy: Laser Magnetic Storage International)*

corded on multiple optical disk cartridges. In the absence of an autochanger, an operator must be constantly available to mount cartridges when requested by individual workstations.

Autochangers have been developed for write-once and rewritable optical disk cartridges of all types and sizes. The broadest selection exists for 5.25- and 12-inch cartridges. Available models range from limited-capacity desktop units to large-scale mass storage systems that provide unattended access to more than one terabyte of information. Autochanger capacity depends on two factors: the number of optical disk cartridges which a given unit can contain and the recording capacity of each cartridge. As might be expected, autochangers for 12- and 14-inch media offer higher storage capacities than those intended for smaller media.

While they operate as online peripheral devices, optical disk autochangers are best described as providing "nearline" access to stored information, since electronic document images or data recorded on a specific optical disk cartridge is not brought online until the cartridge is requested and mounted. Access times are consequently measured in seconds rather than the milliseconds associated with true online access. Interchange times for optical disk cartridges range from six to twenty seconds, with newer models being generally faster than older ones. Some jukebox-type autochangers also include an import/export slot for the manual addition and removal of cartridges.

An autochanger must obviously incorporate an optical disk drive appropriate to the cartridges it contains. Depending on the model, an autochanger may be equipped with a write-once optical disk drive, a rewritable optical disk drive, or a multi-functional optical disk drive. To improve cartridge interchange times, some jukebox-type autochangers are configured with two optical disk drives as standard equipment, thereby allowing a previously mounted cartridge to be removed from one drive while a specified cartridge is being inserted into the other. In other cases, a given autochanger can be optionally configured with multiple drives. Depending on the model, two to five drives may be supported. Because they occupy space that would otherwise be utilized for optical disk cartridges, additional drives invariably reduce an autochanger's storage capacity. As an interesting variation, some autochangers can be equipped with both write-once and rewritable optical disk cartridges. Such devices, which are sometimes describes as multifunctional jukeboxes, must contain one or more multifunctional optical disk drives or a combination of WORM and rewritable drives. In the latter case, the autochanger determines the type of optical disk cartridge required for a particular retrieval operation and inserts it in the appropriate drive.

*CD-ROM*

As briefly noted earlier in this chapter, optical disks are available in read/write and read-only varieties. The latter include videodiscs and compact discs. As their name indicates, the contents of read-only optical disks can be read (that is, retrieved) but it cannot be modified, added to, or deleted. Read-only optical disks are essentially electronic publishing media. Lacking recordable properties, they contain prerecorded information produced by a mastering process; the information must be sent to a factory where it is incorporated into a specially prepared mold or matrix that is used to produce multiple copies for distribution or sale. The complete production sequence involves a complex combination of information formatting, mastering, replication, packaging, and distribution, each of which requires special equipment or system design expertise. These operations are described for various types of read-only optical disks by Andrews (1991), Armstrong (1987), Belani (1991), Isailovic (1985), Marsh (1982), Pahwa and Rudd (1991), Reynolds and Halliday (1987), Rodgers (1990), Thiel et al. (1990), Troeltzsch (1984), and Van Rijsewijk et al. (1982), among many others.

With their high capacities and direct recording capabilities, read/write optical disks are the most widely utilized storage media in electronic document imaging implementations. Read-only optical media may prove useful, however, in applications where copies of a document collection must be distributed to multiple sites and where the recipients will not add new images to the collection. Among read-only optical media, Compact Disc-Read Only Memory (CD-ROM) offers substantial capacity and can store any computer-processible information, including digitized document images. Since the mid-1980s, information specialists have emphasized CD-ROM's advantages as a storage medium for character-coded data and text; it is widely utilized for data base publishing, for example. Recent discussions of multimedia applications, however, have stimulated an interest in CD-ROM for storage of computer-generated graphic images. Digitized page images generated by document scanners are a variety of such computer-generated graphic images.

Any discussion of CD-ROM must begin with definitions that distinguish it from other information storage products. The phrase "compact disc" denotes a group of optical storage formats and products that are based on technology developed jointly by Sony and Philips during the 1970s and 1980s. As a trade name, compact disc is spelled with a "c" rather than the "k" that is used to denote the read/write optical disks discussed above. Introduced in 1980, the most widely encountered type of compact disc is a rigid plastic platter which measures 12 centimeters (approximately 4.75 inches) in diameter and is 1.2 millimeters thick. A 9-cm (approximately 3.5-inch) version was introduced in 1987. While the term compact disc is sometimes loosely applied to 3.5- and 5.25-inch read/write optical disks which are compact in size, such usage is improper. Compact disc is a precisely defined product designation for specific information storage media; 3.5- and 5.25-inch write-once and rewritable optical media do not conform to Sony/Philips specifications for physical characteristics and recording formats of compact discs.

Compact discs feature a reflective metal layer covered with a protective coating. Digitally-coded information is recorded as a series of microscopic pits and adjoining spaces arranged in spiralling tracks. The various compact disc formats are typically categorized by the type of information they contain. The possibilities include audio and video signals, graphics, and computer-processible data and text. The technology's earliest and most widely publicized implementation—properly termed, Compact Disc-Digital Audio (CD-DA) but popularly and simply described as a "CD"—offers a sonically superior alternative to conventional long-playing phonograph records and prerecorded magnetic tape cassettes in consumer audio applications. As originally conceived, the CD-DA standard provided some storage space for computer-processible, character-coded information to identify the individual musical selections on a given compact disc, although such character-coded data is used sparingly as an adjunct to the audio signals which occupy the majority of disc space. CD-ROM, the subject of this discussion, is an implementation of compact disc technology designed specifically for computer-processible information. Like their CD-DA counterparts, CD-ROM discs typically measure 4.75 inches in diameter, although 3.5-inch versions are also available. Regardless of size, CD-ROM discs feature a reflective metal layer covered with a protective coating. Their rugged polycarbonate base material is well suited to a wide range of use environments and permits relatively casual handling, although scratches can render a given disc unusable.

A CD-ROM disc is a single-sided computer storage medium. In the 4.75-inch size, its nominal capacity is 540 megabytes. Several companies have demonstrated CD-ROM recording formats that can double or quadruple a disc's capacity, but such innovations have not been incorporated into commercially available products. The 3.5-inch CD-ROMs can store approximately 180 megabytes of computer-processible data. The 3.5-inch CD-ROMs are utilized in Sony's Data DiscMan, a portable electronic reference book system. Several other vendors have proposed 3.5-inch CD-ROM drives for notebook computer configurations.

As with read/write optical disks, the image storage capacities of CD-ROM media depend on various factors, including the sizes of documents to be recorded, the scanning resolution employed, and the image compression algorithms utilized. A 4.75-inch CD-ROM can store approximately 11,550 letter-size pages scanned at 200 pixels per horizontal and vertical inch, assuming the use of CCITT Group III compression algorithms with an average compression ratio of 10:1. When CCITT Group IV compression algorithms—which provide a typical compression ratio of 15:1—are utilized, the CD-ROM's capacity increases to 17,325 letter-size pages per 4.75 inch disc at the same scanning resolution. If the scanning resolution is increased to 300 pixels per horizontal and vertical inch, a 4.75-inch CD-ROM's capacity falls to 5,130 letter-size pages with Group III compression and 7,700 letter-size pages with Group IV compression. As page sizes increase, the number of pixels to be stored rises at all scanning resolutions and compression ratios, and the page capacity of a CD-ROM declines. A 4.75-inch CD-ROM, for example, can store just 1,250 D-size (24-by 36-inch) engineering drawings scanned at 200 pixels per inch and less than half that number when the scanning resolution is increased to 300 pixels per horizontal and vertical inch.

A CD-ROM disc offers less storage capacity than the majority of double-sided read/write optical disk cartridges described earlier in this chapter. The most widely encountered 5.25-inch write-once and rewritable optical disks offer double-sided capacities that range from 600 megabytes to 1.28 gigabytes. With such media, however, only half of the double-sided capacity is actually online at a given time; 5.25-inch write-once and rewritable drives are single-headed devices which require that an optical disk cartridge be ejected, turned over, and remounted to access information recorded on its opposite side. When online availability is considered, the storage capacity of a 4.75-inch CD-ROM equals or exceeds most 5.25-inch read/write optical disk products. By any measure, however, CD-ROM storage capacity is lower than capacities offered by 12- and 14-inch WORM disks; such media can store up to 10.2 gigabytes per double-sided cartridge. With their smaller surface areas, 3.5-inch CD-ROMs offer one-third the image storage capacities of their 4.75-inch counterparts. Storage capacities of 3.5-inch CD-ROMs exceed those of 3.5-inch rewritable optical disk cartridges which, like CD-ROM, are single-sided media.

The relatively low cost and widespread availability of CD-ROM drives (variously described as CD-ROM players or CD-ROM readers) are potential advantages for electronic document imaging

*Figure 3–5. A CD-ROM drive. (Courtesy: Hewlett-Packard)*

applications. Like their read/write counterparts, CD-ROM drives are computer peripheral devices. They are offered by numerous vendors in internal, external, and portable configurations. Performance characteristics have improved and prices have declined steadily since the mid-1980s. Some models cost less than half as much as the least expensive read/write optical disk drives. As an additional advantage, increased acceptance of CD-ROM standards has promoted the interoperability of equipment and recorded media. The physical characteristics of CD-ROM media are specified in a Sony/Philips document that is popularly described as the "Yellow Book". It standardizes CD-ROM's external dimensions, prescribes its track and sector organization, and defines the recording modes that determine the allocation of bytes for user data, error correction, and control information. Logical file formats for CD-ROM media are specified by the High Sierra Group (HSG) specifi-

cation and its successor the ISO 9660 standard. Those formats specify the characteristics of volume tables of contents and directories to be recorded on CD-ROMs. HSG- and ISO-compliant CD-ROM media are intended for drives equipped with Microsoft Extensions, device-driver software that provides an interface between a CD-ROM drive and the MS-DOS operating system.

Limited availability of high-capacity autochangers is a potential impediment to the use of CD-ROM in electronic document imaging applications. While CD-ROM jukeboxes have been developed for specific installations, they are not as routinely available as jukeboxes for read/write optical disks. Where unattended access to information recorded on multiple CD-ROMs is required, however, several vendors offer specially designed file servers equipped with multiple CD-ROM drives. Some products can be configured with several dozen drives. Where documents are scanned at

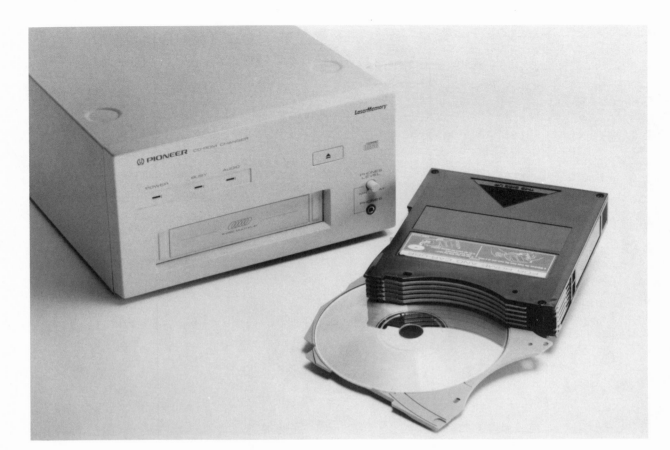

*Figure 3–6. A CD-ROM minichanger with six-disc cartridge. (Courtesy: Pioneer)*

200 pixels per inch with Group IV compression, they provide rapid online access to almost half a million letter-size pages—the equivalent of approximately forty vertical-style, four-drawer file cabinets. For lower-volume applications, magazine-type autochangers can be loaded with interchangeable cartridges, each containing six CD-ROMs. A single cartridge provides unattended access to approximately 3.2 gigabytes of information—sufficient to store more than 103,000 letter-size page images scanned at 200 pixels per inch with Group IV compression. Up to seven autochangers can be attached to a single controller for a total nearline capacity of 22.4 gigabytes.

Equipment characteristics aside, CD-ROM's principal limitation for electronic document imaging implementations derives from its status as a prerecorded medium produced by mastering processes rather than direct recording. The CD-ROM production cycle—from submission of appropri-

ately formatted data to a compact disc factory through receipt of the specified number of disc copies by the customer—can require several weeks to complete, although some compact disc manufacturers offer five-day, three-day, and overnight turnaround times at premium prices. As might be expected of a publishing medium, CD-ROM rates favor document imaging applications which require multiple copies of a document collection for distribution or other purposes. The cost to prepare and produce a CD-ROM master is relatively high; individual copies, however, are inexpensive. Actual mastering and replication rates vary with the amount of data to be recorded and the number of copies required. Some production facilities quote a single price for each copy, including a pro-rated portion of mastering charges; others cite separate prices for mastering and replication.

While CD-ROM is usually categorized as a read-only optical publishing medium, recordable compact disc systems broaden the range of applications which CD-ROM technology can successfully address. Introduced in the late 1980s, such systems support direct recording of computer-processible information, including digitized document images, onto write-once optical media. Recording is performed by a computer peripheral device which includes two components: a data encoder that organizes information into the CD-ROM format and a read/write optical disk drive in the CD-ROM form factor. When write-once optical media are utilized, the recordable CD-ROM format is variously described as CD-WO or CD-WORM. The CD-Recordable (CD-R) designation recognizes the future potential of rewritable media for compact disc recording; rewritable CD-ROM systems, while demonstrated in prototype, were not commercially available at the time this chapter was written.

Recordable technology permits the use of CD-ROM in applications where rapid job turnaround is essential and/or a limited number of required copies does not justify the cost of mastering. They can also be used to produce test media for jobs that will eventually be mastered. Recordable CD-ROM discs conform to the ISO 9660 standard and can be read by CD-ROM drives intended for read-only media. Media produced by recordable CD-ROM systems should not be confused with 5.25-inch WORM or rewritable optical disks. As previously noted, such media are sometimes loosely described as "compact", but they are somewhat larger than true compact discs, do not utilize the CD-ROM recording format, and cannot be read by CD-ROM drives.

*Optical Cards and Tape.*

As noted earlier in this chapter, optical storage products can be packaged as rectangular media (optical cards) and ribbon-shaped media (optical tape). While not as widely encountered as optical disks, optical cards (sometimes termed optical memory cards or optical digital data cards) have been available since the early 1980s. The best known and most widely demonstrated example is the LaserCard developed by Drexler Technology Corporation. It measures approximately 2.1 inches high by 3.4 inches wide by .03 inches thick—the size of a credit card—and employs a proprietary,

*Figure 3–7. An optical card (Courtesy: Drexler Technology Corporation)*

patented write-once optical recording material called Drexon. In its most commonly encountered configuration, a Drexon strip measuring 35 millimeters wide by 75 millimeters long is coated on one side of an optical card. Its storage capacity is 2.86 megabytes.

Optical cards can contain any computer-processible information that might be recorded on other optical or magnetic media. The cards are recorded and read by a laser-based computer peripheral device called an optical card reader/writer or, simply, an optical card drive. Despite an initially enthusiastic reception by computer industry observers, the optical card's progress toward widespread commercial availability has been disappointly slow, partly because reader/writers have not been readily available. Optical cards have been demonstrated in a variety of information management applications, including medical recordkeeping, electronic publishing, software distribution, maintenance logs, identification systems, and financial transactions. While their use as microfiche replacements has been discussed, the relatively low capacity of optical cards limits their potential for electronic document imaging. An optical card can store approximately sixty letter-size pages digitized at 200 pixels per horizontal and vertical inch with Group III compression or eighty-five letter-size pages digitized at 200 pixels per horizontal and vertical inch with

Group IV compression. If the scanning resolution is increased to 300 pixels per horizontal and vertical inch, storage capacities fall to approximately twenty-five letter-size pages when Group III compression is used and thirty-eight pages when Group IV compression is used. By way of comparison, a microfiche can store ninety-eight letter-size pages reduced 24x.

Capacity limitations are not encountered with optical tape systems; in fact, the opposite problem—too much capacity for most electronic document imaging implementations—applies. As a group, optical tapes are intended as high-capacity replacements for magnetic tape in mainframe and minicomputer installations. A write-once optical tape measuring 35 millimeters wide by 880 meters long and packaged on a 12-inch reel can store 1 terabyte (1 trillion bytes) of data, the equivalent of about 5,000 reels of nine-track magnetic tape recorded at 6,250 bits per inch or of one-hundred of the highest-capacity optical disk cartridges. In electronic document imaging applications, such a medium can store approximately thirty million letter-size pages—the contents of 2,500 four-drawer filing cabinets—digitized at 200 pixels per horizontal and vertical inch with Group IV compression. Optical tapes with somewhat lower capacities have been demonstrated in cartridge and cassette formats; optical tape packaged in a 3480-type cartridge, for example, can store 50 gigabytes as compared with the 200 megabytes permitted by magnetic tape in the same format.

From the standpoint of recording and retrieval performance, optical tapes suffer from serial access limitations associated with all ribbon-shaped media. To reach a given location on tape, the recorder's read/write heads must pass through all preceding locations. Optical tapes are consequently unsuitable for applications where electronic document images must be retrieved quickly and in an unpredictable sequence. Platter-shaped media, which support direct access, offer obvious advantages in such situations.

## Magnetic Storage

Magnetic recording devices and media have dominated computer storage technology for four decades. The historical and theoretical foundations of magnetic recording technology are discussed in many publications, including Bhushan (1990), Camras (1988), Jorgensen (1988), Mallinson (1987), Matick (1977), Mee and Daniel (1987), Stevens (1981), and White (1985). Magnetic recording materials consist of atoms that are aligned in microscopic regions called "domains". When the material is in an unmagnetized state, the domains are randomly arranged. To record document images or other digitally-encoded information, an external magnetic field orients the domains in either of two directions—towards the field's north or south pole—to represent one or zero bits. With computer storage devices, the recording field is generated by an electromagnetic mechanism called a read/write head. The same mechanism reads information by determining the orientation of domains. All magnetic recording materials are rewritable; previously recorded information can be erased or overwritten by a magnetic field of sufficient strength.

Magnetic recording materials may be coated on rigid platters (hard disks), flexible circular substrates (floppy disks), thin ribbons of film (magnetic tapes), or rectangular sheets (magnetic cards). The magnetic materials utilized in computer applications are characterized by strong, easily detectable magnetization. Examples of such materials include gamma ferric oxide, the most widely utilized recording material in magnetic tape and disk products; cobalt-alloyed iron oxide, which is employed by videotapes and high-density diskettes; chromium dioxide, which is used by some magnetic tapes; pure iron particles, the recording material for certain videotapes, audiotapes, and high-capacity data cartridges; and barium ferrite compounds, which are utilized by some high-capacity disks. The following discussion examines the potential of magnetic storage devices and media for electronic document imaging implementations, comparing them to optical disks where appropriate.

### Magnetic Disks

As noted in Chapter One, fixed magnetic disk drives, usually described as hard disk drives, are the principal storage devices for the character-coded data bases that support retrieval of electronic document images. Index data entry requires a rewritable medium that can accommodate editing of data base records to correct keystroking errors or otherwise change previously entered field values. Being nonerasable, write-once and read-only optical disks cannot satisfy that requirement. In addition, data base searches and related operations require high-performance devices that provide rapid access to recorded information. As described above, optical disk drives support high-capacity media appropriate to the voluminous storage requirements of electronic document imaging applications, but their other performance characteristics, particularly, their average access times, suffer in comparison with those of hard disk drives.

As direct access storage devices, optical and magnetic disk drives write data onto, and retrieve data from, particular tracks within a given platter's recording surface. To accomplish these tasks, the drive's read/write head assembly must be positioned above the proper track; the platter then revolves to bring the desired track area under the read/write head. Average access time is the total of seek time (the average time required to move the read/write head to the proper track for recording or retrieval) and latency (the average time required for the desired part of the track to revolve around to the read/write head). Average access times for WORM drives range from about one-hundred milliseconds to over 400 milliseconds, depending on the model; as a group, 5.25-inch WORM drives tend to be faster than their 12- and 14-inch counterparts. The fastest CD-ROM drives support an average access time of 300 milliseconds, the approximate speed of floppy disk drives. Both WORM and CD-ROM drives are considerably slower than hard disk drives; average access times for such devices range from less than twenty milliseconds for high-performance models to about fifty milliseconds for the least expensive devices encountered in entry-level microcomputer configurations. Like floppy disk drives, the slow access times associated with optical disk drives are partly attributable to long latencies resulting from slow disk rotation rates, but WORM and CD-ROM drives are also burdened by slow head movement. While new models support progressively faster access times than their predecessors, parity with hard disk drives is not imminent.

Addressing a limitation of WORM and read-only technology, rewritable optical disk drives employ the erasable media required for data base editing. They also support faster access times than write-once and CD-ROM devices, but their performance lags well behind the fastest hard disk drives. Average access times less than one-hundred milliseconds are typical of 5.25-inch rewritable drives. With average access times of forty to seventy milliseconds, some models approach or exceed the performance levels of the slowest hard disk drives. With 3.5-inch rewritable optical disk drives, average access times range from thirty to seventy milliseconds. The fastest models feature split-optics systems which minimize the number of components on the drive's actuator, thereby reducing its mass and speeding its movement.

It must be emphasized that the average access times delineated above assume online media. Fixed magnetic disks are, by definition, online. As removable media, however, optical disks are typically stored outside of their drives when not in use. Additional time will be required to locate and mount a desired disk for recording or retrieval. That time will range from six to twenty seconds for nearline access in autochanger installations. Where optical disks are stored offline on shelves or in cabinets, location and mounting times may be measured in minutes.

The performance advantages outlined above make hard disk drives the storage devices of choice for data bases that support the indexing and retrieval of electronic document images. As computer-processible information, the document images themselves can also be stored on magnetic disks. In most electronic document imaging implementations, hard disk drives provide a staging area for images that will eventually be recorded on optical disks or other media. Following scanning, the digitized document images are routed to hard disk drives for temporary storage. This is often done to minimize inefficiencies associated with the slow recording speeds of some optical disk drives; alternatively, document images may be batched on hard disk drives pending inspection or index data entry. Hard disk drives likewise provide temporary storage for document images retrieved from optical disks or other media. A multi-page document or group of related documents may be transferred to a hard disk drive from which individual pages can be displayed as required. The rapid access times supported by hard disk drives are advantageous in such situations. A given document image can be redisplayed quickly without returning to the optical disk drive. In some installations, hard disk drives store digitized document images during a relatively brief, predetermined period of intense retrieval activity, after which the images are transferred to optical disks or other media. That approach is well suited to certain transaction processing applications where document images will be referenced frequently and must be retrieved quickly for thirty to ninety days following an event, such as the receipt of an order or submission of an insurance claim.

As the preceding examples indicate, magnetic disks typically play a supplementary role in document image storage. Hard disk drives could conceivably be used as the principal storage devices for electronic document images, but this is rarely done. As previously discussed, digitized document images require considerable storage space, even after compression algorithms are applied. Further increasing the storage requirement, electronic document imaging is often employed in complex records management applications involving many pages. Most computer configurations are not equipped with sufficient hard disk capacity to accommodate large quantities of digitized document images. This is most obviously the case in microcomputer configurations, where hard disk drives with sixty to 150 megabytes of capacity are commonplace. While hard disk drives with several gigabytes of capacity are increasingly encountered in file server installations, many document imaging applications require much greater amounts of storage. Based on a scanning resolution of 200 pixels per horizontal and vertical inch with Group IV compression averaging 15:1, a 2GB hard disk drive dedicated entirely to document image storage can accommodate about 60,000 letter-size pages—the approximate contents of just five four-drawer filing cabinets. As with other media, higher scanning resolutions or lower compression ratios will adversely impact storage capacity. While mainframe computer installations can be configured with hundreds of gigabytes of hard disk storage, electronic document imaging must typically compete with many other applications for available capacity.

As an additional constraint, fixed magnetic disk drives can become full, necessitating the purchase of additional drives, the deletion of document images, or the transfer of selected images to other media. Magnetic disk drives that utilize removable media address this problem. Like their optical counterparts, such drives provide infinite storage capacity within a given hardware configuration, although some document images will necessarily be stored offline at any given moment. As a significant limitation for high-volume document imaging applications, removable magnetic disks provide lower online storage capacities than conventional hard disk drives and much lower media capacities than optical disk drives.

Most removable magnetic disk products are intended for standalone microcomputers and local area network installations where they are utilized for data archiving and backup operations. As their name implies, hard disk cartridges feature rigid magnetic-coated platters encapsulated in a protective plastic shell. The highest capacity model employs 5.25-inch media and can store 88 megabytes—30 percent less than the lowest capacity optical disk cartridge. Assuming a scanning resolution of 200 pixels per horizontal and vertical inch with Group IV compression, an 88-megabyte hard disk cartridge can store approximately 2,650 letter-size pages—the equivalent of one file drawer.

Floppy disks are the most widely utilized type of removable magnetic media, but relatively low capacities limit their suitability for document image storage. With a formatted capacity of 1.44 megabytes, for example, a 3.5-inch double-sided, high-density (DS/HD) diskette can store about forty-five letter-size pages digitized at 200 pixels per horizontal and vertical inch with Group IV compression. Among higher-capacity products, so-called "floptical" disks combine magnetic data recording with optically-encoded control signals that permit high-track densities. A 3.5-inch floptical disk cartridge can store 21 megabytes—one-sixth as much as a 3.5-inch rewritable optical disk cartridge. The Bernoulli Box, developed by Iomega Corporation and sold under various private labels, is perhaps the best known example of a high-capacity floppy disk system. Bernoulli cartridges are available in various sizes and capacities. The newest model can store 90 megabytes, a slightly greater amount than the hard disk cartridges described above.

*Magnetic Tape*

Broadly defined, magnetic tapes are ribbon-shaped media coated with a magnetizable recording material. Widely encountered in computer, audio, and video applications, they may be packaged on open reels, in cartridges, or in cassettes of various sizes and shapes. Tape widths range from four millimeters to 1 inch. Lengths vary from format to format and from product to product. In computer applications, magnetic tapes are recorded and read by peripheral devices that are variously described as tape drives, tape recorders, or tape units.

As noted in Chapter One, the concept of tape-based electronic document imaging dates from the 1960s and 1970s, when several companies introduced video recording systems for document storage and retrieval. Those products, which utilized analog coding rather than digitization to represent document images, were ultimately discontinued, but the potential of magnetic tape as an alternative to optical disks in document imaging configurations continues to attract systems integrators, value-added resellers, and other product designers. As a significant development for electronic document imaging, the recording capacities of certain magnetic tape formats have increased steadily and significantly in recent years, and continued improvement is expected. The capacities of some magnetic tapes compare favorably with those of optical disks, and, as an attractive characteristic, magnetic tapes are less expensive than optical media. Capitalizing on these features, several vendors have introduced electronic document imaging systems that employ magnetic tapes as their principal storage media. Such products are marketed as alternatives to optical disk-based imaging systems as well as replacements for microfilm and paper filing systems. The following discussion examines the characteristics, advantages, and limitations of magnetic tapes as storage media in electronic document imaging implementations, emphasizing their competitive relationship with optical disks.

Magnetic tape devices and media vary in storage capacity, the principal determinant of suitability for electronic document imaging. Half-inch magnetic tape mounted on open plastic reels is widely described as nine-track tape because the bits that encode individual characters are recorded in nine parallel tracks across the tape's width. The most widely utilized open reel measures 10.5 inches in diameter and contains 2,400 feet of tape. Several manufacturers use thinner media to store 3,600 feet of tape per 10.5-inch reel. Smaller reels, containing as little as 300 feet of tape are also available.

Nine-track tape is the dominant format for backup operations, data archiving, and software distribution in many minicomputer and mainframe installations, but it does not offer sufficient storage capacity for most electronic document imaging applications. Tape capacity varies with the linear recording density, which is measured in bits per inch (bpi). High-performance nine-track tape drives operate at 6,250 bpi. Allowing space for the interrecord gaps necessary to accommodate the drive's start/stop mode of operation, a 2,400-foot reel of nine-track magnetic tape has a recording capacity of 160 megabytes—sufficient to store about 4,800 letter-size pages digitized at 200 pixels per horizontal and vertical inch with Group IV compression. Among optical disks, only 3.5-inch rewritable media provides less storage capacity.

Capacity limitations similarly limit the utility of 3480-type magnetic tape cartridges in electronic document imaging implementations. Designed as a more compact and convenient alternative to nine-track reels, the 3480-type cartridge takes its name from the IBM tape drive for which it was initially developed, although 3480-type cartridge tape drives have since been introduced for various minicomputers and mainframes. In the standard recording mode, a 3480-type cartridge contains 540 feet of half-inch magnetic tape. It stores 200 megabytes of data—sufficient to accommodate about 6,000 letter-size pages digitized at 200 pixels per horizontal and vertical inch with Group IV compression. As previously discussed, most optical disks offer far greater storage capacities. The 3480-type cartridges with extra-length tape are available. Several vendors also utilize data compression methodologies to increase cartridge capacity, but that technique is not applicable to electronic document images which are already compressed.

Quarter-inch magnetic tape cartridge systems (often described as QIC cartridge systems) are widely utilized for hard disk backup and offline data storage in desktop computer installations and microcomputer-based local area networks. Although described as data cartridges, they are actually cassettes that house both a tape supply and a take-up spool in a single plastic shell. Quarter-inch cartridges are available in two sizes: a standard version measures 4 inches high by 6 inches wide by 0.625 inches deep; the mini data cartridge measures 2 inches high by 3 inches wide by 0.5 inches deep.

QIC cartridge capacities vary with recording formats and tape lengthes. Some older formats stored as little as 45 megabytes per standard-size cartridge. Of particular significance for electronic document imaging, the QIC-1350 provides a formatted capacity of 1.35 gigabytes per standard cartridge utilizing 750-foot tape, while the QIC-2100C format provides a formatted capacity of 2.1 gigabytes per standard cartridge utilizing 925-foot tape. Both formats exceed the capacities of 5.25-inch optical disks. They employ high-coercivity magnetic media which permit greater recording densities; in this context, coercivity denotes the magnetic field strength required to record information. The QIC-1000 format provides 1.01 gigabytes of storage capacity per standard-size 760-foot cartridge, but its relatively slow data transfer rate limits its utility for electronic document imaging implementations.

Among mini data cartridges appropriate for electronic document imaging, the QIC-385M and QIC-410M formats can store 385 megabytes and 410 megabytes, respectively. They provide more than twice the capacity of 3.5-inch rewritable optical disks, but they can store fewer document images than most 5.25-inch optical media. Given the role of QIC cartridges as backup media, capacity improvements are largely driven by the rapidly expanding capacities of hard disk drives employed in local area network installations. QIC product developers have defined a migration path that will ultimately permit quarter-inch data cartridges with 10GB of storage capacity.

The half-inch and QIC magnetic tape systems described above employ longitudinal recording methods. Information is recorded in parallel tracks along the entire length of a tape. An increasingly popular group of magnetic tape systems for computer installations is based on audio and video products originally developed for consumer applications. Such devices utilize helical scan technology to record information in narrow tracks that are positioned at an acute angle with respect to the edges of a tape. Precise head positioning permits high track densities which, when combined with high linear recording densities, yields formidable storage capacities that compare favorably with the capacities of some optical disks.

The most widely implemented helical scan devices record information on 8mm data cartridges or 4mm digital audio tape (DAT). The 8mm data cartridge systems are an adaptation of 8mm videocassette technology for computer installations. The recording medium is a data-grade 8mm videocassette which measures 3.7 inches wide by 2.5 inches high by 0.6 inches deep. The 8mm data cartridges drives are manufactured by Exabyte Corporation, which supplies them to many systems integrators, value-added resellers, and other product developers. They have been incorporated into electronic document imaging configurations. The 8mm cartridges are available in various tape lengths, the maximum being approximately 180 feet (112 meters). Depending on the model selected and the tape length, maximum storage capacities of 2.5 or 5GB per data cartridge are supported. A five-gigabyte data cartridge can store approximately 150,000 letter-size pages digitized at 200 pixels per horizontal and vertical inch with Group IV compression. Autochangers are available for applications requiring unattended access to large quantities of document images or other computer-processable information recorded on 8mm data cartridges.

As their name indicates, digital audiotape systems for computer applications are based on technology that was originally developed for audio recording. The computer storage devices are sometimes described as Data-DAT systems to distinguish them from their audio counterparts. DAT cartridges measure 3 inches wide by 2 inches high by 0.4 inches deep. The tape, as noted above, is 4

*Figure 3-8. An autochanger for 8 millimeter data cartridges. (Courtesy: Exabyte)*

millimeters wide. Cartridge capacity varies with tape length. At the time this chapter was written, 60-meter DAT cartridges could store 1.3 gigabytes, while 90-meter cartridges could store 2 gigabytes. These capacities exceed those of 5.25-inch write-once and rewritable optical disks described earlier in this chapter. Assuming a scanning resolution of 200 pixels per horizontal and vertical inch with Group IV compression, a 2GB-DAT cartridge can store digitized images of approximately 60,000 letter-size pages. The migration path for DAT systems calls for a doubling of media capacity every two years up to a total of 16 gigabytes per cartridge. The higher capacities will be achieved through increased tape length combined with improved media formulations that permit greater recording densities. DAT autochangers are available for applications requiring nearline access to large quantities of computer-processible information.

While they are less widely encountered than 8mm data cartridge drives and DAT systems, other helical scan products can record computer-processible information on VHS-type videocassettes or D2 digital videocassettes. Depending on the model, VHS-type data recorders support storage capacities in excess of 10 gigabytes per T-120 cartridge. The D2 digital cassettes can store up to 165 gigabytes, depending on the tape length. Both media have been utilized in electronic document imaging implementations.

Specific formats aside, magnetic tape hardware and media prices are competitive with those of optical storage devices and media of comparable capacity. At the time this chapter was written, for example, a 5GB, 8mm data cartridge drive could be purchased for one-third to one-half the price of a 5GB, 12-inch WORM drive. Data-grade, 8mm cartridges could be purchased for ap-

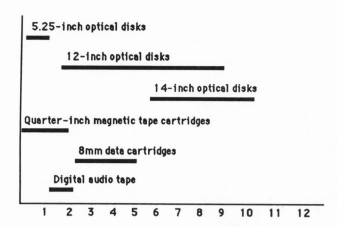

*Figure 3–9. Storage capacities (in gigabytes) of selected optical and magnetic media.*

proximately $30 each or six-tenths of a cent per megabyte. In contrast, prices for write-once optical disk cartridges ranged from less than 6 cents per megabyte to more than 25 cents per megabyte, depending on cartridge size, media capacity, recording technology, and procurement source. Typical media costs for rewritable optical disk cartridges ranged from 25 to 35 cents per megabyte. In high-volume document imaging applications, the use of magnetic tape rather than optical disks can yield substantial savings in media costs.

As might be expected, however, such cost advantages involve significant trade-offs in other aspects of system operation, the most obvious being slow retrieval times for information recorded on magnetic tape. Optical disks are direct access storage devices; while they are slower than their magnetic disk counterparts, their access times are still measured in milliseconds. Magnetic tapes, as previously noted, are limited to serial access. Although direct addressing of data and high-speed search capabilities may be supported, the necessity of physically traversing many feet of tape makes disk-like access speeds unattainable. In some cases, the time required to retrieve an electronic document image recorded on magnetic tape may be measured in minutes. Similar limitations associated with microfilm products have led to their replacement by optical disk-based electronic document imaging systems.

In data processing installations, magnetic tape has historically been reserved for applications where information will be processed in batches and retrieved sequentially, starting at the beginning of a tape and proceeding through to the end without reversing direction. Similarly predictable processing characteristics must be present if magnetic tapes are to be utilized effectively in electronic document imaging implementations. To minimize the disadvantages of serial access, logically-related documents should be grouped into batches prior to scanning and recording on magnetic tape. Document images should be retrieved in batches and in the same sequence in which they were recorded. At retrieval time, a batch of related document images can be transferred from tape to magnetic disks; individual images can then be retrieved in random sequence for display, printing, or other purposes. While such batch-oriented recording and retrieval operations may be possible in some installations, they cannot address the broad spectrum of document imaging requirements. As a result magnetic tape's role as a primary recording medium for electronic document images will be limited to a specific, presumably narrow subset of imaging applications.

Magnetic tapes can play an important role, however, as backup media in electronic document imaging applications that utilize optical disks as their primary recording media. The importance of backup copies of digitized document images recorded on optical disks was discussed earlier in this chapter. Optical disk backup is most easily and conveniently accomplished in a dual-drive equipment configuration with document images being simultaneously recorded on two optical disk cartridges. In many implementations, however, the cost of a second optical disk drive and additional optical storage media exceeds the budgetary allocation for system procurement. As a result, backup components are omitted. In such situations, the incorporation of magnetic tape drives and media can provide back-up protection at a lower cost than is possible with optical storage components. A growing number of electronic document imaging systems support magnetic tape as a back-up option. The QIC-2100C cartridges, 8mm data cartridges and digital audiotapes, in particular, provide storage capacity appropriate to such applications. Depending on the system configuration, they may be able to back-up the contents of two or more optical disk cartridges. As a potentially troublesome limitation, backup copies of document images recorded on magnetic tape must be transferred to optical disks when needed. Depending on the quantity of images involved, this process can prove time consuming. In contrast, backup copies recorded on a duplicate set of optical disks are immediately usable. As a further constraint discussed in Chapter Five, the limited stability of magnetic tapes may not be appropriate for primary recording or backup copies of document images that must be retained for long periods of time.

## References

Andrews, C. (1991). Mastering the CD-ROM mastering and replication process. CD-ROM Professional 4/4: 17-22.

Armstrong, A. (1987). Premastering and mastering. In CD ROM: Optical Publishing. Redmond, WA: Microsoft Press, pp. 217-26.

Bartholomeusz, B. (1989). Thermo-Magnetic marking of rare-earth transition-metal thin films. Journal of Applied Physics 65: 262-65.

Bate, G. (1987). Materials challenges in metallic, reversible, optical recording media: a review. IEEE Transactions on Magnetics 23: 151-61.

Belani, R. (1991). Jane's CD-ROM project: step-by-step through the development process. CD-ROM Professional 4/3: 69-72.

Bhushan, B. (1990). Tribology and Mechanics of Magnetic Storage Devices. New York: Springer-Verlag.

Bracker, W. (1987). Optical data storage: theory, hardware, software, and applications. In Proceedings of the National Computer Graphics Association: Graphics 87—Eighth annual Conference. Fairfax, VA: National Computer Graphics Association, pp. 75-90.

Camras, M. (1988). Magnetic Recording Handbook. New York: Van Nostrand Reinhold.

Chen, M. and Rubin, K. (1989). Progress of erasable phase-change materials. In Proceedings of the SPIE, vol. 1078. Bellingham, WA: Society of Photo-Optical Instrumentation Engineers, pp. 150-56.

Connell, G. (1986). Magneto-optics and amorphous metals: an optical storage revolution. Journal of Magnetism and Magnetic Materials 54: 1561-66.

Cornet, J. (1983). Deformation recording process in polymer-metal bilayers and its use for optical storage. In Proceedings of the SPIE, vol. 420. Bellingham, WA: Society of Photo-Optical Instrumentation Engineers, pp. 86-95.

Crasemann, J. and Hansen, P. (1989). Reversible optical recording on rare-earth-transition-metal disks. Thin Solid Films 175: 261-64.

Croucher, M. and Hopper, M. (1987). Materials for optical disks. Chemtech 17: 426-33.

Emmelius, M. et al. (1989). Materials for optical data storage. Angewandte Chemie: International Edition in English 28: 1445-71.

Freese, R. (1988). Optical disks become erasable. IEEE Spectrum 25/2: 41-45.

Freese, R. et al. (1982). Characteristics of bubble-forming optical direct-read-after-write (DRAW) media. In Proceedings of the SPIE, vol. 329. Bellingham, WA: Society of Photo-Optical Instrumentation Engineers, pp. 174-80.

Funkenbusch, A. (1991). Magneto-optic data storage in the 90s. In Proceedings of the SPIE, vol. 1396. Bellingham, WA: International Society for Optical Engineering, pp. 699-708.

Gravesteijn, D. (1988). Materials developments for write-once and erasable phase-change optical recording. Applied Optics 27: 736-38.

_____. (1989). Phase-change optical recording. Philips Technical Review 44: 250-58.

Gravesteijn, D. and Van Der Veen, J. (1984). Organic dye films for optical recording. Philips Technical Review 41: 325-33.

Greidanus, F. (1990). Status and future of magneto-optical disk drive technologies. Philips Journal of Research 45: 19-34.

Greidanus, F. and Zeper, W. (1990). Magneto-optical storage materials. MRS Bulletin 15/4: 31–39.

Hansen, P. (1990). Magneto-optical recording materials and technologies. Journal of Magnetism and Magnetic Materials 83/1: 6–12.

Harvey, D. and Reinhardt, A. (1990). State of the media. Byte 15: 275-81.

Hecht, J. (1987). Optical memories vie for data storage. High Technology 7/8: 43-47.

Isailovic, J. (1985). Videodisc and Optical Memory Systems. Englewood Cliffs, NJ: Prentice-Hall.

Jorgensen, F. (1988). The Complete Handbook of Magnetic Recording, Third Edition. Blue Ridge Summit, PA: Tab Professional and Reference Books.

Kawabata, H. and Yamamoto, K. (1988). Advances in magnetic and optical recording: recent trends in erasable optical recording media. Journal of the Institute of Television Engineering in Japan 42: 323-39.

Kryder, M. (1990). Advances in magneto-optic recording technology. Journal of Magnetism and Magnetic Materials 83: 1-5.

Lee, W. (1989). Thin films for write-once and reversible optical data storage. In Proceedings of the Sino-U.S. Joint Seminar on Vacuum and Surface Analysis, vol. 2. Singapore: World Scientific, pp. 249-78.

Mallinson, J. (1987). The Foundations of Magnetic Recording. San Diego: Academic Press.

Mansuripur, M. et al. (1985). Erasable optical disks for data storage: principles and applications. Industrial and Engineering Chemistry: Product Research and Development 24: 80-84.

Marsh, F. (1982). Videodisc technology. Journal of the American Society for Information Science 33: 237-44.

Matick, R. (1977). Computer Storage Systems and Technology. New York: Wiley.

Mee, C. and Daniel, E. (1987). Magnetic Recording. New York: McGraw-Hill.

Meikeljohn, W. (1986). Magneto-optics: a thermomagnetic recording technology. Proceedings of the IEEE 74: 1570-81.

Nakane, Y. et al. (1985). Principle of laser recording mechanism by forming an alloy in the trilayer of thin metallic films. In Proceedings of the SPIE, vol. 529. Bellingham, WA: Society of Photo-Optical Instrumentation Engineers, pp. 76-82.

Ojima, M. and Ohta, N. (1988). Erasable optical disk technologies. Hitachi Review 37/3: 139-46.

Pahwa, A. and Rudd, G. (1991). Sending your CD-ROM data for mastering. CD-ROM Professional 4/5: 100-13.

Reynolds, G. and Halliday, J. (1987). Compact disc processing. In Sound Recording Practice, Third Edition. Oxford: Oxford University Press, pp. 440-52.

Rodgers, D. (1990). Step-by-step through the CD-ROM production process. Laserdisk Professional 3/1: 36-39.

Rubin, K. and Chen, M. (1989). Progress and issue of phase-change erasable optical recording media. Thin Solid Films 181: 129-39.

Ryan, B. (1990). Entering a new phase. Byte 15/12: 289-96.

Saffady, W. (1989). Optical Storage Technology: A Bibliography. Westport, CT: Meckler Corporation.

_____. (1992). Optical Storage Technology 1992. Westport, CT: Meckler Corporation.

Sponheimer, E. (1990). Magneto-optical recording technology. Hewlett-Packard Journal 41/6: 8-9.

Stevens, L. (1981). The evolution of magnetic storage. IBM Journal of Research and Development 25: 663-75.

Suh, S. (1985). Writing process in ablative optical recording. Applied Optics 24: 868-74.

Thiel, T. et al. (1990). CD-ROM Mastering for Information and Image Management. Silver Spring, MD: Association for Information and Image Management.

Thomas, G. (1987). Thin films for optical recording applications. Journal of Vacuum Science and Technology, part A, vol. 5, pp. 1965-66.

Troeltzsch, L. (1984). 3M optical videodisc project: part two—preparing the master tape. Videodisc/Videotex 4/1: 54-62.

Urrows, H. and Urrows, E. (1990). Erasable-rewritables now and promised: introductory notes. Optical Information Systems 10/1: 14-27.

Van Rijsewijk, H. et al. (1982). Manufacture of Laser Vision video discs by a photopolymerization process. Philips Technical Review 40: 287-97.

White, R. (1985). Introduction to Magnetic Recording. New York: IEEE Press.

# Chapter Four
# Output

As discussed in Chapter One, improved retrieval when compared to an existing paper- or microfilm-based system, is a strong motive for electronic document imaging implementations. In many installations, it is the principal motive and an anticipated source of enhanced productivity and improved operating efficiency. This chapter examines retrieval characteristics and capabilities of electronic document imaging systems. It begins with a discussion of retrieval software, emphasizing the flexible database search and image delivery features that distinguish electronic document imaging from other document management methodologies. Subsequent sections describe workstation components that permit database searches and display, print, or transmit retrieved document images.

## Retrieval Software

When properly designed and implemented, electronic document imaging systems can satisfy the demanding retrieval requirements of a broad spectrum of information management applications. They can identify pertinent document images and retrieve them quickly, even when complex combinations of retrieval parameters are involved. In some cases, they permit retrieval operations that cannot be conveniently performed, and may not even be possible, with conventional paper filing methodologies or microfilm technology. Once retrieved, document images can be routed to designated workstations or, if desired, to other information processing systems.

As briefly described in Chapter One, an electronic document imaging system's retrieval capabilities are embodied in database management programs. Depending on the system, such programs may be custom-developed for a particular installation or prewritten; some vendors of electronic document imaging systems rely on established data-

base management products (such as Oracle, Informix On-Line, or Paradox) that can be programmed or otherwise modified to address application-specific requirements. As described in Chapter Two, database management software supports the creation of computer-maintained databases that contain descriptive information about, and serve as an index to, digitized document images. In most cases, a separate database is established for each document collection encountered in a given imaging installation. The databases, which usually reside on hard disk drives, contain one record for each indexable item in a given document collection. Database records consist of fields that correspond to indexing parameters determined through analysis of application requirements.

As previously discussed, retrieval operations begin with a search for database records—and, by implication, electronic document images—that satisfy specified parameters. The database records contain pointers to document images stored on optical disks or other media. The nature and complexity of database searches depend on the characteristics of retrieval software supported by a given electronic document imaging system and are important determinants of the system's effectiveness. Commonly encountered characteristics and capabilities of retrieval software are outlined in the following discussion.

### Search Capabilities

Document retrieval operations begin with a reference requirement that can presumably be satisfied by information contained in one or more document images. Characteristics of reference requirements are application-dependent. As discussed by Saracevic (1983), Taylor (1968), and many others, they may vary in scope, specificity, complexity, and clarity of expression. In some cases, a request is made for specific documents that are known to contain required information. With such known-item searches, documents may be identified by authors, dates, or other straightforward parameters. Often, however, a reference requirement is initially expressed as a general question about the availability of documents pertaining to some subject, project, event, transaction, or other matter. In some cases, the reference requirement may be presented in vague terms or otherwise poorly articulated. Such ambiguous requirements must be interpreted, analyzed, and clarified through discussion. While this process, which is sometimes described as question negotiation, can prove time consuming, a properly articulated reference requirement is essential if satisfactory retrieval results are to be obtained.

Once the reference requirement is understood, a retrieval strategy is formulated and expressed as one or more database search statements which are submitted to an electronic document imaging system. As described later in this chapter, the retrieval workstations employed in electronic document imaging installations include a keyboard for the entry of search specifications and a video monitor for the display of database records and document images. Depending on software characteristics, retrieval procedures may be command-driven or menu-based. In the former case, a workstation operator key-enters a database search statement in a specified syntax. The retrieval program may instruct the operator to enter search commands in a particular format. Often, however, a command-driven program simply displays a terse, relatively uninformative prompting symbol indicating its readiness to accept a search statement; the operator must know what to do next. As an obvious disadvantage, command-driven programs require memorization of a usable repertoire of retrieval commands as well as the correct typing of search statements, some of which, as described below, may be long and complicated. Formal operator training, reinforced by practice and readily accessible user manuals, is consequently required.

While a given operator's familiarity with retrieval commands and procedures will typically improve dramatically with experience, novice users are often discouraged by the extensive memorization requirements and long familiarization periods associated with command-driven retrieval programs. For occasional users, the long learning curve may be a fatal impediment to acceptance of electronic document imaging technology. Such users may have searches performed for them by others or ignore the system entirely; preferring the familiar to the effective, they may continue to rely on personal files of paper documents to satisfy their information requirements.

Addressing these concerns, an increasing number of electronic document imaging systems are optimized for ease of use by persons with little or no formal instruction. Designed to minimize memorization requirements, such systems feature menu-driven retrieval software as an alternative or supplement to command-driven approaches. They increasingly rely on the user-friendly interfaces associated with Microsoft Windows, Macintosh systems, Open Look, and other graphical operating environments. Databases, document collections, and application programs are represented by displayed icons. Available retrieval commands are listed in pulldown menus. Dialog boxes provide extensive operator prompting and on-screen instructions. Whenever possible, point-and-click mouse operations are substituted for key-entry of commands. To simplify the formulation of retrieval statements, formatted screens permit the entry of search terms into blank spaces adjacent to labelled fields. As an additional aid, some systems will display lists of field values for user selection. Database records and document images are displayed in multiple windows which may be adjacent, overlapping, or otherwise arranged on the video screen in operator-selectable fashion.

Such menu-driven retrieval programs favor novice or occasional searchers. Experienced users may find them slow and tedious, especially where several levels of menus and dialog boxes must be navigated to complete a given operation. Addressing this problem, some menu-driven programs optionally support a command mode which permits direct entry of search statements without excessive prompting.

Whether command-driven or menu-based approaches are utilized, a search statement typically includes a field name and a textual or quantitative field value to be matched, linked by a relational expression that specifies the type of match desired. In a correspondence control application, for example, a search statement of the form:

AUTHOR = SMITH

will initiate a search for database records that contain the character string "SMITH" in the author field. The equals sign, or a textual equivalent such as "EQ," is the most meaningful relational expression for database searches involving character strings. In most cases, the equals sign specifies an exact match of a designated field value. The relational expression "not equals,"which may be represented by the abbreviation "NEQ" or by the symbol "≠," is its opposite. For numeric field values, most retrieval software supports other relational expressions, including greater than, represented by the symbol > or the abbreviation GT; less than, represented by the symbol < or the abbreviation LT; greater than or equal to, represented by the symbol ≥ or the abbreviation GTE; and less than or equal to, represented by the symbol ≤ or the abbreviation LTE. These relational expressions can also be applied to character strings; a field value that is greater than a specified character string, for example, follows it in alphabetic sequence. When combined with the Boolean operators described below, relational expressions permit range searches which can identify field values that fall between an upper and lower numeric or alphabetic limit.

As an initial response to a search statement of the type presented above, most electronic document imaging systems display a count of the number of database records, and, by implication, the number of electronic document images, that satisfy the retrieval specification. That response, which is sometimes termed "hit prediction", allows the operator to reconsider the search statement, broadening it if too few records are identified or narrowing it if the number of retrieved items is excessive. Such search modifications typically rely on the so-called Boolean operators—AND, OR, and NOT are the most commonly encountered examples—which permit the logical coordination of two or more search statements in a single retrieval specification. Because their underlying principles are based on formal logical concepts and the algebra of sets, Boolean operations are sometimes de-

scribed as Boolean logic or Boolean algebra. Their advantages and limitations in computer-based information retrieval are discussed in many publications, including Anick et al. (1989), Bataineh et al. (1991), Bookstein and Cooper (1976), Das-Gupta (1987), De Stricker (1988), Heine (1982), Latham and Phil (1991), Oldroyd and Schroder (1982), Ornager and Johne (1983), Paice (1984), Radecki (1982, 1983, 1988), Scheffler et al. (1972), Verhoeff et al. (1961), and Vigil (1982). While they have been criticized as difficult to understand, particularly for novice users, Boolean operators are essential to effective searching in electronic document imaging installations. Collectively, they permit complex retrieval operations that are not possible with conventional paper filing systems. Alternatives have been suggested, but none are widely implemented in electronic document imaging systems.

The AND operator, the best known and most widely implemented of the Boolean operators, is indispensible for effective retrieval operations in electronic document imaging installations. It is supported by virtually all electronic document imaging systems, although it may be more or less convenient to use in a given implementation. With some systems, the Boolean AND operator must be explicitly included in retrieval specifications; in other cases, successively entered search statements are automatically placed in an AND relationship to one another. Regardless of implementation pattern, the Boolean AND operator is typically used to limit the scope of a given search by linking two or more retrieval specifications, both of which must be satisfied. In a correspondence control application, for example, a search statement of the form:

AUTHOR=SMITH AND RECIPIENT=JONES

will restrict retrieval to database records that contain the value "SMITH" in the author field and the value "JONES" in the recipient field. In effect, the retrieval specification presented above establishes two sets, one consisting of database records where SMITH is the author and the other consisting of database records where JONES is the recipient. In this context, the term "set" denotes a group of database records that contain a designated value in a specified field. The Boolean AND operator seeks the logical conjunction or intersection of two sets defined in a retrieval specification; that is, it identifies those records that are members of both sets.

The Boolean OR operator, in contrast, broadens a database search by specifying two or more retrieval conditions, either of which must be satisfied. Thus, a search statement of the form:

AUTHOR=SMITH OR AUTHOR=JONES

will retrieve database records that contain either of the two indicated values in the author field. The Boolean OR operator establishes a logical union of two sets. It merges the two sets into a new set consisting of database records that are members of either set. Duplicate records are eliminated in the process. The Boolean OR operator is particularly useful for subject searches based on synonymous terms. It can also facilitate retrieval of documents with multiple authors. While it offers very convenient and highly desirable capabilities, the Boolean OR operator is not indispensible, since the same results can be achieved by conducting separate searches based on successively entered retrieval specifications.

The Boolean NOT operator, which may be implicitly or explicitly combined with the AND operator, will narrow a database search by excluding records that contain specified values in designated fields. In an electronic document imaging application involving technical reports, for example, a search statement of the form:

AUTHOR=SMITH AND NOT DATE < 1992

will restrict retrieval to those database records that contain the value "SMITH" in the author field and any value later than 1991 in the date field. The NOT operator seeks the logical negation or complement of two sets. It identifies records that are members of a given set but not also members of another designated set.

Depending on the system, several Boolean operators may be combined in a given search statement, thus permitting very complex retrieval operations involving multiple field matches. Thus, in a correspondence control application, a statement of the form:

(AUTHOR=JONES OR AUTHOR=SMITH)
AND DATE=9/19/92 AND

(SUBJECT=PROJECT 1250 OR SUBJECT=PROJECT 1251)

will retrieve database records for those documents that were written by either Jones or Smith on September 19, 1992, concerning either Project 1250 or Project 1250. Such complicated search capabilities are most often associated with command-driven retrieval programs. They are intended for experienced users. As depicted in the above example, parentheses are typically utilized to control the sequence in which particular Boolean operations will be performed. Operations within parenthesis are performed first. In the absence of parentheses, Boolean operations are performed in a default sequence defined by the retrieval program itself. Usually, NOT and AND operations are performed before OR operations. In such cases, the searcher's intent may be misinterpreted and inappropriate results obtained. Without parentheses, the foregoing search statement would retrieve documents written by Smith on 9/19/92 concerning Project 1250 or

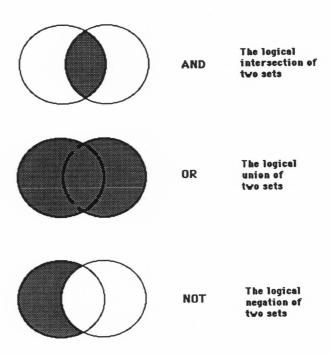

*Figure 4–1. Boolean operators.*

all documents written by Jones, regardless of date or subject, or all documents concerning Project 1251, regardless of author or date.

To enhance retrieval flexibility, some electronic document imaging systems support additional search capabilities as a supplement or alternative to Boolean operations. In addition to retrieving database records that match exact field values specified in search statements, some electronic document imaging systems can identify field values that begin with, contain, or end with specified character strings. As a group, such capabilities can be used to broaden retrieval specifications. Searches for field values that begin with a specified character string are particularly useful for retrieving subject terms, personal names, or corporate names with common roots, as well as single and plural forms of field values. Thus a search statement of the form:

SUBJECT = IMAG?

will identify database records that contain "IMAGE", "IMAGES", and "IMAGING", among other values, in the subject field. Such retrieval operations are sometimes described as "right trunctation" or "root word searches." With some electronic document imaging systems, right trunctation must be explicitly stated, using a designated operator such as the question mark employed in the above example. In other cases, right trunctation is implicit; field values that begin with a specified character string are invariably retrieved unless an exact match is specified.

Retrieval operations based on left truncation (that is, searches for field values that end with a designated character string) are not as broadly useful or widely supported as those based on right trunctation. They can produce unique retrieval results in certain situations, however. In an application involving pharmaceutical research reports that are indexed with drug names, for example, a search statement of the form:

SUBJECT = ?MYCIN

will retrieve database records that contain certain antiobiotic names (such as aureomycin, streptomycin, and terramycin) in the subject field.

Retrieval operations based on embedded character strings (sometimes described as "substring searches") will match field values that contain a specified sequence of characters, which may be preceded or followed by other characters. Thus, a search statement of the form:

SUBJECT CONTAINS TAPE

will retrieve database records that contain "VIDEOTAPE", "VIDEOTAPES", and "TAPE RECORDER", among other values, in the subject field. In some cases, substring searches can yield irrelevant or otherwise unintended results; the foregoing search statement, for example, will retrieve database records containing "TAPESTRY" in the subject field.

Wildcard characters broaden retrieval specifications by using designated non-alphabetic symbols, such as asterisks or question marks, to denote positions within designated field values that can be matched by any character. Thus, a search statement of the form:

SUBJECT = DIS*S

will retrieved database records with subject field values that begin with "DIS", followed by any character, and ending in an "S". Such a statement will retrieve any records that contain the values "DISKS" or "DISCS" in the subject field. As this example indicates, wildcard searches are particularly useful for subject terms with variant spellings. Depending on the system, wildcard symbols may be used to match a single character in a designated position, multiple characters, or one or more characters from a specified list. With some systems, for example, a search statement of the form:

SUBJECT = DIS*CK*S

will match subject field values that begin with "DIS", followed by either a "C" or a "K", and ending in "S."

As a relatively new development, several electronic document imaging systems have introduced "fuzzy" search capabilities which will retrieve database records with field values that are similar to, but do not exactly satisfy, a designated search specifications. As originally conceived by Zadeh (1965) and elaborated by Bookstein (1980, 1980a, 1985), Kaufmann (1975), Kerre et al. (1986), Kraft and Buell (1983), Lucarella and Morara (1991), Negoita and Flonder (1976), Prade and Testemale (1987), Radecki (1979, 1981), Sachs (1976), Tahani (1976, 1977), and others, fuzzy retrieval concepts recognize a continuum of possibilities when field values are matched against character strings. Distinctions between field values that match or do not match designated character string are not delineated precisely. Partial matches are permitted. With some programs, the operator can control the fuzziness of a search by entering a numeric value between two extremes to indicate the desired conformity of field values to search strings; the value 1, for example, may designate a very loose match, while the value 10 may specify an exact match. Like the wildcard symbols described above, fuzzy searches are particularly useful for subject terms with variant spellings. They can also be used to retrieve misspelled field values or personal names of uncertain spelling. In electronic document imaging installations that utilize auto-indexing techniques based on optical character recognition, fuzzy searches can be used to match field values that contain incorrectly recognized characters.

Specific search features aside, retrieved database records may be displayed as formatted screens with labelled fields or in tabular listings with labelled columns. Depending on program capabilities and the application designer's specifications, the displayed information may contain all or selected fields from within database records. If optical disk cartridges or other image storage media must be manually mounted for retrieval, the displayed records will include cartridge numbers or other media identifiers. Retrieved database records can usually be sorted by an operator-designated field value in a specified sequence prior to display or printing. The most sophisticated database management programs also include elaborate report-generation capabilities that can produce highly formatted output, although such capabiiities will typically prove more useful for general data processing applications than in electronic document imaging installations.

Depending on the type of video monitor utilized, database records and their associated document images may be displayed simultaneously in adjacent or overlapping windows. Document images may be enlarged, reduced, rotated, or otherwise manipulated for display in a designated screen area. Among unusual features, some electronic document imaging systems offer document annotation capabilities that allow users to type brief comments, instructions, corrections, or other notes to be appended to specific images. A note indicator appears when its associated document image is retrieved; if desired, the note can be displayed on command. Several electronic document imaging systems also support an optional voice annotation capability that stores remarks spoken into a microphone as digitized audio signals. Like key-entered notes, the remarks are appended to designated document images for subsequent retrieval.

*Workflow Programming*

Workflow programming is one of the most widely publicized software capabilities of electronic document imaging systems. As its name suggests, a workflow implementation provides automatic control and coordinated management of the document flow associated with specific information processing tasks. In a workflow implementation, electronic document images associated with particular transactions or tasks are automatically routed in the proper sequence to those workstations that require them. Designated workstation operators examine the routed images to obtain information required to complete an assigned portion of a task.

Workflow capabilities are neither provided nor required in every electronic document imaging installation. In the right situation, however, they offer considerable potential for work streamlining and productivity improvement. Workflow implementations are, by definition, applicable only to multi-workstation electronic document imaging configurations. They are principally intended for transaction-processing or production-oriented information management applications that are governed by clearly defined procedures for document preparation, review, and approval. Examples include the processing of payment orders, loan applications, customer inquiries, personnel forms, insurance claims, and pension records. In such applications, documents are typically routed from one worker to another in order to complete a transaction or other operation. Often, information is extracted from documents to complete business forms associated with particular transactions. Many workflow implementations similarly involve the completion of displayed workforms using information obtained from retrieved document images. They are consequently described as "autoform" or "intelligent form" implementations.

Workflow concepts and workflow-based electronic document imaging implementations are described in many publications. Examples include Edelstein (1991), Fisher and Gilbert (1987), Irwin (1992), McCready (1989), Neiberding (1990), Nelson (1989), Newcombe (1991), Plesums and Bartel (1990), Seigle (1987), and Trammell (1989). In most cases, workflow programming is an extra-cost feature made possible by an optional software module. While customer-originated configurations are possible, workflow-based electronic document imaging implementations usually involve consulting services provided by a value-added reseller or systems integrator. Such services, while subject to considerable application-dependent variation, can significantly increase the complexity, time, and cost of a given electronic document imaging installation.

Workflow implementations must be preceded by a thorough analysis of the target application to identify the specific document images and work-steps necessary to complete a transaction, as well as the sequence and timeframes in which the work-steps must be performed. The displayed work-forms to be completed during transaction processing must be designed. Using a scripting language, a programmer or other application designer must specify the flow of workforms and document images among designated workstations based on the previously analyzed sequence of operations. The resulting workflow program is a set of rules that defines the way in which images are to be routed, as well as the specific operations to be performed at each stage in the route. Depending on system capabilities and the application being automated, workflow routing rules may be based on document types, on the activities to be performed, on field values contained in database records, or on external events, such as elapsed time or the arrival of new documents. While it is not as difficult as conventional computer programming, the preparation of workflow scripts for complex applications may require familiarity with variable types, conditional branching, and other programming concepts. The newest workflow programming languages employ symbols and other graphic components that simplify the designation of workstation roles and charting of document routes.

As a simple example of a workflow implementation, invoice documents received by the accounts payable department of a project-oriented engineering organization might be processed by a workflow program in the following sequence:

- Incoming vendor invoices and supporting documents are scanned and indexed by purchase order number, customer invoice number, vendor name, date, and an identifying number for the project to which they pertain. Index records, as previously discussed, are maintained in a database that resides on a hard disk drive. The document images are recorded on optical disk cartridges which are maintained in an autochanger.

- A workflow program automatically routes document images to an accounts payable queue for the indicated project. A designated clerk retrieves images from the queue and checks each invoice for completeness of information. If additional information is required, a notice is printed and sent to the vendor that submitted the invoice. Further processing of that invoice is suspended, pending receipt of the additional information.

- When an invoice is judged complete, the pertinent document images are routed to a designated project manager who confirms delivery of the invoiced goods or services and completes a displayed workform to approve payment. If the goods or services were not delivered as invoiced, an exception workform is prepared and routed, with the document images, to the accounts payable clerk who notifies the vendor or takes other appropriate action. Processing is suspended until the exceptional condition is resolved.

- When delivery of the invoiced items is confirmed, the document images are routed to a disbursements supervisor who authorizes check writing. Database records are updated to indicate that the invoice was paid.

The most effective workflow programs check to determine that a given process has been completed before routing an image to the next workstation. They can perform simultaneous routing of images for tasks which need not be performed in a prescribed sequence. Dates, times, and workstation identifiers are recorded for all image retrievals and workform entries, thereby creating an audit trail. Workflow programs monitor the progress of transaction processing to detect and report delays. Document images routed to specific queues can often be prioritized for processing in a designated sequence. A dynamic routing feature allows a workstation to specify a successor where document flow is unpredictable or the normal flow must be suspended.

## COLD

The discussion to this point has emphasized retrieval of document images and their associated database records. As a standard or optional feature, some electronic document imaging systems can also store and retrieve page-formatted computer output. As such, they incorporate capabilities offered by so-called Computer Output Laser Disk (COLD) systems which record computer-generated information on read/write optical disks. COLD products offer an online alternative to computerized report production methodology, including paper printouts and computer-output microfilm (COM). COLD systems accept information generated by batch-oriented application programs operating on mainframes or minicomputers. The information is recorded in the character-coded form associated with data and text files rather than as electronic document images. Unlike conventional data files, however, the information is formatted as report pages, just as it would be transmitted to a paper printer or COM recorder. Some systems can also store images of business forms or organizational logos. Such images are superimposed on report data at the time specific pages are retrieved, in the manner of form slides employed by COM recorders.

COLD systems include software which indexes the downloaded information in a specified manner. Once indexed, the report pages are recorded on write-once or rewritable optical disks. Among their functional advantages, COLD systems store information in compact character-coded form. Many pages can be recorded on a single optical disk cartridge. Assuming a typical computer printout format of sixty lines per page (at six lines per vertical inch) with a maximum of 132 characters per line (at ten characters per horizontal inch), a 5.25-inch WORM or rewritable optical disk cartridge with 600 megabytes of double-sided recording capacity can store at least 75,000 report pages—the equivalent of approximately 280 COM-generated, 48x microfiche. Because report data is often formatted in columns which are separated by blank spaces and tab commands, the number of characters per line is usually less than 132, and the page capacity per optical disk will consequently prove much higher than the total indicated above. Some systems use data compression algorithms to achieve even greater media capacities.

COLD technology provides convenient online access to computer-generated reports, thereby eliminating the time and labor associated with physical distribution of COM-generated microforms or paper printouts to user sites. Because they are stored in character-coded form rather than as graphic images, report pages can be accessed by conventional terminals and microcomputers; special workstations with high-resolution display components are not required. Reference copies of specified pages can be produced by conventional dot matrix, ink-jet, laser, or other printers.

The most flexible COLD systems include powerful retrieval software that permits extensive page indexing by designated key fields. The retrieval software usually supports relational expressions and Boolean operations. Once a report page is retrieved and displayed, commands can be used to browse through preceding and following pages in a given report or series of reports. As a potentially useful capability, report pages can be exported to other application programs; a table from a computer-generated report can be incorporated into a word processing document, for example, or manipulated by a spreadsheet program.

## Retrieval Workstations

Retrieval workstations provide the necessary hardware interface between an electronic document imaging system's users and the information retrieval and workflow capabilities described in preceding sections. As discussed in Chapter One, electronic document imaging systems are often implemented as paperless replacements for conventional filing systems. Retrieval operations consequently rely on video monitors for "softcopy" display of database records and document images. The video monitors are usually configured as computer terminals with keyboards for entry of retrieval commands, activation of menu selections, or other interaction with retrieval software. Single-workstation configurations also include a laser printer for output of database records and document images. In multi-workstation systems, print servers typically provide shared access to hardcopy production capabilities, although desktop printers may be provided at selected workstations. Characteristics and capabilities that influence the suitability of display devices and printers for electronic document imaging are described and explained in the following discussion.

### Display Devices

In electronic document imaging installations, it is common to distinguish image-capable workstations from those that are not image-capable. An image-capable workstation includes a graphics-type video monitor and keyboard; often, a mouse or other pointing device is provided. As their name suggests, image-capable workstations can display digitized document images that are generated by scanners or retrieved from optical disks or other storage media. They can also display the character-coded information contained in database records. In contrast, non-image-capable worksta-

tions lack graphic display components; their displayable repertoire is limited to character-coded data and text. A non-image-capable workstation includes a conventional alphanumeric video monitor that is suitable for data entry and database searching, but it cannot display document images or other computer-generated graphics. Non-image-capable workstations are obviously limited-purpose retrieval devices in electronic document imaging installations. They can be utilized to determine the existence of potentially relevant document images and, software permitting, to route those images to a printer for hardcopy output. As such, they are suitable for users with occasional document retrieval requirements.

The graphic display devices included in image-capable workstations are sometimes described as bit-mapped video monitors. They store bit patterns for digitized document images in internal memory circuits and selectively illuminate or darken portions of the monitor's screen to match light and dark areas within the source documents from which the images were produced. Digitized document images are, in effect, redrawn on the video monitor. Most of the bit-mapped monitors employed in electronic document imaging installations are CRT-based, monochrome display devices. With CRT displays, an electron beam scans a phosphorescent glass panel and creates an image by illuminating selected spots in a predetermined pattern of lines and pixels. Digitized document images are usually displayed in the same polarity as the source documents from which they were produced; dark areas in source documents appear as dark pixels on the video monitor, while background areas are represented by light pixels. With most office documents, for example, digitized images consist of black text on a white background, a practice which reverses the most commonly encountered display pattern in conventional data and text processing applications where video monitors feature light characters on a dark background.

The monochrome bit-mapped displays utilized in electronic document imaging applications usually employ a white phosphor that effectively emulates the appearance of paper documents. Such displays are often described as "paper white." Color bit-mapped monitors are increasingly available in models appropriate for electronic document imaging. While prices have fallen significantly since the 1980s, they are more expensive than monochrome devices of comparable size and resolution. Their use is consequently limited to those imaging applications that involve colored source documents, such as photographs and reproductions of art works. Grayscale monitors are also available for the display of photographic images generated by grayscale scanners. Nugent (1991) discusses display requirements for such applications.

Liquid crystal displays (LCDs) and other flat panel display technologies have attracted considerable attention as alternatives to cathode-ray tubes in computer applications. They are occasionally encountered in electronic document imaging installations. When compared to CRTs, flat panel displays offer the advantages of compact dimensions, light weight, low power consumption, and freedom from radiation emissions, but small screen sizes and relatively low resolutions currently limit their suitability for electronic document imaging. Utilization of flat panel displays may increase, however, as the technology improves and as portable computers are incorporated into electronic document imaging configurations.

Display technology aside, the bit-mapped video monitors employed in image-capable workstations can be divided into two groups: (1) devices intended specifically or primarily for electronic document imaging and other applications requiring high-resolution display capabilities; and (2) general-purpose video monitors that are capable of displaying various types of computer-generated graphics, including digitized document images. Within each group, available products differ in screen size, screen orientation, resolution capabilities, and ergonomic features. Wood (1991) examines the importance of these characteristics for document imaging applications.

An image-capable video monitor must be large enough to display document images in a manner appropriate for reference or other purposes. In some cases, retrieval operations require the simultaneous display of document images and other information, such as database records, forms to be completed in workflow implementations, or a terminal emulation window that permits interaction with an external computer. As with television receivers, the screens of bit-mapped video moni-

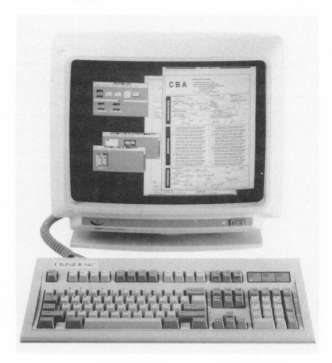

*Figure 4–2. An image-capable workstation. (Courtesy: Sigma Imaging)*

tors are measured diagonally. Bit-mapped monitors designed specifically for document imaging applications are widely available in two screen sizes: 15 inches and 19 inches. Larger sizes are selectively available for applications involving large documents, such as engineering drawings. With 15-inch models, the display area is approximately equivalent to a letter-size page. The 15-inch devices are often described as full-page or single-page monitors, because they can display one complete letter-size page image at a time. They are also described as vertically-oriented or portrait-mode monitors, because they are taller than they are wide—like the canvases that artists use for portraits.

Employed by the earliest optical-disk based electronic document imaging systems, 15-inch portrait-mode monitors are increasingly being supplanted by larger horizontally oriented, landscape-mode displays with 19-inch, diagonally measured screens. As their name suggests, such devices are wider than they are tall—like the canvases that artists use for landscapes. With a display area that measures approximately 11 inches high by 14 inches wide, they are sometimes described as dual-

*Figure 4–3. Retrieval workstation components may include bitmapped and conventional monitors, portable terminals with LCD displays, fax machines, touch-tone telephones, and barcode recognition devices. (Courtesy: Intellus)*

*Figure 4–4. A portrait-made monitor intended for document display. (Courtesy: Bell and Howell)*

page monitors because they are large enough to display two digitized document images side by side. In most applications, however, a document image is displayed in one half of the screen and a data entry window, a database search window, a terminal emulation window, or other information is displayed in the other half. As their most attractive feature, 19-inch landscape-mode video monitors permit the simultaneous display of document images and related information with little or no overlapping. With 15-inch, portrait mode monitors, database search windows or other information must overlap and consequently obscure portions of displayed document images.

As noted above, many 19-inch bit-mapped video monitors are designed specifically for document imaging applications. With general-purpose bit-mapped video monitors, the most common screen size is 14 inches, although 17-inch models are increasingly available. Both sizes are widely encountered in desktop computer installations; the VGA monitors employed by IBM-compatible microcomputers are the best known example. In electronic document imaging installations, general-purpose bit-mapped video displays are sometimes described as landscape-mode, partial-page monitors. As with television receivers, their horizontal-

to-vertical aspect ratio is 4:3, that is, the display area's width is 1.33 times greater than its height. The display area is approximately 8 inches high by 10.6 inches wide. Due to resolution constraints described below, most general-purpose bit-mapped video monitors are limited to partial-page displays of letter-size or larger document images. Database search windows and other information will typically overlap displayed images.

Screen sizes aside, bit-mapped video monitors intended specifically for electronic document imaging applications are sometimes described as high-resolution monitors to distinguish them from general-purpose bit-mapped display devices which operate at lower resolutions. In this context, resolution denotes the number of pixels that a given monitor can address and, consequently, the amount of image detail that it can display. Conceptual and technical aspects of display resolution are delineated and discussed in various publications, including Bechis (1991), Cushman and Miller (1988), Infante (1985), Keller (1986), MacNaughton (1991), Murch and Virgin (1985), Rosen (1987), Thoone (1982), and Wilson (1987).

The resolution of a given bit-mapped video monitor may be expressed in either of two ways: (1) as the number of pixels along the display

*Figure 4–5. A large-screen landscape-mode monitor. (Courtesy: Cimage)*

area's horizontal and vertical dimensions, or (2) as the number of pixels or dots per inch that are displayable within a digitized document image. The first method of expressing resolution indicates the number of pixels per line followed by the number of lines per display area; 640 by 480, the familiar resolution of VGA monitors, is an example. Video monitors capable of displaying 1,000 pixels along the vertical dimension have been available since the 1970s; sometimes described as 1,000-line monitors, their resolution is equivalent to 90 to 100 pixels per horizontal and vertical inch. Through the mid-1980s, various vendors of electronic document imaging systems offered 15-inch, portrait-mode, bit-mapped video monitors with a display resolution of 2,200 lines with 1,700 pixels per line, the equivalent of 200 pixels per horizontal and vertical inch. As discussed in Chapter Two, that resolution is supported by most document scanners and is widely utilized in many electronic document imaging installations. Where such is the case, digitized document images can be displayed at the same resolution at which the source documents were scanned.

As previously noted, many electronic document imaging systems are designed to minimize or eliminate paper documents, replacing them with softcopy displays of digitized document images. In the mid-1980s, it was assumed that successful implementation of such paperless document manage-

ment systems required the highest quality display components. While the 200-pixel-per-inch displays described above offered satisfactory resolution for most applications, many product developers and industry analysts predicted that video monitors capable of displaying 300 or more pixels per inch would eventually become commonplace. Such products were introduced in the late 1980s, but they have had relatively little impact in electronic document imaging installations. Reversing the predicted trend toward higher image quality, the bit-mapped video monitors employed in newer electronic document imaging installations typically operate at lower resolutions than display devices employed in the mid to late 1980s. The widespread utilization and relatively unquestioned acceptance of such monitors suggests that display resolutions of 200 pixels per inch or higher exceed many application requirements and customer expectations. As a significant incentive to acceptance, monitor prices vary directly with resolution; by sacrificing some quality without impairing the utility of displayed document images, customers can save money, particularly in multi-workstation installations.

As previously noted, 19-inch, landscape-mode, bit-mapped video monitors are increasingly supplanting 15-inch, portrait-mode devices in electronic document imaging installations. Most 19-inch, landscape-mode monitor operate at resolutions of 110 to 150 pixels per inch. Resolutions in

*Figure 4–6. Document images and computer interaction displayed in overlapping windows. (Courtesy: IBM Corporation)*

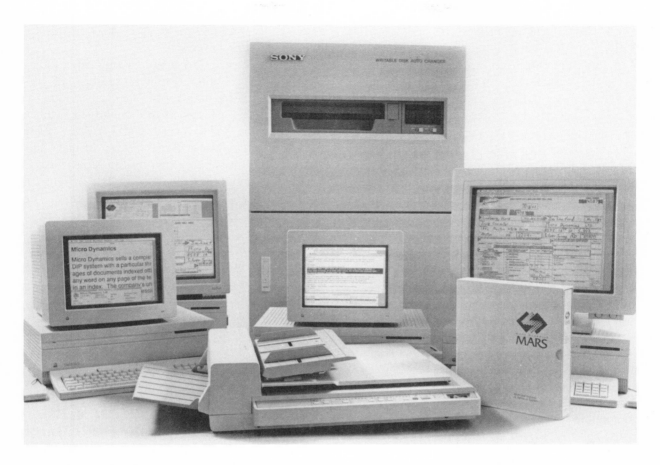

*Figure 4–7. Macintosh monitors displaying portions of document images. (Courtesy: Micro Dynamics Limited)*

that range permit the legible display of 6-point type—the smallest size encountered in most office documents. At 120 pixels per inch, the display area of a 19-inch, landscape-mode monitor contains 1,280 lines with 1,600 pixels per line for a total of 2,048,000 pixels per image. At 150 pixels per inch, the display area contains 1,538 lines with 2,048 pixels per line for a total of 3,149,824 pixels per image. Digitized document images, however, typically contain more than that number of pixels; a letter-size page scanned at 200 pixels per horizontal and vertical inch, for example, contains 3,740,000 pixels. In such cases, the digitized image must be scaled for display at a lower resolution. Scaling is also used to display document images that exceed the screen's dimensions. Such scaling may be performed by specially-designed circuit boards or by image processing software.

A number of image-capable workstations incorporate general-purpose, bit-mapped video monitors (IBM-compatible VGA monitors, for example) as document display devices. This is increasingly the case with entry-level microcomputer-based electronic document imaging systems. As an obvious advantage, VGA monitors are much less expensive than the special-purpose bit-mapped displays described above. VGA monitors are also utilized as display devices in LAN-based electronic document imaging installations. In such situations, application planners typically want to utilize their already installed base of microcomputers as image-capable workstations, particularly for those users whose occasional document retrieval requirements do not justify the purchase of a special-purpose bit-mapped monitor.

General-purpose bit-mapped video monitors can be used as image-capable workstations in electronic document imaging installations, but the results may prove unacceptable for some purposes. As a group, such devices operate at lower display resolutions than bit-mapped monitors designed specifically for document imaging applications. The VGA monitors employed in most newer IBM microcomputer installations, as pre viously noted, can display 480 lines with 640 pixels per line for a total of 307,200 pixels per image. The same resolution is supported by Macintosh II computer systems. When a letter-size page is displayed in its entirety, the effective resolution is approximately 45 pixels per inch. The resulting images will be recognizable but not readable, that is, paragraphs and other formatting characteristics will be detectable, but their textual content will not be legible. For character legibility, document images must be displayed in a partial-page format which necessitates panning and scrolling, an inconvenient and tedious process.

In some applications, however, VGA monitors can provide sufficient viewability to confirm the correct retrieval of document images which will subsequently be printed at a higher resolution for reference purposes.

Among other bit-mapped display formats for IBM-compatible microcomputers, EGA (640 by 350 pixels) and CGA (640 by 200 pixels) provide lower resolution than the VGA format. They are generally unacceptable for document imaging applications and are not supported by most electronic document imaging systems. At 512 by 342 pixels, the resolution employed by the Macintosh Classic product line is likewise poorly suited to document image display. For IBM-compatible microcomputers, the Video Electronics Standards Association (VESA) has endorsed a Super VGA format with a resolution of 800 by 600 pixels—the equivalent of approximately 55 pixels per inch. That resolution, while too low for legible display of a broad range of document images, yields a noticeable improvement over the conventional VGA format. The Super VGA format is supported by some microcomputer-based electronic document imaging systems. Super VGA adapters and video monitors are increasingly available, but prospective purchasers are warned that product-specific variations in scan rates, video drivers, and other characteristics can pose compatibility problems in some installations. Users considering the use of previously purchased Super VGA devices in an electronic document imaging configuration should confirm compatibility in advance of procurement.

Some Super VGA adapters and video monitors support a higher display resolution of 768 lines with 1,024 pixels per line for a total of 786,432 pixels per displayed image—2.5 times more than the VGA format and 1.6 times more than the conventional Super VGA format. The same resolution is supported by the XGA format, which was announced by IBM in late 1990 as a higher quality alternative to the VGA format. The equivalent of approximately 70 pixels per inch, it can legibly display many document images.

The substitution of displayed images for paper documents raises questions and concerns about the prolonged use of video monitors and its impact on worker productivity, health, and safety. Such questions and concerns are not unique to electronic document imaging installations; they apply to all computer applications. They have been defined and discussed in many publications; examples, representing various viewpoints, include Campbell and Durden (1983), Cushman (1986), Cushman and Miller (1988), Dain et al. (1988), Gould et al. (1987), Gur and Ron (1992), Isensee and Bennett (1983), Landau and Jaercke (1987), Matthews and Mertins (1987), Matula (1981), Mourant et al. (1981), Ong et al. (1988), Stark (1984), Van Overbeck (1991), and Wilkinson and Robinshaw (1987). While screen size and resolution are important determinants of image quality and viewability, various technical and ergonomic factors can have a significant impact on the effective utilization of bit-mapped video monitors in electronic document imaging installations. The screen refresh rate, sometimes termed the vertical scan rate, is a frequently overlooked factor in monitor selection. As previously described, CRT-based monitors generate document images by selectively energizing spots within a phosphorescent glass panel. In most cases, the displayed image lasts only a fraction of a second, and the screen phosphors must be repeatedly re-illuminated or "refreshed" to sustain a viewable image. The screen refresh rate, which is measured in hertz, denotes the number of times a given video display is re-illuminated per second. A high refresh rate, 70 hertz or greater, is essential to avoid perceptible flicker and resulting operator fatigue. Some video monitors employ refresh rates of 50 to 60 hertz, which may not be sufficient to prevent flicker at low luminances. Perceptible flicker is also affected by the refesh methodology. Non-interlaced monitors refresh the entire display at the indicated rate, while interlaced monitors refresh odd and even numbered scan lines in alternating operations. Non-interlaced monitors are preferred for flicker-free display.

Video display devices have been the subject of widely publicized complaints about eyestrain, headaches, and other symptoms of visual fatigue. Such symptoms are often attributable to glare from light that is reflected by the monitor's screen. To minimize this problem, some bit-mapped video monitors employed in electronic document imaging configurations incorporate an anti-glare filter as a standard or optional feature. Some models are likewise equipped with swivelling and/or tiltable screens that can be positioned to reduce glare while minimizing musculo-skeletal fatigue resulting from static postures. Such features are mandatory in many European installations where human engineering considerations reflected in government regulations play a decisive role in equipment selection. Since a video monitor's keyboard and exterior surfaces can also be a source of disturbing glare, some models are finished in materials and colors that are designed to minimize reflectivity.

In electronic document imaging installations, great differences in luminance between a monitor's immediate work area and the surrounding environment can lead to discomfort glare. In most offices, ambient light levels are too high for comfortable use of video displays. General room illumination ranging from 24 to 50 footcandles is recommended. The luminance difference ratio between the monitor's work area and surrounding room environment should not exceed 3:1. Artificial and natural light should be diffused. Video monitors should be located as far away from windows as possible, and operators should never face windows or other bright surfaces.

The most serious and ominous health-related questions about video monitors concern potential hazards associated with radiation emissions. Cathode-ray tubes emit various types of radiation, including visible, infrared, and ultraviolet rays; microwaves; radio frequency waves; and x-rays.

These emissions have been named as suspect agents in several court cases involving health problems of video display operators, but there has been no conclusive evidence establishing a causative relationship. On the contrary, various studies have concluded that the radiation emitted by CRT displays is within levels defined as safe by the U.S. government; but the issue cannot be put to rest. Recently, concerns have been voiced about the potential harmful effects of extremely-low-frequency (ELF) and very-low-frequency (VLF) electromagnetic waves. While a relationship between low-frequency emissions and specific health problems has not been established by scientific studies, the issue has been widely publicized, particularly in the case of emissions from power transmission lines.

Addressing customers' concerns, some manufacturers of bit-mapped video monitors for electronic document imaging configurations offer special shielding against ELF and VLF emissions. An increasing number of companies advertise their products as meeting specifications for safe levels of low-frequency emissions defined by SEMKO, the Swedish National Board for Testing and Measurement, which has established stringent regulations concerning such emissions. Various after-market products for emission reductions, such as specially-designed filters that attach to a video monitor's screen, are also available.

## Laser Printers

As noted above, many electronic document imaging systems are designed to replace paper documents with softcopy displays, but it is a rare application that does not require some paper copies of digitized document images or database records for reference or other purposes. Half a century of experience with microfilm systems implemented as an alternative to conventional paper files suggests that hardcopy production capability is essential for both functionality and user acceptance. Diminished reliance on paper copies, rather than their outright abolition, is a realistic goal for the imaging systems planner.

Electronic document imaging installations consequently include one or more printers for paper output, the familiar combination of lasers and xerography being the preferred printer technology. Hardcopy output is especially important where retrieval workstations include low-resolution or partial-page displays. In such cases, as previously noted, an image-capable workstation may serve as a locating device for document images that will be routed to a printer. Paradoxically, some installations employ electronic document imaging technology to facilitate and automate the production of paper copies.

As with video monitors, the laser printers employed in electronic document imaging configurations differ in their operating characteristics and output capabilities. Most models support black-and-white printing resolutions up to 300 pixels (dots) per horizontal and vertical inch. The resulting output quality is more than acceptable for most electronic document imaging applications. Higher-resolution devices (printers operating at 600 pixels per inch, for example) are increasingly available but rarely required, since scanning resolutions seldom exceed 300 pixels per inch. Color printers, employing laser and other technologies, are likewise available, but they play a limited role in electronic document imaging installations; as previously discussed, most source documents consist of black text on a white background.

*Figure 4–8. A standalone electronic document imaging system configured with a document scanner, image-capable monitor, and laser printer. (Courtesy: Tab Products)*

Since resolution is virtually identical across the product group, individual laser printers are widely categorized by operating speed, which is usually measured in pages per minute. As might be expected, the least expensive electronic document imaging systems are configured with relatively slow laser printers. Such devices are encountered in entry-level, single-workstation, microcomputer-based document imaging configurations. In multi-workstation systems, they may be installed on the desktops of users who require local printing capabilities. In either case, the volume of output such devices can support is constrained by their relatively low printing speeds. They can usually produce four to six letter-size pages per minute and have a duty cycle comparable to that of a desktop copier; they can produce several thousand copies per month with reliable operation, but are not built for high volumes of printing activity. Most models feature a single paper tray capable of containing up to 250 sheets. Output is typically limited to letter-size pages.

Faster, more expensive printers typically operate as shared peripherals in multi-workstation electronic document imaging configurations. Medium-speed laser printers, which often function as print servers in LAN-based electronic document imaging installations, can produce twelve to twenty-four pages per minute. As an alternative to parallel and serial ports, some models are equipped with Ethernet or IBM Token Ring interfaces for direct connection to local area networks. They are more ruggedly constructed than the lower-speed models described above; typical duty cycles range from 50,000 to 75,000 pages per month. To simplify operation, minimize interruptions in print jobs, and enhance throughput, some models are equipped with multiple paper trays capable of containing up to 5,000 sheets of paper.

High-speed laser printers, some of which can operate at rates exceeding fifty pages per minute, are obviously intended for very high-volume, centralized output in large-scale, multi-workstation electronic document imaging configurations. They are usually encountered in minicomputer- and mainframe-based document imaging installations where they may also serve the output requirements of other applications.

## Microform Output

While rarely implemented as an output option, electronic document images can be recorded on microfilm, microfiche, aperture cards, or other microforms. This alternative to full-size paper copies converts digitized document images to miniaturized photographic images, making it appear that the digitized images were first printed onto paper and then microfilmed by a source document camera. The technology that permits such conversion is computer-output microfilm (COM). The conversion is performed by a computer peripheral device called computer-output microfilmer or COM recorder. Combining the attributes of a microfilm camera and a computer printer, it records machine-readable digital information as human-readable page images in microform without creating an intervening paper copy. Specific operating characteristics and output capabilities vary from model to model. Most COM recorders produce microfiche, sheets of film that measure 105 by 148 millimeters and contain the equilvanet of 420 letter-size pages or 270 computer-printout-size pages recorded at an effective reduction of 48x. Other COM recorders can produce 16- and 35-mm roll microfilm or 35-mm aperture cards.

As output media for electronic document images, COM-generated microforms offer several attractive advantages:

- They permit compact dissemination of large quantities of printed images to users who are external to a given electronic document imaging installation. Because they are highly miniaturized copies, microform images require magnification for viewing or printing, but devices for those purposes are readily available from many sources.

- As discussed more fully in Chapter Five, electronic document imaging systems record digitized images in machine-readable formats that depend on the continued availability of specific hardware and software components for retrieval. If a given product line or individual system component is discontinued, the utility of recorded images may be imperilled.

COM-generated images, in contrast, contain human-readable information. The content of such images can be displayed by relatively simple magnifying devices that will presumably be available for the foreseeable future.

- Microforms are more stable than the optical and magnetic media that store digitized document images. They are excellent storage media for document images that must be retained for long periods of time. When processed and stored in a manner specified in American National Standards, polyester-based silver gelatin microforms—the type utilized by many COM recorders—have a lifetime estimate exceeding 500 years. Diazo and vesicular microforms, which are used for duplication rather than original recording, have lifetime estimates of one-hundred years. As discussed in Chapter Five, lifetime estimates for most optical and magnetic media are much shorter.

Despite these advantages, the incorporation of microforms as output alternatives for electronic document images is impeded by the limited availability and high cost of the COM recorders required for such implementations. Computer-output microfilm is a well-established technology that offers a fast, reliable, potentially cost-effective alternative to paper printers in a variety of data processing applications. COM production equipment has been in widespread use, at customer sites and through microfilm service bureaus, for over a quarter of a century. The majority of available COM recorders, however, are alphanumeric devices. Their printable repertoire includes alphabetic characters, numeric digits, punctuation marks, and other symbols commonly encountered in textual documents. Because they lack graphic output capabilities, they are unsuitable for the applications discussed here. The conversion of electronic document images to microform requires a graphics COM recorder. Such devices can generate microforms from raster-format, bit-mapped images as well as alphanumeric information. Sometimes described as COM plotters, graphic COM recorders are most often encountered in computer-aided design (CAD) installations. As a signficant complication for electronic document imaging implementations, graphic COM recorders are manufactured by a small number of companies and are much more expensive than their alphanumeric counterparts.

*Image Transmission*

As outlined above, viewing and printing are the most common output options in electronic document imaging installations. Retrieved document images may be displayed on a video monitor or dispatched to a local or shared printer for hardcopy output. In some cases, however, document images retrieved at a given workstation must be transmitted to other workstations within a given electronic document imaging installation. The ability to transmit digitized images between system components is one of the principal advantages of electronic document imaging technology. Unlike paper documents and microfilm images which require conversion to electronic formats prior to transmission, digitized document images are transmission-ready.

Image transmission is an obvious component of workflow programming, which provides automatic routing of document images based on a predefined script. Apart from coordinated workflow implementations, document images retrieved by a given user may be appended to electronic messages and dispatched through an electronic mail system to other workstations for action or reference purposes. Alternatively, retrieved documents images may be transmitted to external computer systems or to fax machines.

Multi-workstation electronic document imaging configurations typically rely on local area networks (LANs) to link individual components at a given site. Such networks support the intra-site transmission of document images. Wide-area networks (WANs) permit the transmission of document images to external devices. In both cases, the communication links must offer sufficient bandwidth to accommodate the large number of bits that encode individual document images. As discussed in Chapter Three, a letter-size page digitized in the binary mode at 200 pixels per horizontal and vertical inch with Group IV compression averaging 15:1 contains approximately 31,000

bytes. At 8 bits per byte, that image is composed of 248,000 bits. Most LAN-based electronic document imaging systems are designed for Ethernet or IBM Token Ring installations. Ethernet networks, which conform to IEEE 802.3 standards, exist in several varieties: thick Ethernet (10 BASE 5), which uses RG-11 coaxial cable as its communication medium; thin Ethernet (10 BASE 2), which uses RG-58 coaxial cable; and twisted-pair Ethernet (10 BASE T), which uses twisted-pair wiring. All varieties transmit data at 10 million bits per second. While Ethernet's theoretical maximum network throughput is 600 million bits per hour, all communication networks operate at some fraction of maximum efficiency. Throughput is invariably degraded by inefficiencies inherent in network access protocols, the limited transmission speeds of network interface cards, and other factors; operating efficiency at 30 percent of the theoretical maximum throughput is typical. At that rate, Ethernet throughput is 180 million bits per hour, which is sufficient to support image transmission traffic of 725 pages per hour. If retrieval activity averages ten pages per workstation per hour, an Ethernet network can support an electronic document imaging installation with seventy-two workstations, assuming that the network is dedicated to image transmission and does not support other applications. IBM Token Ring networks, which conform to IEEE 802.5 standards, support transmission rates of 4 or 16 million bits per second. In the latter case, a Token Ring network supports a theoretical maximum throughput of 960 million bits per hour. At 30 percent efficiency, however, the maximum throughput is 288 million bits per hour, which is sufficient to transmit 1,160 pages per hour—again assuming that network traffic consists exclusively of document images. In their 4-megabit implementations, IBM Token Ring networks may prove too slow for document image transmission in some installations. At 30 percent efficiency, their maximum throughput is 72 million bits per hour, which is sufficient to transmit just 290 pages per hour. Other local area networks (including ARCNet, StarLAN, AppleTalk, and such entry-level LANs as Artisoft's LANtastic) operate at even slower rates.

As discussed in Chapter Three, page size, digitization mode, scanning resolution, and com-

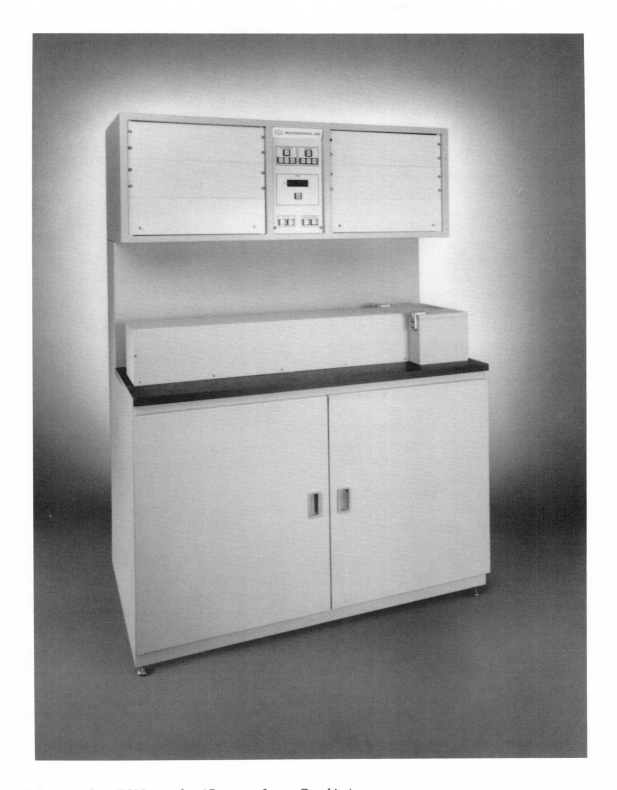

*Figure 4–9.  A graphics COM recorder. (Courtesy: Image Graphics)*

pression algorithms have a widely recognized impact on storage requirements and media capacity in electronic document imaging implementations; their significance for image transmission and network throughput, while equally important, is often overlooked. The foregoing discussion of network throughput is based on letter-size pages digitized in the binary mode at 200 pixels per inch with Group IV compression—one of the most favorable scenarios for image transmission. A given network's image transmission capabilities will be degraded by increases in page size and scanning resolution, by grayscale or color mode digitization which utilize multiple bits to encode each pixel, by the use of Group III rather than Group IV compression algorithms, and by document characteristics which may limit the effectiveness of compression algorithms, regardless of type. Where letter-size pages are scanned in the binary mode at 300 pixels per horizontal and vertical inch with Group III compression, for example, each page consists of approximately 105,000 bytes or 840,000 bits. Where those conditions apply, an Ethernet installation operating at 30 percent efficiency can transmit just 215 page-images per hour, assuming that the network is dedicated to document image transmission. As a significant complicating factor, some electronic document imaging systems are implemented as an addition to a previously installed local area network that is utilized by other applications. In such cases, the increased competition for transmission resources engendered by an imaging implementation can degrade the performance of all applications operating on the network.

Throughput limitations in LAN-based document imaging implementations may be alleviated by future implementations of fiber optic networks. The FDDI (Fiber Distributed Data Interface) protocol supports a nominal transmission rate of 100 million bits per second. Such high transmission rates are particularly important for electronic document imaging installations with large numbers of workstations with very high reference activity; large documents, such as engineering drawings; or documents digitized in grayscale or color modes.

Throughput limitations are a potentially greater concern in implementations where electronic document images must be transmitted over long-distance communication facilities, which usu-

*Figure 4–10. A LAN-based document imaging installation. (Courtesy: Sigma Imaging)*

ally operate at slower rates than their LAN counterparts. T1 lines, for example, support transmission at 1.544 million bits per second, and other types of leased lines may be considerably slower. Much long-distance transmission of electronic document images relies on facsimile technology, which operates over conventional dial-up telephone lines at speeds up to 9,600 bits per second. As a standard or optional feature, many electronic document imaging systems support a facsimile gateway consisting of a fax modem and its associated software. The fax modem and software may be installed in a single-workstation electronic document imaging system or in a network server that can be accessed by multiple workstations. In the latter case, the server may be dedicated to facsimile transmission or used for other purposes. Specific configurations aside, a facsimile gateway can transmit one or more retrieved document images directly to a Group III fax machine or to a computer equipped with a Group III-compatible fax modem, thus eliminating the need to print the image for transmission through an external facsimile transceiver. Several electronic document imaging systems also support the use of fax machines as remote scanners. Incoming facsimile images can be indexed and recorded in the same manner as digitized images produced by locally-installed scanners. As a cautionary note, however, the scanning resolutions supported by Group III fax machines may not satisfy the quality requirements of a given electronic document imaging implementation. In the fine mode, the highest setting for Group III machines, facsimile resolution is 200 pixels per inch, but most facsimile transmission occurs at the normal-mode resolution of 200 by 100 pixels per inch. While the resulting images may be legible, they cannot be used for auto-indexing via optical character recognition. Most OCR programs, as noted in Chapter Two, require images digitized at 300 pixels per inch.

## References

Anick, P. et al. (1989). A direct manipulation interface for Boolean information retrieval via natural language query. In Proceedings of the 13th International Conference on Research and Development in Information Retrieval. New York: Association for Computing Machinery, pp. 135-50.

Bataineh, A. et al. (1991). Parallel Boolean operations for information retrieval. Information Processing Letters 39/2: 99-108.

Bechis, D. (1991). CRT technology survey. Information Display 7/12: 8-12.

Bookstein, A. (1980). Fuzzy requests: an approach to weighted Boolean searches. Journal of the American Society for Information Science 31: 240-47.

_____. (1980a). Fuzzy requests. Journal of the American Society for Information Science 32: 257-59.

_____. (1985). Probability and fuzzy-set applications to information retrieval. In Annual Review of Information Science and Technology, vol. 20. White Plains, NY: Knowledge Industry Publications, pp. 118-51.

_____. and Cooper, W. (1976). A general mathematical model for information retrieval systems. Library Quarterly 46: 153-67.

Campbell, F. and Durden, K. (1983). The visual display terminal issue: a consideration of its physiological, psychological and clinical background. Ophthalmic and Physiological Optics 3: 175-92.

Cushman, W. (1986). Reading from microfiche, a VDT, and the printed page: subjective fatigue and performance. Human Factors 28: 65-72.

Cushman, W. and Miller, R. (1988). Resolution and gray-scale requirements for the display of legible alphanumeric characters. In 1988 SID International Symposium: Digest of Technical Papers. Playa del Rey, CA: Society for Information Display, pp. 432-34.

Dain, S. et al. (1988). Symptoms in VDU operators. American Journal of Optometry and Physiological Optics 65/3: 162-67.

Das-Gupta, P. (1987). Boolean interpretations of conjunctions for document retrieval. Journal of the American Society for Information Science 38: 245-54.

De Stricker, U. (1988). A menu interface to formulate Boolean logic: can it be done? Information Service and Use 8/1: 39-46.

Edelstein, H. (1991). Imaging shifts emphasis to workflow management. Software Magazine 11/13: 96-105.

Fisher, W. and Gilbert, J. (1987). FileNet: a distributed system supporting WorkFlo, a flexible office procedures control language. In IEEE Computer Society Office Automation Symposium.

Washington, DC: IEEE Computer Society Press, pp. 226-33.

Gould, J. et al. (1987). Reading is slower from CRT displays than from paper: attempts to isolate a single-variable explanation. Human Factors 29: 269-99.

Gur, S. and Ron, S. (1992). Does work with visual display units impair visual activities after work? Documenta Ophthalmologica 79: 253-59.

Heine, M. (1982). A simple, intelligent front end for information retrieval systems using Boolean logic. Information Technology: Research and Development 1/4: 247-60.

Infante, C. (1985). On the resolution of raster-scanned CRT displays. Proceedings of the S.I.D. 26/1: 23-36.

Irwin, G. (1992). Royal Life's FileNet pilot. Information Management and Technology 25/2: 78-80.

Isensee, S. and Bennett, C. (1983). Perception of flicker and glare on computer CRT displays. Human Factors 25: 177-84.

Kaufmann, A. (1975). Introduction to the Theory of Fuzzy Subsets. New York: Academic Press.

Keller, P. (1986). Resolution measurement techniques for data display cathode ray tubes. Displays, Technology, and Applications 7/1: 17-29.

Kerre, E. et al. (1986). The use of fuzzy set theory in information retrieval and databases: a survey. Journal of the American Society for Information Science 37: 341-45.

Kraft, D. and Buell, D. (1983). Fuzzy sets and generalized Boolean retrieval systems. Internal Journal of Man-Machine Studies 19: 45-56.

Landau, K. and Jaercke, F. (1987). The analysis of stress and strain at the videotex workplace. Behaviour and Information Technology 6: 327-35.

Latham, S. and Phil, M. (1991). Beyond Boolean logic: probabilistic approaches to text retrieval. Law Librarian 22/3: 157-63.

Lucarella, D. and Morara, R. (1991). Fuzzy information retrieval system. Journal of Information Science 17/2: 81-91.

MacNaughton, B. (1991). What to look for when choosing your high res display. Advanced Imaging 6/9: 34-40.

Matthews, M. and Mertins, K. (1987). The influence of color on visual search and subjective discomfort using CRT displays. In Proceedings of the Human Factors Society: 31st Annual Meeting. Santa Monica, CA: Human Factors Society, vol. 2, pp. 1271-75.

Matula, A. (1981). Effects of visual display units on the eyes: a bibliography (1972-1980). Human Factors 23: 581-86.

McCready, S. (1989). Workflow software: a highway to productivity. Inform 3/1: 12-16.

Mourant, R. et al. (1981). Visual fatigue and cathode ray tube display terminals. Human Factors 23: 529-40.

Murch, G. and Virgin, L. (1985). Resolution and addressability: how much is enough? In 1985 SID International Symposium: Digest of Technical Papers. New York: Pallisades Institute Research Services, pp. 101-103.

Negoita, C. and Flonder, P. (1976). On fuzziness in information retrieval. International Journal of Man-Machine Studies 8: 711-16.

Neiberding, M. (1990). Image processing of health insurance claims. IMC Journal 26/2: 16-18.

Nelson, N. (1989). Maimonides Medical Center uses workflow management system. Computers in Healthcare 10/3: 45, 50-52.

Newcombe, F. (1991). Why workflow? Inform 5/6: 10-12, 18.

Nicklin, B. and Stoeppel, G. (1991). High resolution display systems: only with the right tools. Advanced Imaging 6/9: 46-49.

Nugent, W. (1991). Electronic imaging in high-resolution gray-scale for fine art and salon photography. Document Image Automation 11/5: 284-87.

Oldroyd, B. and Schroder, J. (1982). Study of strategies used in online searching: 2. Positional logic—an example of the importance of selecting the right Boolean operator. Online Review 6/2: 127-33.

Ong, C. et al. (1988). Review and reappraisal of health hazards of display terminals. Displays, Technology and Applications 9/1: 3-13.

Ornager, S. and Johne, M. (1983). Changes in thesaurus construction caused by the use of Boolean searching. In Seventh International Online Information Meeting. Oxford: Learned Information, pp. 167-73.

Paice, C. (1984). Soft evaluation of Boolean search queries in information retrieval systems. Information Technology: Research Development Applications 3/1: 33-41.

Plesums, C. and Bartel, R. (1990). Large-scale image systems: USAA case study. IBM Systems Journal 29: 343-55.

Prade, H. and Testemale, C. (1987). Fuzzy relational databases: representational issues and reduction using similarity measures. Journal of the American Society for Information Science 38: 118-26.

Radecki, T. (1979). Fuzzy set theoretical approach to document retrieval. Information Retrieval and Management 15: 247-59.

_____. (1981). Outline of a fuzzy logic approach to information retrieval. International Journal of Man-Machine Studies 14: 169-78.

_____. (1982). Similarity measures for Boolean search request formulations. Journal of the American Society for Information Science 33/1: 8-17.

_____. (1983). Generalized Boolean methods of information retrieval. International Journal of Man-Machine Studies 18: 407-39.

_____. (1988). Trends in research on information retrieval: the potential for improvements in conventional Boolean retrieval systems. Information Processing and Management 24: 219-27.

Rosen, B. (1987). Raster displays hit 3000-line resolution. ESD: the Electronic System Design Magazine 17/7: 91-95.

Sachs, W. (1976). An approach to associative retrieval through the theory of fuzzy sets. Journal of the American Society for Information Science 27: 85-87.

Saracevic, T. (1983). On a method for studying the structure and nature of requests in information retrieval. In Proceedings of the American Society for Information Science, vol. 20. White Plains, NY: Knowledge Industry Publications, pp. 22-25.

Scheffler, F. et al. (1972). An experiment to study the use of Boolean NOT logic to improve the precision of selective dissemination of information. Journal of the American Society for Information Science 23: 58-65.

Seigle, D. (1987). Document-image processing: breaking the productivity barrier in today's office. IMC Journal 23/4: 55-57.

Stark, L. (1984). Visual fatigue and the VDT workplace. Visual Display Terminals: Usability Issues and Health Concerns. Englewood Cliffs, NJ: Prentice-Hall, pp. 229-69.

Tahani, V. (1976). A fuzzy model of document retrieval systems. Information Processing and Management 12: 177-88.

_____. (1977). A conceptual framework for fuzzy query processing: a step toward very intelligent database systems. Information Processing and Management 13: 289-303.

Taylor, R. (1968). Question negotiation and information seeking in libraries. College and Research Libraries 29: 178-94.

Thoone, M. (1982). A very high resolution document display. In International Conference on Electronic Image Processing. London: IEE, pp. 6-10.

Trammell, B. (1989). Too little, too late? Not at USAA: big and early describes this organization's efforts in document processing. Inform 3/7: 24-26, 50-52.

Van Overbeck, T. (1991). Hi-res displays: the serious health and comfort issues. Advanced Imaging 6/9: 42-44, 98.

Verhoeff, J. et al. (1961). Inefficiency of the use of Boolean functions for information retrieval systems. Communications of the Association for Computing Machinery 4: 557-59.

Vigil, P. (1982). Utilization of Boolean NOT to facilitate online searching effectiveness and comprehension. In Information Interaction: Proceedings of the 45th ASIS Annual Meeting, vol. 19. White Plains, NY: Knowledge Industry Publications, pp. 316-19.

Wilkinson, R. and Robinshaw, H. (1987). Proofreading: VDU and paper text compared for speed, accuracy and fatigue. Behaviour and Information Technology 6: 125-33.

Wilson, S. (1987). Specifying the resolution of a color CRT. In MCC '87: Military Computing Conference, Proceedings. Palo Alto, CA: EW Communications, pp. 68-75.

Wood, D. (1991). Specifying requirements for document displays. Inform 5/6: 22-24.

Zadeh, L. (1965). Fuzzy sets. Information and Control 8: 338-53.

*Chapter Five*
# Issues

While electronic document imaging systems offer attractive information storage and retrieval capabilities, important and challenging questions have been raised about the document management implications and limitations of specific system characteristics. Records managers and others responsible for the retention of information need for legal reasons, business reference, or other purposes are understandably concerned about the continued retrievability of document images associated with potentially short-lived hardware and software environments. Similar concerns have been expressed about the stability of optical and magnetic media used for document image storage and about their admissibility as evidence in judicial proceedings. Various application developers and system planners have expressed an interest in integrating electronic document imaging with other document management technologies, such as micrographics and text-oriented storage and retrieval systems. Finally, the costs associated with innovative technologies and their justification are ever-present concerns in automated document storage and retrieval implementations. These issues are examined in this chapter.

## Continued Retrievability

Continued retrievability refers to the future ability to identify and retrieve potentially relevant document images for display, printing, or other purposes. Information systems analysts, records managers, computer systems specialists, and others responsible for planning, selecting, implementing, and operating electronic document imaging systems are understandably concerned about the continued retrievability of digitized images, particularly as it relates to retention periods defined for specific groups of documents. Such retention periods may be based on recordkeeping requirements

contained in legal statutes and government regulations or on reference or research considerations. Depending on their information content and the applications in which they are utilized, some documents will be retained for several months or years; others may remain useful indefinitely.

As described in Chapter Three, electronic document images may be recorded on optical disks, magnetic disks, or magnetic tapes. The continued retrievability of document images is obviously affected by the stability of such recording media. In this context, stability denotes the retention of chemical properties and physical characteristics appropriate to a given medium's intended purpose. For the optical and magnetic media employed in electronic document imaging systems, the intended purposes are recording of new information and playback (retrieval) of previously recorded information. The stable life—or lifetime estimate—of a given medium is the period of time during which it can be used for reliable recording and playback. Continued retrievability is a concern when a given medium's lifetime estimate is shorter than the retention periods for document images that the medium contains. Because electronic document images are recorded in computer-processable form, their retrievability also depends on the continued availability of hardware and software components required for data base searching, image display, document printing, and other operations. These issues are discussed in the following subsections.

### Media Stability

As noted above, lifetime estimates define the time periods during which optical and magnetic media will support reliable retrieval of document images or other recorded information. With electronic media, reliability is determined by the preservation of signal strength and the absence of permanent read/

write errors during recording and playback. In the computer industry, the de facto standard of reliable operation specifies that media contain less than one permanent read/write error per trillion recorded bits. Since most commercially available optical and magnetic media contain fewer than one trillion bits (approximately 12.2 gigabytes) of recording capacity, any given medium should be free of errors during its claimed stability period.

Lifetime estimates are most relevant to removable storage media, such as optical disk cartridges and magnetic tapes. While rigid, fixed magnetic disks are the storage media of choice for data base records that serve as an index to electronic document images and, occasionally, for the document images themselves, information recorded on them is continuously vulnerable to damage from head crashes or other disk drive malfunctions. Data base records and document images recorded on hard disks must consequently be copied onto removable media for backup protection. In some applications, electronic document images are recorded on hard disks during a relatively brief period of frequent reference, after which they are transferred to optical disk cartridges or magnetic tapes. In such situations, the brevity of hard disk storage renders stability concerns irrelevant—provided, of course, that appropriate backup procedures are implemented.

The stability of a given information storage medium depends on several factors, including the medium's chemical composition and the conditions under which it is stored and used. These factors have been delineated and discussed in various scientific monographs, technical reports, journal articles, and conference papers. Examples are surveyed by Saffady (1991). Unlike national and international standards that address the stability of paper and photographic media, lifetime estimates for the optical disks and magnetic tapes employed in electronic document imaging configurations are principally based on media manufacturers' claims, which are occasionally supported by published studies or independent investigations. While optical disks and magnetic tapes are sometimes described as archival media, they do not offer the permanence implied in that description. On the contrary, optical and magnetic media are vulnerable to significant time-dependent degradation

through environmental effects. Such degradation will ultimately impede the reliable retrieval of recorded information.

Most read/write optical disks, for example, feature metallic thin films as their recording materials. Many write-once optical disks are composed of tellurium alloys, as are rewritable phase-change media. Rewritable magneto-optical recording materials similarly include various combinations of rare-earths and transition metals. As a group, such metallic thin films are susceptible to oxidation resulting from exposure to air. Over time, oxidation promotes pinhole formation and other forms of corrosion which can significantly alter the reflectivity, transmissiveness, signal-to-noise ratios, pit formation characteristics, bit-error frequencies, and other recording and playback properties of optical media. As a further complication, optical recording materials are coated on glass or plastic substrates which contain rough spots, strains, and other defects that can promote localized corrosion. In addition, plastic substrates tend to absorb moisture.

The degradative impact of oxidation on write-once and rewritable optical disks is well documented in published studies. For the most part, such works report the results of accelerated aging tests performed in research laboratories, combined with accumulated knowledge about the chemical behavior of specific optical recording materials; tellurium, for example, was discovered in the late eighteenth century and its vulnerability to oxidation has long been recognized. Optical media manufacturers increasingly incorporate oxidation-resistant alloys and barrier coatings into their products, but such measures only retard deteriorative processes. Media degradation, with consequent loss of recorded information, is ultimately inevitable.

Generalizations about the stability of optical disks are complicated by several factors. As discussed in Chapter Three, available optical storage products employ a variety of technologies, each involving different recording materials, substrates, processes, and equipment. Write-once and rewritable optical disks may be composed of metal alloys, metal/polymer combinations, or dye-based materials coated on glass or plastic substrates. Information may be recorded by forming microscopic pits, bubbles, or bumps; by diffusion of dyes; by crystalline-to-amorphous transitions, or vice versa; or through a combination of heat and magnetism. In addition, specific implementations of a given optical recording technology vary from manufacturer.

The relative newness of optical storage media prevents stability evaluation estimates based on direct observation. In their technical specification sheets and other product literature, manufacturers of write-once and rewritable optical media often provide lifetime estimates based on accelerated aging tests. Such tests are usually performed by the media manufacturers themselves. Their outcomes may or may not be published in scientific journals. Where they are, it is often difficult to relate the published findings to specific optical storage products, since accelerated aging tests may be performed during the product development stage on laboratory disks rather than commercially available media. With these cautionary observations in mind, the following discussion summarizes manufacturers' lifetime estimates for playback stability of write-once and rewritable optical disks that utilize specific recording technologies. Playback stability denotes the period of time during which document images or other recorded information can be reliably retrieved. Readers are cautioned that such lifetime estimates are subject to revision, usually in the direction of longer life, as media manufacturers.

Manufacturers of tellurium-based, write-once optical disks for ablative recording variously claim playback stability of ten to forty years from the date a given disk was manufactured. Lifetime estimates for most newer tellurium-based media range from thirty to forty years; ten-year stability claims were characteristic of first-generation tellurium-based disks. Manufacturers of write-once media for thermal-bubble recording typically claim playback stabilities of ten to fifty years from the manufacturing date, with the longer period being characteristic of newer media. Manufacturers of dye-based and phase-change media for write-once recording claim a playback stability period of fifteen years. Sony, the only manufacturer of dual-alloy media, provides a lifetime estimate of one-hundred years for its write-once optical disks.

Lifetime estimates for rewritable optical disks are sometimes shorter than those for write-once media. Manufacturers of magneto-optical disks with plastic substrates typically claim playback stability of ten to fifteen years. For magneto-optical disks with glass substrates, typical lifetime estimates range from twenty to thirty years, glass substrates being less prone to degradative moisture absorption than their plastic counterparts. Manufacturers of rewritable phase-change media claim playback stability of ten years.

Because lifetime estimates are based on media manufacturing dates, large quantities of write-once or rewritable optical disks should not be purchased in anticipation of future use. Unrecorded media should be purchased new shortly before the time it will be used.

Stability claims for CD-ROMs and other read-only optical media vary. As previously described, read-only optical disks are non-recordable copies produced by mastering processes. They consist of a plastic substrate with a thin reflective metal layer and protective coating. The reflective layer is usually composed of aluminum, although several compact disc manufacturers have experimented with gold, silver, platinum, and other metals. The protective overcoat is a layer of acrylic or lacquer. Most producers indicate that read-only optical media will remain playable for at least twenty-five years from their manufacturing dates. As with read/write optical disks, their reflective layers are vulnerable to oxidation, and their plastic substrates can absorb moisture. Possible degradative effects include internal cracking, shrinkage, changes in tensile strength, and the formation of water-filled pockets, any of which can alter a medium's optical characteristics.

In the case of magnetic tapes, anecdotal evidence based on operational experience with media in prolonged use suggests the possibility of long life. Audio and video tapes manufactured more than a quarter century ago remain playable today. Computing facilities have likewise successfully retrieved data from magnetic tapes that have been in storage for more than a decade. Contradicting such claims, however, audible and visible distortions attest to the deterioration of many older audio and video tapes, while questions have been raised about the retrievability of information recorded on magnetic tape maintained in large data archives. Many personal computer users have had the disturbing experience of being unable to retrieve information recorded on magnetic tapes or disks,

**Table 5-1. Manufacturer's Lifetime Estimates for Read/Write Optical Disks**

| Recording Technology | Lifetime Estimate |
| --- | --- |
| Ablative recording | 10-40 yrs |
| Thermal bubble | 10-50 yrs |
| Dual alloy | 100 yrs |
| Dye-based | 15 yrs |
| Magneto-optical | 10-30 yrs |
| WORM phase change | 15 yrs |
| Rewritable phase change | 10 yrs |

even though recording may have been performed just a short time before the failed retrieval attempt.

As storage media in electronic document imaging installations, magnetic tapes are vulnerable to accidental erasure of recorded information and to the migration or print-through of previously recorded signals from one part of a given medium to another. With the exception of the magneto-optical variety of rewritable media, information recorded on optical disks is unaffected by magnetic fields. Retrievability of information is also imperiled by changes in the physical characteristics and chemical composition of magnetic tapes. The most significant physical changes are attributable to rough or careless media handling, to damage from improperly maintained equipment, and to abrasive media wear resulting from contact with magnetic read/write heads during recording and playback— a problem that does not affect optical disks, which are recorded and read by lasers without contact. Both physical deformations and chemical degradation may be induced by improper storage environments. In particular, the polyurethane binders that cause magnetic recording materials to adhere to tape substrates are easily damaged by inappropriate environmental conditions. At high humidity, polyurethanes are subject to hydrolytic degradation and decomposition processes which promote particle shedding and impair retrievability.

Given their longstanding and widespread use for information recording, it is surprising that so few sources provide lifetime estimates for magnetic tapes. Available information suggests useful lifetimes that are shorter than the optical disk estimates cited above. Geller (1983), the most frequently cited authority on longevity of magnetic tapes in data processing applications, claims that magnetic tapes can retain their playback utility for a period of ten to twenty years when stored under appropriate environmental conditions and handled carefully. Smith et al. (1986) likewise estimate a useful lifetime of twenty years for computer tapes. Both studies deal exclusively with nine-track computer tapes, which feature gamma ferric oxide as their magnetic recording material. Because their recording capacities are relatively low, such tapes are seldom utilized for document image storage. Other magnetic media employ different recording materials, such as chromium dioxide in the case of IBM 3480-type cartridges and cobalt-substituted iron oxide in the case of high-density quarter-inch data cartridges. Manufacturers seldom provide lifetime estimates for such media, and few publications address their stability characteristics. As discussed in Chapter Three, some electronic document imaging systems employ 8-mm data cartridges or digital audiotapes as image storage media. Those tape formats feature metal-particle recording materials. Manufacturers of such products claim a useful lifetime of thirty years for their newest media.

*Hardware/Software Dependence*

As discussed above, lifetime estimates for optical and magnetic media vary considerably from product to product. Playback stability periods range from ten years for magnetic tapes and some rewritable optical disk cartridges to one-hundred years for one type of write-once optical disk cartridge. Within that broad range, lifetime estimates of 15 to forty years are typical for most optical and magnetic storage media employed in electronic document imaging configurations. Some document imaging system vendors claim a competitive advantage based on the longer period of continued retrievability associated with more stable media. They contend, for example, that media with lifetime estimates of thirty or forty years are preferable to those with lifetime estimates of ten or fifteen years.

As computer storage media, however, optical disks and magnetic tapes are designed for use with specific hardware and software components which will usually have shorter service lives than the media themselves. While a given optical disk may remain stable for thirty years or longer, there is no historical precedent, for example, for computer storage peripherals remaining in use for that length of time. Most optical disk drives and magnetic tape units are engineered for a maximum service life of ten years, and the frequency of repair and high maintenance costs associated with aging equipment will typically necessitate replacement before that time. The availability of new models with improved cost-performance characteristics, coupled with changing application requirements, also encourages replacement at relatively short intervals, within five years or less in many cases.

Successive generations of optical disk and magnetic tape equipment have supported higher density recording formats than their predecessors. The earliest 12-inch write-once optical disk drives, for example, supported double-sided media capacities of 2 to 3 gigabytes; the latest models can record more than that amount of information on one side of a 12-inch WORM cartridge. To preserve the utility of previously recorded media, successor products usually offer backward compatibility, that is, they can retrieve information from media recorded by predecessor models in a given manufacturer's product line. There is no guarantee, however, that such backward compatibility will be continued in all future products. On the contrary, the history of computer storage peripherals suggests that backward compatibility provides a bridge between one or, at most, two generations of equipment. Eventually, support for older media and recording formats is phased out, necessitating the transfer of information to newer media for continued retrievability. As an example, low-density nine-track magnetic tape formats, such as 200 and 550 bits per inch, are no longer supported by magnetic tape units. Even the 800 bits-per-inch format, which was widely utilized in the 1970s and early 1980s, is no longer supported by some newer tape drives. As a further constraint, backward compatibility does little, if anything, to address retrievability problems associated with discontinued or obsolete products. 8-inch disks, for example, dominated word-processing installations in the 1970s; many organizations continue to store such media, but given the virtual demise of 8-inch floppy disk drives, the information recorded on them is effectively "lost." Similarly, there is no guarantee, and probably little likelihood, that the current variety of optical disk sizes and formats will be supported by equipment available in the twenty-first century.

As an additional complication, electronic document images and their associated data base records are designed for retrieval or other processing by specific systems and application software. Even more than hardware components, such software may be updated or otherwise changed in a manner that can render previously recorded information unusable.

As the foregoing discussion suggests, electronic document imaging systems cannot satisfy multi-decade reference and retention requirements with a single set of optical or magnetic media. Some industry analysts and information specialists note, however, that computer-based systems are routinely upgraded or replaced at short intervals to take advantage of improved technology embodied in new products. Since an electronic document imaging system installed today is likely to be replaced or significantly upgraded within five years, they contend that the stability of particular storage media has little practical significance—provided, of course, that information from existing optical or magnetic media can be conveniently and reliably transferred to the replacement system, that the costs associated with such transfer is not prohibitive, and that the required media conversions can be incorporated into an organization's work routines.

System replacement aside, the retrievability of electronic document images recorded on optical disk cartridges or magnetic tapes can be extended by copying the images onto new media at intervals determined by a given medium's claimed stability period or by the service life of compatible hardware and software components, whichever is shorter. This procedure is analogous to recopying methodologies that are currently implemented in many data processing installations where magnetic tapes are routinely duplicated on an annual or biannual basis. The time and effort required to accomplish the periodic transfer of document images to new media should not be trivialized, however.

As noted above, the transfer procedures must be incorporated into an organization's work routines; as the number of documents recorded on optical or magnetic media grows, successive transfers will involve an increasingly large volume of images and will require more time to complete. To further minimize the impact of hardware and software dependence and to prevent the irrevocable loss of information recorded on obsolete or discontinued media, application planners may choose to implement a dual-format system in which documents recorded as electronic images on optical or magnetic media are also retained in human-readable form on paper or on microfilm.

## Legality

The available of electronic document imaging systems as alternatives to conventional paper files has raised questions about the status of digitized images as legally-acceptable substitutes for the paper documents they are supposed to supplant. Specific concerns include the ability of digitized images to satisfy legally-mandated recordkeeping requirements, as well as the admissibility of digitized images as evidence in court trials, administrative hearings, and other judicial proceedings. These concerns are obviously greatest where paper documents will be destroyed following digitization, leaving electronic images recorded on optical or magnetic media as the only available versions of documents.

As discussed by Skupsky (1991) and Williams (1987), current assumptions about the legal acceptability of digitized document images recorded on optical or magnetic media are based on the status of those images as true copies of the documents from which they were made. As described in Chapter Four, the retrieval operations supported by electronic document imaging systems typically culminate in the display or printing of digitized images. The displayed images (soft copies) or paper prints (hard copies) are subject to those legal statutes and provisions of case law which pertain to duplicate records.

For purposes of this discussion, a true copy is one that contains all significant details from an original document. Technologies widely recog-

nized as producing true copies include xerography, the most widely utilized photocopying process, and microfilming. Skeptical observers have objected to the inclusion of electronic document imaging among such technologies, contending that the use of compression algorithms to reduce image storage requirements or of enhancement algorithms to improve image quality compromises the status of electronic document images as true copies. If that contention is correct, it would certainly complicate the legal status of electronic document images and potentially invalidate much of the following discussion. While it may arguably be valid for enhanced images, the contention appears to be groundless for the most common instances of image compression. As discussed in Chapter Three, the image compression methodologies employed by most electronic document images are based on CCITT Group III and Group IV algorithms. Those algorithms are sometimes described as "lossless" because they yield compressed images that preserve the entire contents of the object being compressed. Some other compression algorithms, however, employ so-called "lossy" methodologies which achieve high compression ratios by omitting information from images. Electronic document images produced by such algorithms may not qualify as true copies.

The following discussion summarizes statutes and opinions that bear on the legal status of electronic document images with respect to both recordkeeping requirements and admissibility in evidence. The discussion emphasizes U.S. legal statutes and rules of evidence. As noted by Skupsky (1991), most other countries have yet to address the legality of electronic document images; in some countries, the legal status of photocopies and microfilm remains unclear.

### Recordkeeping Requirements

As discussed above, various legal statutes and government regulations specify recordkeeping requirements and retention periods for documents associated with particular activities. Such laws and regulations apply to all private and public organizations that operate within a specific governmental jurisdiction. Skupsky (1989) provides an excellent overview, with well-chosen examples based on recordkeeping requirements contained in U.S. federal laws and regulations.

In the United States, the Uniform Photographic Copies of Business and Public Records as Evidence Act, commonly abbreviated as the UPA, permits the substitution of photocopies for original documents to satisfy legally mandated recordkeeping requirements, except where retention of the original documents is specifically required by law. As its title indicates, the UPA applies to copies of public records maintained by government agencies as well as to copies of business records maintained by corporations, non-profit institutions, and other non-governmental organizations. In every case, the copies must have been produced in the regular course of business as part of an organization's established operating procedures. Where retention of the original documents is not required by law, the UPA permits—but does not mandate—their destruction and the substitution of copies. Although the UPA does not specify procedures for the destruction of original documents, such destruction should be performed in conformity with an organization's formally established schedules for record retention. Such schedules should clearly state that original documents from specified record series are to be converted to electronic images for recording on optical or magnetic media at predetermined intervals as part of an organization's regular business procedures and that the original documents are to be destroyed following such conversion and recording.

Written in 1949, the UPA predates the commercial availability of electronic document imaging systems discussed in this book, but it can be applied without change to digitized images recorded on optical or magnetic media. While it specifically mentions photocopying and microfilming, it does not provide an exhaustive list of acceptable reprographic technologies, nor does it exclude technologies that are are not mentioned. The UPA applies to any copying process that "accurately reproduces or forms a durable medium for so reproducing" original documents. That definition encompasses electronic document imaging technology, provided—as previously indicated—that image compression or other image processing does not compromise the accuracy of reproduction.

As one of the so-called "uniform" laws, the UPA applies only in those legal jurisdictions where it has been adopted. At the time this report was prepared, it had been adopted by the federal judiciary and by more than two-thirds of the states. In other jurisdictions, state-specific statutes may contain similar provisions. In some cases, however, such state-specific statutes restrict the legal status of duplicate records for admissibility in evidence or to satisfy legally-mandated recordkeeping requirements. Some states, for example, prohibit the destruction of original documents held in a custodial or fiduciary capacity. As a much publicized development, several states have recently passed or are considering laws that deal specifically with electronic document imaging technology. The scope of such laws is necessarily restricted to those documents (such as state agency and local government records) over which a given state government has jurisdiction. Specific statutes are often narrowly focused. The Texas government code, for example, recognizes electronic document images as an acceptable storage medium for local government records with retention periods shorter than ten years.

Certain government regulatory agencies have formulated guidelines or issued opinions concerning the use of copies to satisfy recordkeeping requirements associated with particular regulated activities. Such guidelines and opinions may address the acceptability of electronic document images as copies.

### Images as Evidence

Broadly defined, the purpose of evidence is to prove or clarify points at issue in court trials, administrative hearings, or other judicial or quasi-judicial proceedings. Documents are widely employed as evidence in such situations, often as a complement or supplement to testimony. Evidence, including documents, which a judge or jury can properly consider is termed "admissible". Records managers, corporate and institutional attorneys, and others responsible for planning and implementing recordkeeping systems that will effectively support legal actions are understandably concerned about the admissibility of electronic document images recorded on optical or magnetic media. Typically, admissibility issues center on paper copies produced from electronic document images. As noted above, admissibility concerns are greatest where original documents are discarded following conversion to electronic images. Several states have recently modified their rules of evidence to include provisions that specifically mention copies produced by electronic document imaging systems. In most cases, however, admissibility will be based on considerations that apply to copies of documents, regardless of reprographic technology or format.

Admissibility is determined by rules of evidence that are embodied in legal statutes and court decisions. To be admissible as evidence, copies produced from electronic document images must satisfy two foundation requirements associated with all documents: (1) they must be relevant to the matter at issue; and (2), their authenticity must be firmly established. Relevance determinations are case specific. Based on the content rather than the format of documents, they fall outside the scope of this discussion. Authentication, however, is a direct concern of those responsible for planning and implementing electronic document imaging systems.

The purpose of authentication is to demonstrate the reliability of evidence (in the case of this discussion, copies produced from electronic document images and, by implication, the images themselves) to a court's satisfaction. Certain general authentication considerations apply to all documents, regardless of format. To be considered reliable, a document must have been made at or near the time of the event that is the subject of litigation. It must have been created by a person with knowledge of the event and maintained in the regular course of an organization's business activities. If these requirements are met, the documents, or copies of electronic images of them, will be admitted as evidence unless the opposing party in a legal action raises a valid objection. Objections to the admissibility of electronic document images, or to paper copies made from such images, are likely to be based on the rule against hearsay or the best evidence rule.

Hearsay is an out-of-court statement that pertains to some matter raised in court. Because hearsay is not subject to cross-examination by the opposing party in a legal action, it is generally inadmissible under the Federal Rules of Evidence (FRE), Uniform Rules of Evidence (URE), and state-specific rules of evidence. Since electronic document images, like their paper counterparts, are usually created out of court, they are considered hearsay and will not be admitted in evidence unless they fall within one of the various exceptions to the rule against hearsay. Such exceptions exist for both business and public records.

In federal courts, the most broadly applicable example is Rule 803(6) of the Federal Rules of Evidence (the so-called business records exception to the hearsay rule), which is based on the premise that records created in the normal course of business possess a circumstantial probability of trustworthiness; since organizations that create such records must rely on them to support their business operations, their accuracy is presumed. The business records exception to the hearsay rule covers records "in any form" and interprets business records broadly to include those created and maintained by government agencies, institutions, associations, and non-profit organizations. At the state level, an identical business records exception is included in the Uniform Rules of Evidence, which have been adopted by approximately 60 percent of the states. A business records exception to the hearsay rule is similarly included in the Uniform Business Records as Evidence Act (URBREA) and in various state-specific statutes. The FRE and URE also provide a public records exception for documents created by government agencies, although the business records exception will typically suffice for government documents. Various other provisions for overcoming hearsay objections, sometimes collectively described as "residual exceptions," may be applicable in specific circumstances.

Objections to the admissibility of copies produced from electronic document images may also be raised under the best evidence rule which stipulates that an original record rather than a copy must be admitted in evidence unless the absence of the original can be satisfactory explained. If the original record is unavailable, a trustworthy copy may be received in evidence. In electronic document imaging installations, the original record is usually a paper source document; the copy to be admitted in evidence, as previously noted, is a paper print produced from a digitized image recorded on optical or magnetic media. Original records may be unavailable for various reasons. In electronic document imaging installations, the destruction of original source documents in the regular course of business following digitization and image recording is typically considered a satisfactory explanation. An organization is on safest ground when document destruction is performed in conformity with formally established and approved retention schedules.

Among statutory provisions that can be used to overcome best evidence objections to the admissibility of copies produced from electronic document images, the previously discussed Uniform Photographic Copies of Business and Public Records as Evidence Act, as its name indicates, covers the admissibility of copies of documents in evidence in judicial proceedings as well as their ability to satisfy legally-mandated recordkeeping requirements. Rule 1003 of the Federal Rules of Evidence and Uniform Rules of Evidence permits the admission of duplicate records in evidence as substitutes for originals unless serious questions are raised about the authenticity of the original records or, in specific circumstances, it is judged unfair to admit a copy in lieu of an original. As with the UPA, the FRE and URA predate the commercial availability of electronic document imaging systems. The Uniform Rules of Evidence Act was written in 1953 and revised in 1974. The Federal Rules of Evidence were passed by Congress in 1975. Both laws mention some photographic copying processes specifically but do not exclude copies made by other technologies.

By recognizing the admissibility of copies, Rule 1003 of the FRE and URE places the burden of argument on the party seeking to exclude a copy rather than the party seeking to admit it. Under Rule 1003, existence of an original record does not preclude the admissibility of a copy. Even if an organization has retained its original source documents, copies made from electronic document images can be admitted in evidence; in most cases, such copies are more quickly and conveniently retrievable than the originals.

The foregoing discussion surveyed rules of evidence and related considerations which determine admissibility in court trials. A large percentage of legal proceedings, however, are held before federal and state administrative agencies where court-oriented rules of evidence do not apply. Federal administrative agencies, for example, are bound by the Administrative Procedures Act which gives such agencies considerable discretion in determining admissibility. A number of federal administrative agencies have informal rules of evidence which must be evaluated on a case-by-case basis to determine their applicability to copies produced from electronic document images. At the state government level, the admissibility of evidence in administrative proceedings is typically governed by state administrative procedures acts and procedural rules that apply to individual agencies. Significant variations are possible from state to state and, within a given state, from agency to agency.

*Facilitating Authentication*

As noted above, the admissibility of copies produced from electronic document images is contingent upon the authentication of such copies as reliable reproductions of original source documents. Certain procedures can facilitate authentication, thereby increasing the likelihood of admissibility.

A written policy statement, approved by an appropriate corporate or institutional officer, should formalize the conversion of source documents to digitized images recorded on optical or magnetic media as part of an organization's regular business practices. The statement should enumerate the specific types of documents to be included in a given electronic document imaging implementation. Document digitization, and the destruction of original source documents where applicable, should be designated in retention schedules. The retention schedules should be formally approved as an organization's policy.

Authentication procedures for copies produced by electronic document imaging systems will typically involve foundation testimony by a qualified witness who is familiar with the procedures and circumstances under which the copies were produced. An administrator should consequently be designated for each electronic document imaging system implemented by an organization. The administrator, who will typically be a management-level employee, should be identified by job title rather than personal name. He or she will be responsible for the system's operation and, through direct involvement with all system components and activities, will be able to provide the foundation testimony required for authentication purposes.

In various court cases, questions and concerns have been raised about the reliability of equipment and programs that record and store computer-processible information. Such questions have been most commonly associated with emerging technologies. To facilitate the authentication of electronic document images, a given system's hardware and software components should be documented in a manner that fully describes their characteristics and purposes. The documentation should indicate the types, brand names, and model numbers of all equipment and recording media encountered in a given installation, together with the dates that specific components were put into and taken out of service. Technical specification sheets provided by vendors will typically provide sufficiently detailed information to satisfy hardware documentation requirements. To confirm that hardware is being maintained in proper working condition, records should be kept of inspections, repairs, and preventative maintenance. Software documentation should include names and version numbers for all programs that support document scanning, image recording, data entry, and other system operations, as well as implementation dates for all software upgrades. If application software developed on a customized basis, flowcharts, source code, and other developmental documentation should be included.

Scanning, data entry, quality control, and other worksteps should be delineated in written procedures for each electronic document imaging application. Detailed instructions should be prepared for all equipment and imaging operations. A logbook should indicate the names of persons who oprated equipment on specific dates. Quality control procedures should likewise be specified in writing and a quality control logbook maintained. The logbook should indicate the inspections and other quality control procedures performed on specific dates.

Concerns about the improper alteration of electronically stored information have been widely publicized in discussions of computer crime. With paper documents and microfilm, such modifications can prove difficult to make and may be detectable by forensic scientists, auditors, or even casual observers. In contrast, computer-processible information recorded on erasable media can be deleted, changed, or otherwise manipulated without a trace. In timeshared and networked computer installations, recorded information may be altered by a remote perpetrator, thereby evading restrictions on physical access that can thwart attempted tampering with paper files. In electronic document imaging implementations, concern is warranted where rewritable optical disks and magnetic tapes are utilized for image storage. While the use of erasable media does not impeded admissibility in evidence, the possibility of tampering raises obvious questions about the trustworthiness of recorded information. Such concerns do not apply to document images recorded on write-once optical disks which, as previously noted, are not erasable.

To facilitate the authentication of electronic document images recorded on erasable media, security provisions, access control procedures, and other safeguards against tampering must be fully documented. A list of all authorized users and their access privileges should be maintained. The list should differentiate those users who are authorized to record or erase data base records and electronic document images from those who are restricted to data base searches and retrieval of designated document images in designated applications. System security should be audited on a regular basis. Audit findings should document the implementation of corrected actions.

## Integration with Other Technologies

Application developers and systems planners are increasingly interested in the integration of electronic document imaging with other information management technologies. As their principal advantage, such integrated implementations permit more effective information processing operations based on the combined strengths of their constituent technologies. They may also provide useful so-

*Figure 5–1. A hybrid document imaging system incorporating electronic and micrographic components. (Courtesy: Minolta)*

lutions to information management problems that cannot be addressed by electronic document imaging alone. The following discussion examines the potential for integrating electronic document imaging with micrographics and text-based storage and retrieval systems, two technologies which predate electronic document imaging and offer potentially significant document management capabilities.

*Micrographics*

The characteristics, advantages, and limitations of electronic document imaging and micrographics systems have been widely compared, contrasted, and otherwise analyzed at professional meetings and in various information management publications. Obvious similarities between the two technologies invite such analysis. Both electronic document imaging and micrographics systems, for example, convert source documents to compact facsimiles, thereby providing significant savings in floor space when compared to paper filing systems. Relying on image display devices, both technologies permit paperless records management implementations; both also support printing equipment, however, for production of reference copies. Like electronic document imaging systems, computer-assisted microfilm retrieval systems (so-called CAR systems) employ a computer-maintained data base as an index to document images. Saffady (1988, 1992) reviews other commonalities and provides a point-by-point comparison of specific system components and capabilities, including document conversion methods, media capacities and characteristics, and retrieval features.

Similarities aside, such comparative analyses have been characterized by strongly held, often provocative opinions about the nature and future of the two technologies. Their competitive relationship has been dramatically depicted by electronic document imaging's advocates as a contest between a high-performance, functionally superior challenger that incorporates the latest advances in computerization and a well-established, but old-fashioned, technology rooted in photography. That viewpoint is reflected in optimistic sales forecasts and market projections for electronic document imaging systems, many of which emphasize microfilm replacement. Equally important, but not quantified by market analysts, is the deterrent impact of electronic document imaging on new or expanded micrographics implementations. For every electronic document imaging installation or microfilm-to-electronic document imaging conversion reported in publications and at professional meetings, there are probably dozens of prospective micrographics users who are deferring procurements because of concern and confusion about the future viability of an apparently threatened technology. Evidently taking the competitive threat seriously, many micrographics equipment manufacturers and dealers have added electronic document imaging systems to their product lines.

While competitive evaluations necessarily emphasize the role of electronic document imaging as a micrographics alternative, various information specialists and industry analysts have noted their potential for complementary implementations based on the special information management attributes of the each technology. Such ideas were initially voiced in the early 1980s, when electronic document imaging systems, particularly those that employ optical disks as image storage media, were just emerging as a serious threat to micrographics technology. Kalthoff (1983, 1985), for example, categorized microforms and optical disks as subgroups of optical mass memory technology, noting that they can be effectively combined in a variety of information management applications. Bogue (1985) similarly described optical disks as components in a continuum of document storage products that also includes micrographics. Emphasizing the primary importance of document indexing and retrieval software, Newman (1985, 1986) suggested that microforms and optical disks can each be employed effectively as storage media in conceptually similar document management systems. Wolf (1984) noted

that the installation of efficient document management systems, regardless of the specific storage technology employed, will facilitate upgrading to new media when they become available. Banks (1985), Meth (1986), and Zagami (1987) discussed the complementary potential of computer-assisted microfilm retrieval and optical disk-based electronic document imaging systems. Among recent commentators, Andrews (1990, 1990a), Black (1989), Blake (1990), Burger (1990), Gallenberger (1989), and Gallenberger and Batterton (1989) have advocated mixed media systems (sometimes described as "hybrid" implementations) that combine integrate electronic document imaging and micrographic components.

Such hybrid document storage and retrieval implementations are based on previously noted similarities between computer-assisted microfilm retrieval and electronic document imaging systems, particularly the use of a computer-maintained data base that contains pointers to the storage locations of document images associated with specific index values. In a hybrid implementation, document images may be stored on either microforms or electronic media, such as optical disks or magnetic tapes. A single data base serves as an index to both types of media. A data base search reveals the microform and/or electronic media locations of document images pertinent to specific retrieval requirements. In the simplest and least expensive hybrid configurations, an operator manually locates and loads the successively designated electronic media and microforms which contain pertinent images. Retrieval workstations include display and printing components for both types of media. Bit-mapped video monitors display digitized document images stored on optical disks or other electronic media, while laser printers provide hardcopy capabilities. Reader/printers support the display and printing of microform images.

More complex and expensive hybrid configurations combine optical disk autochangers and specially designed microform retrievers for completely automated media handling. In such installations, optical disk cartridges are stored in a jukebox or magazine-type autochanger, the characteristics of which were described in Chapter Three. Cartridges identified by a data base search are automatically located and mounted in an optical disk drive for rapid retrieval of specific digitized images. The retrieved images are transferred to a host computer for display on a bit-mapped video monitor. Microforms, indexed by the same data base, are likewise stored in an automated retrieval unit. Depending on the device, 16mm microfilm cartridges, microfiche, or aperture cards may be accommodated. Microforms that contain images identified by a data base search are located and automatically removed from their storage locations by a robotic extractor. The retrieved microforms are inserted into a scanning mechanism, and the desired document images are digitized for transmission to a host computer. The digitized images are displayed at the same high-resolution video monitors employed for images recorded on optical disk cartridges. Laser printers can be used to produce hardcopy output from document images recorded on either media. Since digitized images are displayed and printed in identical formats regardless of source, any given document's storage medium is transparent and irrelevant to the requestor.

Taking a less automated, but less costly, approach to microform retrieval and scanning, several micrographics equipment manufacturers have recently introduced reader/scanners that will display microimages in the manner of a conventional microfilm reader and, at the operator's option, digitize them for transmission to a computer, printer, or fax machine. Depending on the device, such reader/scanners may accept 16mm microfilm cartridges, microfiche, or other microforms. If transmitted to a computer, the digitized microimages can be displayed on a bit-mapped video monitor. They can also be transferred to optical disks or other electronic media for storage.

As with all multi-technology systems, the hybrid configurations described above offer potentially more effective approaches to a broader range of information management tasks than can successfully be accommodated by either electronic document imaging or micrographics technology alone. Drawing on advantages noted in preceding chapters, a hybrid system's electronic document imaging components offer very high media capacity, the immediate availability of digitized document images, convenient access to both index data and document images from a single display device, rapid display and printing capabilities for ac-

tively referenced documents, and the ability to transfer digitized images to other workstations, to facsimile machines, or to other systems. Among their advantages, micrographics components offer low media cost and easy and inexpensive media duplication for vital records protection or physical distribution to multiple sites. For documents with long retention periods, microforms offer greater stability than electronic media; when properly processed and stored, certain microforms will retain their original information-bearing characteristics for centuries. Microforms also store document images in a human-readable format that is minimally affected by the hardware and software dependencies discussed earlier in this chapter. Recognizing these advantages, some electronic document imaging implementations employ microforms as complementary or supplementary storage media for long-term storage, backup, or other purposes. To facilitate such implementations, several companies have recently introduced scanner/cameras that simultaneously digitize source documents and record them on microfilm.

As an equally important consideration, hybrid systems offer an effective method of implementing electronic document imaging technology in applications where large numbers of documents were previously recorded on microfilm. While microform images can be converted to digitized form for storage on electronic media, the required scanning procedures can prove time consuming in high-volume document storage and retrieval installations. As an example, the scanning of one million pages recorded on 400 microfilm cartridges would require at least 1,000 hours. A hybrid implementation can incorporate such microimages without conversion, allowing electronic document imaging to be utilized for current documents. As time passes, electronic document images will account for an increasingly large percentage of the total document collection. In some applications, the microform component can be phased out by recording digitized microimages on optical disks or other electronic media when they are retrieved. Microform images that have not been converted to electronic media within a predetermined period of time (three to five years, for example) presumably have limited reference value and can be retired from the system.

*Figure 5–2. A microfilm reader/scanner. (Courtesy: Eastman Kodak)*

## Text Retrieval

A text retrieval system—variously called a text storage and retrieval system (TSRS), a text information management system (TIMS), a text base management system (TBMS), or a text data management system (TDMS)—is a computer-based information storage and retrieval system that stores the text of documents in machine-readable, character-coded form for retrieval or other processing. The text may be generated by word processing programs, electronic messaging systems, or other computer applications. Alternatively, the contents of paper documents may be converted to text files by key entry or optical character recognition. The technology has been described in numerous publications, including Ashford and Matkin (1982), Blumer et al. (1987), Colvin (1986), Croft and Pezarro (1981), Dubois (1987), Gill and Woll (1986), Jones and Bell (1984), and Rowland (1987). Saffady (1989) provides additional references to tutorial articles, research reports, and case studies.

Like electronic document imaging systems, text retrieval provides a completely computerized approach to document storage and retrieval, but the two technologies encode and store documents in completely different ways. Electronic document imaging systems, as previously described, store documents as digitized facsimiles. Text retrieval systems, in contrast, store the content of documents; they do not preserve their appearance. Individual characters are represented by combinations of bits defined by computer coding schemes, such as the American Standard Code for Information Interchange (ASCII) or the Extended Binary Coded Decimal Interchange Code (EBCDIC). As their name suggests, text retrieval systems are limited to textual information that is composed of letters of the alphabet, numeric digits, punctuation marks, and other symbols normally encountered on typewriter or computer keyboards. Text retrieval systems are obviously unsuitable for graphic documents, such as photographs, engineering drawings, circuit diagrams, or maps. They provide, at best, a partially effective information management methodology for textual documents that include embedded illustrations, signatures, and other significant graphic components. Such documents, sometimes described as compound documents, are encoun-

tered in many work environments. Text retrieval systems are usually implemented as prewritten software packages for designated computer platforms.

Versions for mainframes, minicomputers, and microcomputers are offered by several dozen vendors. As prewritten software products, text retrieval systems are a variant form of data base management system. Like other data base management programs, they create, maintain, and manipulate files of computer-processible records, but the records contain the unstructured, often voluminous contents of complete documents. Conventional data base records, in contrast, are customarily organized into fields with predefined characteristics that limit their length and content. While relatively long fields may store abstracts or other document surrogates, conventional data base management programs can rarely accommodate the entire text of documents.

Compared to electronic document imaging systems, text retrieval systems require much less media space to store a given quantity of documents. As an example, a typewritten, double-spaced, letter-size page stored as character-coded text will occupy about 1,700 bytes; as previously discussed, the same page stored as a digitized image may occupy 30,000 to 50,000 bytes, depending on document characteristics, scanning resolution, and compression methodology. Among other advantages, character-coded text can be displayed by conventional alphanumeric video monitors; digitized images, in contrast, require more expensive bit-mapped display devices. Because they are smaller, character-coded pages require much less transmission time than digitized images—an important consideration where the volume of transmission is high and/or communication bandwidth is limited.

As their most distinctive feature and principal attraction for most users, however, text retrieval systems support automated document indexing with resultingly powerful retrieval capabilities. For each application, a text retrieval program maintains two files: (1) a text file, which contains the complete text of source documents; and (2) an index to every significant word in the text file. Index entries are automatically extracted from character-coded source documents, individual words being identified as character strings separated by spaces, punctuation marks, or other delimiters. In most cases, a stoplist is used to exclude prepositions, conjunctions, interjections, adverbs, and other words of limited retrieval significance.

With most text retrieval systems, the index file employs an inverted structure. It contains an alphabetized list of words with pointers to their locations in an associated text file. In effect, the index file replicates the contents of its associated text file—minus stoplist words—in a different sequence. Because inverted indexes permit searches based on document contents rather than assigned index values, text retrieval systems are often described as full-text or free-text retrieval systems, and their indexing methodologies are sometimes described as full-text indexing. Names aside, index searches permit the rapid identification of documents that contain specified character strings. The retrieved documents can be displayed or printed to satisfy particular retrieval requirements. Some text retrieval programs initially display sentences, paragraphs, or other parts of retrieved documents that contain designated search terms and their contexts. As a convenient feature, search terms may be highlighted within the displayed text.

Most text retrieval programs support a broad range of search capabilities, including some that are not offered by conventional data base management programs. Term truncation and wildcard characters in search strings are commonly encountered features. Boolean operators can be used to broaden or narrow retrieval specifications. As a distinctive and useful alternative or complement to Boolean operators, most text retrieval programs can locate documents that contain two or more words in a specified proximity relationship. Depending on the program, proximity commands may be able to retrieve documents containing two words in the same paragraph, in the same sentence, or within a specified number of words of one another. Adjacency commands permit phrase searching. An increasing number of text retrieval programs offer hypertext capabilities which link interrelated documents and allow words in previously retrieved text segments to be utilized as search terms. Some text retrieval systems will rank documents by their presumed relevance, based on the proximity and frequency of search terms they contain.

As a document management technology, text retrieval competes with electronic document imaging systems in applications where computer-based information storage and retrieval is desired, the documents to be stored are textual in content, and preservation of the documents' appearance is not essential. Where document appearance must be preserved, as is the case with the compound documents described above, the two technologies can be effectively combined in electronic document imaging implementations that incorporate automatic indexing and full-text retrieval capabilities. In such implementations, source documents are scanned, converted to digitized images, and recorded on optical or magnetic media in a manner delineated in preceding chapters. The digitized images are processed by optical character recognition (OCR) algorithms that convert their contents to one or more text files. The text files, which usually contain ASCII-coded characters, may be recorded on optical or magnetic media. The digitized document images are unaffected by OCR processing; they remain on their original recording media.

As discussed in Chapter Two, a given system's optical character recognition capabilities (sometimes described as its OCR engine) may be hardware- or software-based. Among hardware-based OCR devices, several vendors offer document scanners that can generate digitized images and perform optical character recognition in a single pass. With software-based OCR components, character recognition may be performed immediately after scanning or at some later time. If application requirements warrant, OCR processing can be applied to digitized images recorded weeks, months, or years previously.

Regardless of the interval between document digitization and character recognition, the resulting text files serve as input to a text retrieval program which creates an inverted index with entries for every significant word in the text files. The index entries contain pointers to the digitized document images from which the text files were produced. At retrieval time, the inverted index is searched to identify document images that contain specified character strings. Those images can then be displayed or printed. Depending on the application, document indexing may depend entirely on full-text indexing. Alterntively, text retrieval components may be combined with conventional data base management software. In such cases, document images are indexed by assigned field values, as described in Chapter Two. Full-text searching provides an additional retrieval capability.

When properly implemented, the integration of electronic document imaging and text retrieval components can enhance the capabilities and extend the range of both technologies. By preserving the appearance of source documents, electronic imaging systems can capture graphic information that is necessarily omitted from text-only representations. They consequently permit the application of text retrieval to compound documents which contain embedded illustrations, signatures, and other significant graphic elements. As a potentially important advantage for electronic document imaging implementations, full-text indexing offers enhanced search capabilities when compared to indexing based on assigned field values. Various researchers have suggested that text retrieval systems offer improved subject searching when compared to systems based on a limited number of assigned index terms. In particular, the ability to search for words contained in documents can yield higher recall rates, where recall, as defined in Chapter Two, is the ability to retrieve the maximum number of relevant documents from a given collection. Full-text indexing permits retrieval of documents that treat specific topics peripherally, while indexing systems that rely on a limited number of assigned subject terms must necessarily emphasize major concepts. Full-text and assigned term indexing are not mutually exclusive approaches. Some text retrieval systems combine fully indexed text segments with structured field-oriented records, the latter containing assigned index values that represent subject terms or other predefined data elements. Most text retrieval systems also permit the augmentation of text files through the addition of subject terms not contained in documents themselves.

As an additional advantage, the auto-indexing feature of text retrieval programs can simplify document indexing and its associated data entry operations in electronic document imaging installations. As described in Chapter Two, conventional indexing methodologies based on assigned field values are time consuming and labor intensive. This is particularly true of subject index-

ing, which is intellectually demanding and often requires detailed analysis of source documents. A medium-size pharmaceuticals manufacturer, for example, may produce 15,000 chemical compound analyses, toxicology reports, microbiology reports, clinical protocols, technical memoranda, and other documents per year. If indexers average 10 minutes selecting subject terms for each document, 2,500 hours (aproximately 1.25 person-years) will be required to index the annual accumulation of documents. Given their time-consuming nature, such subject indexing methods are poorly suited to applications where large numbers of documents must be indexed in a short period of time. Some electronic document imaging applications involve large backfiles which may require many person-years of effort to index by conventional methodologies. In such situations, indexing backlogs can delay a system's implementation or limit its operational effectiveness.

Text retrieval programs, as previously described, address this problem by automatically extracting index terms from input documents. As an additional advantage, keyboard-oriented data entry operations, perhaps the most time consuming input workstep in electronic document imaging implementations, are eliminated. Auto-indexing based on the full text of documents is particularly effective in applications where rapid implementation of subject retrieval capabilities is essential, as with the backfile conversions described above. As a cautionary note for application planners, OCR processing of digitized document images and the creation of inverted indexes by text retrieval programs can require considerable computer time, but they are invariably much faster than manual indexing and data entry methodologies. To avoid degradation of response time during periods of peak retrieval activity, optical character recognition and auto-indexing may be performed during evening and nighttime hours. Alternatively, one or both activities may be relegated to a dedicated processor.

Application planners should also be aware that the voluminous inverted indexes generated by text retrieval programs can require considerable storage space, particularly where large quantities of source documents are involved. In most cases, the indexes are maintained on hard disk drives for rapid searching. Storage requirements for a full-text index to a given document collection can be calculated by the following formula:

$$S = P * N * O$$

where:

S = the storage requirement in bytes;
P = the average number of characters per page, including alphanumeric characters, punctuation marks, other symbols, and embedded blank spaces;
N = the number of pages in the document collection; and
O = an overhead factor allocated for inverted indexes and working files.

Inverted indexes, as previously described, include words extracted from documents plus pointers to their associated images. Additional disk space is required for the text retrieval program itself and its working files. While overhead requirements vary from one text retrieval program to another, a factor of 2.5 will provide an appropriate allocation of storage space in most cases. Applying the above formula to a collection of 100,000 double-spaced letter-size pages containing an average of 1,700 characters each, the calculation:

$$S = 1700 * 100000 * 2.5$$

yields a storage requirement of 425 megabytes for inverted indexes and text files. In some electronic document imaging applications, the text files can be deleted, with a corresponding reduction in storage space consumption, following index generation. These calculations do not include storage requirements for electronic document images or for field-oriented data base records associated with a particular application.

## Costs

Information management systems are rarely designed from the ground up with electronic document imaging in mind. In most applications, electronic document imaging is a replacement technology for previously implemented paper-based recordkeeping methodologies or, as noted above, micrographic systems. In either case, the existing system enjoys the advantage of inertia associated with all incumbent methodologies; the proposed replacement must offer an affordable, demonstrably cost-effective alternative. Cost analysis is consequently an important part of the planning and evaluation process for electronic document imaging implementations.

Cost analysis is typically performed in two stages: cost calculation and cost justification. In the first stage, the cost of a proposed electronic document imaging system is determined, and an implementation budget and annualized cost estimate are prepared. Cost calculation involves the identification and estimation of start-up (implementation) and on-going (operating) costs associated with a given electronic document imaging system. Such costs include, but are by no means limited to, equipment and software prices, recording media and other supply costs, service charges, and wages. In the cost-justification stage, the estimated costs are evaluated to determine whether a proposed electronic document imaging system is cost-effective. A cost-effective electronic document imaging system is one that fully addresses the requirements of a given application at a cost lower than that of other technologies or methodologies. Cost justification involves the preparation of realistic, reliable comparisons between a proposed electronic document imaging system and alternative methodologies, typically emphasizing the methodology that the electronic document imaging system is intended to replace.

The following discussion outlines cost analysis principles, delineates cost components, and examines cost justification concepts applicable to electronic document imaging implementations. The discussion is illustrated with hypothetical but hopefully realistic examples. As an unavoidable limitation of any published analysis, costs are subject to variations and changes that may affect the cost calculations and justifications presented here. Prices for equipment, software, and recording media often vary with the circumstances of specific procurements. Competitive bidding, for example, may result in lower costs for particular electronic document imaging configurations. Vendors sometimes offer incentive pricing to obtain initial installations in large corporations and other customers with potential for additional procurements. Certain organizations, such as government agencies and educational institutions, may be able to purchase complete electronic document imaging systems or selected components at substantial discounts. In addition, some costs, such as wage rates, are subject to significant local and regional variations. Rather than providing universally valid calculations and comparisons of specific costs for electronic document imaging implementations, the following discussion emphasizes cost calculation methods and cost justification approaches that are based on widely employed systems analysis principles. The discussion should consequently retain its conceptual validity and utility despite variations or changes in prices.

## Cost Calculation

As noted above, electronic document imaging installations will incur a combination of start-up and on-going costs. The former, as their name implies, are one-time charges associated with initial system implementation. Examples include the purchase price of electronic document imaging hardware and software, vendor charges for application-specific software modifications, and charges for data communication facilities, electrical improvements, or other site modifications required to prepare work areas for equipment installation. Start-up costs are usually fixed costs. A notable exception is service bureau charges for backfile conversions performed in advance of system operation. Such charges vary with the quantity of documents to be digitized and indexed.

Table 5-2 enumerates start-up and on-going cost components for electronic document imaging systems in a worksheet format. The worksheet, which is divided into several parts, is designed to simplify and facilitate cost calculations for electronic document imaging systems with user-specified characteristics. The following discussion presents a line-by-line explanation of the worksheet entries.

### Line 1

The purchase price of electronic document imaging hardware and software is considered a soft-ware cost if the hardware and software are purchased and as an annual fixed cost if the hardware and software are leased or rented. Entries made in Part A of the worksheet apply to purchased equipment only; payments for leased and rented equipment are to be entered in Part B, lines 12 and 14 as described below.

As the most visible start-up costs in electronic document imaging installations, hardware and software prices typically dominate implementation budgets. The total purchase price for hardware and software components dedicated exclusively to electronic document imaging, as opposed to components that are shared with other computing applications, is entered on line 1 of the worksheet. Such prices are usually provided by vendors in response to requests for proposals, requests for quotations, invitations to bid, or less formal customer inquiries. Unfortunately, generalizations about hardware and software prices are complicated by variations in marketing approaches, system implementation patterns, and vendor pricing schemes. Electronic document imaging systems may be marketed directly by their manufacturers or indirectly by authorized dealers, systems integrators, business partners, or other resellers, some of whom add "value," in the form of additional components or consulting services, to basic configurations. Some vendors publish price lists for their offerings, while others invariably prepare customized quotations for specific situations. The following examples represent three typical pricing scenarios, each of which is subject to considerable variation:

1. Some electronic document imaging systems, as noted in Chapter One, consist of preconfigured combinations of computer hardware and software offered as turnkey configurations at an all-inclusive price. Such turnkey systems include computers and peripheral devices plus prewritten indexing and retrieval software, cabling, and documentation sold as a "plug-and-play" package. Options, such as OCR capabilities or fax modems, are priced separately as add-on components, where available. Some turnkey system vendors also offer substitution products, such as faster document scanners or higher capacity optical disk drives, at alternative prices.

**Table 5-2: Cost Calculation Worksheet**

PART A: Start-up Costs

| | | | |
|---|---|---|---|
| 1. | Purchase price of hardware and software used exclusively for electronic document imaging | 1. | $_____ |
| 2. | System-related charges not included in line 1 | 2. | $_____ |
| 3. | Cost of site preparation for system installation | 3. | $_____ |
| 4. | Cost of backfile conversion and related services | 4. | $_____ |
| 5. | Purchase price of hardware and software shared with other applications | 5. | $_____ |
| 6. | Percentage of amount on line 6 attributable to electronic document imaging | 6. | 0._____ |
| 7. | Amount on line 6 multiplied by decimal value on line 7 | 7. | $_____ |
| 8. | Total of amounts on lines 1, 2, 3, 4, and 7 | 8. | $_____ |
| 9. | Estimated useful life of imaging system, in years | 9. | _____ |
| 10. | Amount on line 9 divided by value on line 11; this is the annualized value of start-up costs for electronic document imaging | 10. | $_____ |

PART B: Annual Fixed Costs

| | | | |
|---|---|---|---|
| 11. | Lease or rental payments for hardware and software used exclusively for electronic document imaging | 11. | $_____ |
| 12. | Cost of maintenance contracts for electronic document imaging hardware and software | 12. | $_____ |
| 13. | Annual value of floor space occupied by hardware used exclusively for electronic document imaging | 13. | $_____ |
| 14. | Lease or rental payments for hardware and software shared with other applications | 14. | $_____ |
| 15. | Cost of maintenance contracts for hardware and software shared with other applications | 15. | $_____ |
| 16. | Annual value of floor space occupied by hardware shared with other applications | 16. | $_____ |
| 17. | Total of amounts on lines 14, 15, and 16 | 17. | $_____ |

18. Percentage of amount on line 14     18.    <u> 0.     </u>
    attributable to electronic
    document imaging

19. Amount on line 17 multiplied by     19.   $ <u>        </u>
    decimal value on line 18

20. Total of amounts on lines 11,     20.   $ <u>        </u>
    12, 13, and 19; this is the
    annual fixed cost for electronic
    document imaging

## PART C: Annual Variable Costs — Image Storage Media

21. Capacity of one unit of image     21.     <u>        </u>
    storage media in megabytes

22. Number of images per megabyte     22.     <u>        </u>
    (from table x-x)

23. Value on line 21 multiplied by     23.     <u>        </u>
    value on line 22; this is the
    image capacity of one unit of
    document storage media

24. Number of pages to be converted to     24.     <u>        </u>
    document images per year

25. Value on line 24 divided by value     25.     <u>        </u>
    on line 23; this is the number of
    media units required

26. Cost per unit for image storage     26.   $ <u>        </u>
    media

27. Value on line 25 multiplied by     27.   $ <u>        </u>
    amount on line 26

28. Number of back-up or distribution     28.     <u>        </u>
    copies to be produced for each medium

29. Cost per unit for back-up or distribu-     29.   $ <u>        </u>
    tion copies

30. Value on line 28 multiplied by amount     30.   $ <u>        </u>
    on line 29

31. Total of amounts on line 27 and line     31.   $ <u>        </u>
    30; this is the annual cost of docu-
    ment storage media, including back-up
    and distribution copies

## PART D: Annual Variable Costs — Document Conversion Labor

32. Document preparation rate in pages     32.     <u>        </u>
    per hour

33. Value on line 24 divided by value     33.     <u>        </u>
    on line 32

34. Hourly wage rate for document     34.   $ <u>        </u>
    preparer

35. Value on line 33 multiplied by amount     35.   $ <u>        </u>
    on line 34; this is the annual labor
    cost for document preparation

36.  Document scanning rate in pages
     per hour

36.  _____

37.  Value on line 22 divided by value
     on line 34

37.  _____

38.  Hourly wage rate for scanner
     operator

38.  $ _____

39.  Value on line 37 multiplied by amount
     on line 38; this is the annual labor
     cost for scanner operation

39.  $ _____

40.  Percentage of document images to be
     inspected (if 100 percent, enter
     1.00)

40.  _____

41.  Value on line 24 multiplied by deci-
     mal value on line 40; this is the
     number of pages to be inspected

41.  _____

42.  Image inspection rate in pages per
     hour

42.  _____

43.  Value on line 41 divided by value
     on line 42

43.  _____

44.  Hourly wage rate for document image
     inspector

44.  $ _____

45.  Value on line 43 multiplied by
     amount on line 42; this is the
     annual labor cost for document
     image inspection

45.  $ _____

46.  Total of amounts on line 35, line
     39, and line 45; this is the annual
     labor cost for document conversion

46.  $ _____

PART E: Annual Variable Costs — Document Indexing and Data Entry

47.  Average number of pages per
     document (decimal values per-
     mitted)

47.  _____

48.  Value on line 24 divided by value
     on line 47; this is the number of
     indexable documents per year

48.  _____

49.  Average time, in minutes, required
     to index a document

49.  _____

50.  Value on line 49 multiplied by
     value on line 48

50.  _____

51.  Value on line 50 divided by 60;
     this is the document indexing
     time per year in hours

51.  _____

52.  Hourly wage rate for document
     indexer

52.  $ _____

53.  Amount on line 52 multiplied by
     value on line 51; this is the
     annual labor cost for document
     indexing

53.  $ _____

54.  Average number of characters per
     database record

54.  _____

55. Value on line 48 multiplied by       55. _____
    value on line 54; this is the
    annual keystroking workload

56. Data entry rate in keystrokes per     56. _____
    hour

57. Value on line 55 divided by value     57. _____
    on line 56; this is the annual
    data entry workload in hours

58. Hourly wage rate for data entry       58. $ _____
    clerk

59. Value on line 57 multiplied by        59. $ _____
    amount on line 58; this is the annual
    labor cost for entry of database records

PART F: Annual Variable Costs — Document Retrieval

60. Number of retrieval transactions      60. _____
    per year

61. Average time per retrieval            61. _____
    transaction, in minutes

62. Value on line 61 multiplied by        62. _____
    value on line 60

63. Value on line 61 divided by 62;       63. _____
    this is the retrieval time per
    year in hours

64. Hourly wage rate for retrieval        64. $ _____
    personnel

65. Value on line 63 multiplied by        65. $ _____
    amount on line 64; this is the
    annual labor cost for document
    retrieval

66. Average number of images printed      66. ___.____
    per retrieval transaction
    (decimal values permitted)

67. Value on line 66 multiplied by        67. _____
    value on line 60

68. Cost per print for paper and          68. $ _0._____
    other supplies

69. Amount on line 68 multiplied          69. $ _____
    by value on line 67; this is
    the annual cost of print supplies

70. Total of amounts on line 65           70. $ _____
    and line 69; this is the total
    annual cost for document retrieval

PART G: Total Annual Cost Calculation

71. Total of amounts on lines 10,         71. $ _____
    20, 31, 46, 53, 59, and 70;
    this is the total annual cost
    of an electronic document imaging system

2. Generally, systems integrators and other value-added resellers sell information management capabilities and services rather than preconfigured systems. To support the delivery of such capabilities and services to the broadest clientele, they typically offer a selection of hardware components at various price points. Often, the reseller is an authorized dealer for, or has some other type of business relationship with, specific computer and peripheral equipment manufacturers. Hardware configurations may be flexibly defined, with alternative components and prices delineated. In some cases, customer-owned equipment, such as microcomputers or document scanners, can be substituted for vendor-supplied hardware. Data base management software serves as the development vehicle for indexing and retrieval capabilities that are tailored to specific applications. Detailed analysis of application requirements and customized programming are often involved. The customer pays for consulting and software development services, accompanied—in some cases—by software license fees.

3. As an alternative to hardware/software combinations, electronic document imaging products are increasingly marketed as prewritten software packages for use with customer-supplied computers and peripheral devices of a specified type. Software costs are usually covered by published price lists. The customer is free to purchase compatible hardware components from the most competitive source. In some cases, electronic document imaging software is sold by authorized resellers who also market document scanners, optical disk drives, and other peripherals.

Subject to caveats necessitated by the divergent marketing approaches described above, broad price ranges can be delineated for particular electronic document imaging configurations. The cost of entry-level, single-workstation electronic document imaging systems has fallen steadily and significantly since their introduction in the mid-1980s, largely because of the increasingly attractive price/performance characteristics of microcomputers and peripheral devices employed in such configurations. At the time this chapter was written, a useful system could be configured from separately purchased hardware and software components for less than $20,000. From the hardware standpoint, such a system would include an 80386- or 80486-based IBM-compatible microcomputer with 4 megabytes of random-access memory, a 100MB hard disk drive, a floppy disk drive, a 5.25-inch write-once or rewritable optical disk drive, a VGA video adapter and 14-inch color monitor, a flatbed document scanner capable of digitizing a letter-size page in approximately fifteen seconds, and a laser printer capable of producing four copies per minute. Data base management and imaging capabilities are provided by a prewritten software package designed to run under MS-DOS and Microsoft Windows.

An implementation budget of $40,000 to $60,000 will purchase a single-workstation, microcomputer-based, turnkey electronic document imaging system with preconfigured hardware and software components. Compared to the less expensive configuration described above, such a system would include a sheet-fed document scanner capable of digitizing a letter-size page in three to five seconds; a 19-inch, landscape-mode video monitor with a display resolution of 150 pixels per inch; and a faster laser printer (eight pages per minute). As a turnkey system, all hardware and software components would be pretested for compatibility, purchased from a single source, ready to use, and supported by a single vendor. The purchase price will typically include vendor installation, user documentation, and customer training. In contrast, the less expensive entry-level configuration described above requires customer installation of separately purchased components. Documentation is component-specific. Training is not provided.

Multi-workstation electronic document imaging systems may consist of microcomputers linked by a local area network which includes servers for image storage, printing, and other specialized operations. Alternatively, multi-workstation configurations may be implemented as minicomputer- or mainframe-based timeshared systems. In either case, most installations include an optical disk autochanger for unattended access to document images. Typical procurement budgets range from $150,000 to $200,000 for a five-workstation configuration, including two input stations equipped with sheet-fed document scanners and high-resolution video monitors, three retrieval stations equipped with high-resolution video monitors and low-speed laser printers, and a file server equipped with a twenty-cartridge autochanger for 5.25-inch optical disks. The system price includes data base management and document imaging software, system installation, documentation, and customer training. Application set-up, customized programming, and other consulting services are usually offered for an additional fee. The customer must provide a local area network or other data communication facilities to connect the system's components. The costs cited above can be reduced by employing fewer workstations, slower document scanners, VGA displays rather than high-resolution monitors, and lower capacity desktop autochangers. Implementation costs below $100,000 are attainable in some situations.

A five-workstation configuration of the type described above might meet the needs of a single office or small department. Implementation budgets for larger multi-workstation electronic document imaging systems can range from $300,000 for a ten-workstation system designed to serve several departments to tens of millions of dollars, for an ambitious enterprise-wide installation encompassing several hundred workstations in a corporate or institutional headquarters, office building complex, or campus. High-volume applications may require very high-speed document scanners, heavy-duty laser printers, and 12- or 14-inch optical disk drives and autochangers, which are significantly more expensive than 5.25-inch models. Large-scale document imaging implementations typically involve lengthy systems analysis, complex application set-up, and customized programming. The implementation budget must consequently include allocations for consulting services and software development.

### Line 2

Start-up costs for electronic document imaging products and services other than those included in line 1 are entered in line 2. In some cases, charges for system installation, application analysis, data base set-up, customer training, and other services are embedded in the purchase price of electronic document imaging hardware and software. Many systems integrators and value-added resellers, however, enumerate such charges separately. Separate pricing is particularly common for customized software development, such as workflow programming or the integration of electronic document imaging with existing computer applications. Similarly, some turnkey electronic document imaging systems systems are marketed by value-added resellers who offer consulting services and training on a fee basis.

### Line 3

As is often the case in computer installations, implementation and operation of an electronic document imaging system may require significant building modifications or other site preparation. Examples of such site preparation include construction or movement or interior walls to create or demarcate an installation area; electrical improvements to accommodate hardware components; installation or upgrading of air conditioning and other environmental controls required for reliable operation of computer equipment; and installation of data communication facilities, such as twisted-pair wiring or coaxial cable, to interconnect system components. Some multi-workstation electronic document imaging systems, as previously noted, operate in local area network environments, the installation of which is the customer's responsibility. Site preparation charges are treated as start-up costs to be entered on line 3.

### Line 4

In some electronic document imaging installations, large quantities of paper documents or microforms must be converted to digitized images and indexed in advance of system operation. Rather than performing such backfile conversions in-house, application planners may contract with a document imaging service bureau. The service bureau charges are treated as a start-up cost to be entered on line 4.

Broadly defined, a document imaging service bureau is a private business or other organization that performs image creation and related services using a customer's own documents, data, or other source materials. Backfile conversions typically involve some combination of document preparation, document or microform scanning, image recording, index data entry, quality review, and source file reassembly. Work may be performed at the service bureau's facilities or at a customer's site. Digitized images and data base records are delivered on optical or magnetic media in a format suitable for input to the customer's system. Rates vary with job characteristics and customer requirements.

Document imaging service bureaus can supplement an organization's own scanning and data entry capabilties. They are particularly useful for high-volume work, such as backfile conversions, which must be completed in a short time or for applications, such as microform conversions, which require special equipment or technical expertise that are unavailable in-house. The nature and acceptability of services to be rendered are a matter for individual negotiation between the customer and service bureau. Important criteria for service bureau selection include a demonstrated understanding of the customer's conversion requirements, familiarity and experience with the conversion operations to be performed, the ability to deliver output in a format compatible with the customer's system, and the ability to provide conversion services within the time allotted.

### Lines 5, 6, and 7

Most turnkey systems and certain customized configurations are utilized specifically and exclusively for electronic document imaging operations. As provided on line 1, their entire cost is charged to a given document imaging implementation. Some electronic document imaging implementations, however, share computers and peripheral devices (including hard disk drives, magnetic tape units, and printers) with other applications. This is the case, for example, where document imaging software is implemented in a timeshared minicomputer or mainframe environment. Similarly, LAN-based document imaging configurations may incorporate microcomputer-based workstations that are used for other purposes, such as word processing, spreadsheet manipulation, or message transmission.

In such situations, the purchase price of shared components (including the cost of any site preparation or special services associated with implementation of the components) must be apportioned to the electronic document imaging implementation, based on the estimated percentage of the shared components' resources utilized by document imaging applications. The estimated percentage is entered as a decimal value on line 6. If 25 percent of a timeshared computer's resources are used for document image input, storage, and retrieval and the remaining 75 percent of resources support other applications, the value to be entered on line 6 is 0.25. The allocation of resources might be determined by the amount of central processor time spent on electronic document imaging as opposed to other applications, by the number of workstations engaged in document imaging operations, by the percentage of available storage resources consumed by document images, or by a combination of these and other factors. In any case, the decimal value on line 6 is multiplied by the amount on line 5 to obtain a dollar value attributable to electronic document imaging. That amount is entered on line 7.

### Line 8

Start-up costs for a given electronic document imaging implementation are the sum of the purchase price of hardware and software dedicated to imaging operations (line 1), other system related charges (line 2), site preparation costs (line 3), the cost of backfile conversion where applicable (line 4), and the apportioned cost of shared system components (line 7). That total is entered on line 8.

### Lines 9 and 10

To facilitate cost justification analysis based on comparisons with an existing paper-based filing system or micrographics system, start-up costs for electronic document imaging systems are usually converted to an annualized amount which can be added to annual operating costs to obtain a total annual cost. Such annualization is accomplished by amortizing the start-up costs for a given system; that is, by dividing the start-up costs calculated on line 8 by the system's estimated useful life, in years as entered on line 9.

The resulting annualized amount, which is entered on line 10, will vary inversely with the length of the estimated useful life selected for a given system. The useful life is the period of time between a given system's procurement and its replacement. Long amortization periods, which are sometimes employed in cost justification analyses prepared by electronic document imaging system vendors, can yield attractively low but potentially misleading annualized start-up costs. The continually improving cost/performance characteristics of computer equipment and software encourages the replacement of older devices and programs by newer products at relatively short intervals. For most computer-based information systems, including electronic document imaging systems, an estimated useful life of three to five years is appropriate. Longer amortization periods are not advisable. A three-year amortization period recognizes the inevitability of equipment and software upgrades in most installations. While some system components may remain operable for longer than five years, changing application requirements or the introduction of attractive new products may warrant replacement at shorter intervals. If an electronic document imaging system is leased or rented, amortization is unnecessary. Annualized costs are easily calculated from monthly lease or rental charges.

### Line 11

Part B of the worksheet covers annual fixed operating costs encountered in electronic document imaging installations. Examples include payments for leased or rented equipment and charges for equipment maintenance and software upgrade contracts. Like their start-up counterparts, annual fixed costs are incurred regardless of application characteristics.

Annual lease and/or rental payments for hardware and software intended specifically and exclusively for electronic document imaging are entered on line 11. As noted above, electronic document imaging systems may be leased or rented as an alternative to outright purchase. Combinations of purchased, leased, and rented equipment may be encountered in a given installation. For purposes of this discussion, leasing is defined as a multi-payment purchase methodology that is designed to eliminate the substantial capital outlay associated with the outright purchase of an electronic docu-

ment imaging system. The leasing party agrees to make payments of a specified amount and frequency for an agreed upon term, at the end of which time it obtains ownership of the leased system. Lease payments include an interest charge.

Rental plans similarly involve multiple payments of a specified amount, frequency, and duration. In a conventional rental, however, no part of the payments are applied toward ownership of an electronic document imaging system. The renting party can cease payments and return the system with appropriate notice. Rental plans provide a method of acquiring equipment for which the customer has a short-term need; document scanners might be rented for a six-month backfile conversion project, for example. A variation, called a rental-purchase, allocates a specified percentage of rental payments toward purchase of equipment if the purchase is made within a specified period of time.

### Line 12

Maintenance contract charges (including the cost of equipment repair contracts, software license renewals, and software upgrade contracts) are treated as an annual fixed cost for purchased, leased, and rented system components. The total of annual payments for such contracts is entered on line 12. To ensure proper maintenance of system components in which they retain a property interest, some vendors require the purchase of annual maintenance contracts for leased and rented equipment. In some cases, the cost of maintenance contracts is embedded in the lease or rental payments entered on line 11, making a separate entry on line 12 unnecessary. If maintenance contracts are not purchased, an amount equal to their annual cost should be budgeted for system repair on a per-call basis. That amount should be entered on line 12.

### Line 13

The annual value of floor space occupied by computers, scanners, video monitors, printers, and other equipment dedicated exclusively to electronic document imaging is entered on line 13. For electronic document imaging systems installed in leased and rented buildings, this amount is calculated by determining the total square footage occupied by dedicated hardware components and multiplying by the annual lease or rental payment per square foot. For owned buildings, the amortized value of the floor space, on a cost-per-square-foot basis, must be determined.

### Lines 14, 15, 16, and 17

Annual lease or rental charges for hardware and software components shared with other applications are entered on line 14. The annual cost of hardware maintenance and software upgrade contracts for such shared components is entered on line 15. The annual value of floor space occupied by shared equipment, such as microcomputers utilized for image retrieval as well as other applications, is entered on line 16. The annual total of lease and rental charges, maintenance contract payments, and floor space costs for shared components is calculated by adding lines 14, 15, and 16. The result is entered on line 17.

### Lines 18 and 19

For shared system resources, the percentage of lease or rental payments for system components, maintenance contracts charges, and floor space costs attributable to electronic document imaging is entered as a decimal value on line 18. Methods of determining percentages for the allocation of such shared resources were previously explained in the discussion for line 6. The dollar value of shared system resources, maintenance contracts, and occupied floor space is calculated by multiplying the total on line 17 by the decimal value on line 18. The result is entered on line 19.

### Line 20

Total annual fixed costs for electronic document imaging are calculated by adding the annual amounts for lease or rental payments for hardware and software components dedicated to electronic document imaging (line 11), maintenance contracts for such dedicated components (line 12), the value of the floor space occupied equipment used exclusively for electronic document imaging (line 13), and the portion of shared component costs attributable to electronic document imaging (line 19).

### Lines 21, 22, and 23

Variable costs depend on specific application characteristics, such as the volume of document images to be recorded and the frequency of reference activity, for both their occurence and their amount. Part C of the worksheet covers variable costs for document storage media.

As discussed elsewhere in this book, most electronic document imaging systems use optical disk cartridges, magnetic tapes, or other removable media for image storage. The capacity, in megabytes, of one unit of storage media is entered on line 21. In the case of double-sided optical disk cartridges, the unit capacity is the total of both sides.

The image capacity of a given storage medium is affected by page sizes, scanning resolutions, and compression algorithms. Taking these factors into account, Table 5-3 indicates the approximate number of images that can be recorded per megabyte of media. For letter-size pages scanned at 200 pixels per horizontal and vertical inch, for example, typical capacities are twenty pages per megabyte with Group III compression and thirty pages per megabyte with Group IV compression. The value appropriate to a particular application is to be determined and entered on line 20. The image capacity of one unit of storage media is calculated by multiplying the value on line 21 by the value on line 22. The result is entered on line 23.

### Lines 24 and 25

The estimated number of pages to be converted to digitized images per year is entered on line 24. The entered value must represent pages rather than documents; the latter may contain multiple pages. Double-sided pages are counted as two pages.

The number of media units required per year is calculated by dividing the value on line 24 by the value on line 23. The result is entered on line 25.

### Lines 26 and 27

The unit cost of optical disk cartridges, magnetic tapes, or other media is entered on line 26 and multiplied by the estimated number of media units required per year (line 25) to calculate the annual

**Table 5-3. Approximate Image Capacities per Megabyte**

| Page Size | 200 Pixels per Inch | | 300 Pixels per Inch | |
|---|---|---|---|---|
| | Group III | Group IV | Group III | Group IV |
| 8.5 x 11 | 20 | 30 | 8 | 13 |
| 8.5 x 14 | 17 | 25 | 7 | 11 |
| 11 x 14 | 13 | 19 | 6 | 9 |
| 11 x 17 | 11 | 16 | 5 | 7 |
| 18 x 24 | 5 | 7 | 2 | 3 |
| 24 x 36 | 2 | 3 | 1 | 1.5 |
| 34 x 44 | 1.3 | 2 | 0.6 | 0.9 |

cost of image storage media. The result is entered on line 27.

### Lines 28, 29, and 30

The preceding entries in Part C of the worksheet pertain to the first copy of storage media produced by an electronic document imaging system. Many applications require additional copies for back-up or distribution purposes. The number of such additional copies is entered on line 28. If the number is zero, lines 29 and 30 can be skipped; otherwise, the estimated unit cost of each additional copy is to be entered on line 29. In most cases, the entry on line 29 will be identical to the amount on line 26. The annual cost of additional copies is calculated by multiplying the amount on line 28 by the amount on line 29. The result is entered on line 30.

### Line 31

The total annual cost of image storage media for a given electronic document imaging implementation is calculated by adding the cost of the first copies (line 27) and the cost of the additional copies (line 30). The result is entered on line 31.

### Lines 32, 33, 34, and 35

In most electronic document imaging applications, the digitization and indexing of source documents involves substantial labor costs. As with the image storage media discussed above, labor costs are var-

iable costs. Their importance in a given electronic document imaging installation varies with the volume of source documents to be digitized and indexed. As the volume of work increases, labor costs will account for a progressively greater percentage of total system costs. In high volume applications, labor costs can exceed the annual fixed costs discussed above.

Part D of the cost calculation worksheet covers annual variable costs for labor associated with document conversion in electronic document imaging installations. Such costs are incurred in conjunction with specific document conversion tasks, such as document preparation, scanner operation, and image inspection. Entries on lines 32 through 35 of the worksheet calculate the annual cost of labor for document preparation. The anticipated document preparation rate, in pages per hour, is entered on line 32. That value is divided into the estimated number of pages to be digitized per year, as previously entered on line 24. The result, to be entered on line 33, is the number of hours required for document preparation. The hourly wage, including fringe benefits, for document preparation employees is entered on line 34 and multiplied by the estimated number of preparation hours (line 33). The result is the estimated annual labor cost for document preparation. It is entered on line 35.

### Lines 36, 37, 38, and 39

Entries on lines 36 through 39 calculate the annual labor cost for scanner operation. The anticipated scanning rate, in pages per hour, is entered on line 36. That value is divided into the estimated number of pages to be recorded per year, as previously entered on line 24. The result, to be entered on line 37, is the number of hours required for document scanning. The hourly wage, including fringe benefits, for scanner operators is entered on line 38 and multiplied by the estimated number of hours required for document scanning (line 37). The result is the estimated annual labor cost for scanner operation. It is entered on line 39.

### Lines 40 and 41

In some electronic document imaging installations, all digitized images are inspected following scanning. In other cases, image inspection is limited to a sampling of documents—a practice that is most likely to be encountered in very high-volume applications where the inspection of every image would prove prohibitively time consuming. The percentage of document images to be inspected is entered as a decimal value on line 40 of the worksheet. If all images will be inspected, the entered value should be 1.00. The entry on line 40 is then multiplied by the estimated number of pages to be recorded per year, as previously entered on line 24. The result is the total number of document images to be inspected per year. It is entered on line 41.

### Lines 42, 43, 44, and 45

Entries on lines 42 through 45 calculate the annual cost of labor for document image inspection. The anticipated inspection rate, in pages per hour, is entered on line 42. That value is divided into the estimated number of images to be inspected per year, as previously entered on line 41. The result, to be entered on line 43, is the number of hours per year required for document image inspection. The hourly wage, including fringe benefits, for image inspection personnel is entered on line 44 and multiplied by the estimated number of hours required for image inspection (line 43). The result is the estimated annual labor cost for image inspection. It is entered on line 45.

### Line 46

The total annual labor cost for document conversion is the sum of the annual costs for document preparation (line 35), scanner operation (line 39), and image inspection (line 45). The total is entered on line 46.

### Lines 47 and 48

Annual media and labor costs for image entry, as calculated in Part C and Part D of the worksheet, are based on estimates of the number of pages to be converted in a given electronic document imaging installation. In contrast, annual labor costs for document indexing and the entry of data base records are based on the number of documents rather than the number of pages encountered in a particular installation. In most electronic document imaging installations, multi-page documents are treated as single items for indexing and data entry purposes.

The average number of pages per document is entered on line 47. Decimal values are permitted and, for many document collections, appropriate. In an application where one-third of the documents are two pages in length and the remainder consist of a single page, for example, the average number of pages per document is 1.33. To calculate the number of indexable items, the number of pages to be recorded, as previously entered on line 24, is divided by the average number of pages per document (line 47). The result is entered on line 48.

### Lines 49, 50, 51, 52, and 53

Entries on lines 49 through 53 of the worksheet calculate the cost of labor for document indexing, that is, for the analytical tasks that culminate in the selection of subject terms or other index values as discussed in Chapter Two. In some applications, index values are selected by document originators or other personnel who are not a part of the electronic document imaging implementation. Alternatively, the auto-indexing techniques described elsewhere in this book may be utilized. In such cases, document indexing costs may be difficult to determine or inapplicable, causing lines 49 through 53 to be skipped.

The average time, in minutes, required to select index values for a single document is entered on line 49. That value is multiplied by the number of documents to be indexed per year, as previously calculated on line 48. The result, which represents the annual time requirement for indexing labor in minutes, is entered on line 50. It is divided by 60 to convert the annual labor requirement to hours. The result is entered on line 51. The hourly wage, including fringe benefits, for document indexers is entered on line 52 and multiplied by the number of indexing hours on line 51. The result is the estimated annual labor cost for document indexing. It is entered on line 53.

### Lines 54 and 55

In electronic document imaging systems, as previously described, a computer-maintained data base serves as an index to digitized images. The data base contains one record for each indexable document plus pointers to media where the document's images are stored. Each data base record is divided into fields that represent indexing categories used to describe the documents. The size of each data base record—the sum of the average number of characters in all fields—is entered on line 54. That value is multiplied by the number of indexable documents, as previously entered on line 48. The result is the annual workload, in keystrokes, for entry of data base records. It is entered on line 55.

### Lines 56, 57, 58, and 59

Entries on lines 56 through 58 calculate the cost of labor for entry of data base records pertaining to electronic document images. The anticipated data entry rate, in keystrokes per hour, is to be entered on line 56. If keystroke verification (double-keying) of entries will be employed, the estimated rate should be halved. The value on line 56 is divided into the estimated keystroking workload, as previously entered on line 55. The result, to be entered on line 57, is the number of hours required for entry of data base records. The hourly wage, including fringe benefits, for data entry personnel is entered on line 58 and multiplied by the value on line 57. The result is the estimated annual labor cost for entry of data base records. It is entered on line 59.

### Lines 60, 61, 62, and 63

Part F of the worksheet covers annual variable costs for document retrieval. Such costs consist of labor costs for data base searching and image retrieval and supply costs for printing of retrieved images.

Lines 60 through 63 calculate the annual time required for document retrieval. The estimated number of retrieval transactions per year is entered on line 60. A retrieval transaction is defined as any system operation that involves data base searching and/or image retrieval for display or printing. The estimated average time, in minutes, required to complete a retrieval transaction is entered on line 61. The elapsed time per transaction is measured from the initiation of a data base search through termination of the retrieval operation. It includes the time required for display and printing of document images.

A given retrieval transaction may require several data base searches and examination of multiple document images. The value on line 60 is multiplied by the value on line 61. The result, to be entered on line 62, is the annual retrieval time in minutes. The value on line 62 is divided by 60 to calculate the annual retrieval time in hours. The result is entered on line 63.

### Lines 64 and 65

The hourly wage for retrieval personnel, including fringe benefits, is entered on line 64. Where retrieval will be performed by personnel of different employment ranks, an average of their wage rates, weighted to reflect their relative retrieval activity, should be utilized. In an installation where two-thirds of retrieval transactions are performed by clerical personnel at an hourly rate of $15 and the remaining one-third are performed by managerial personnel at an hourly rate of $36 per hour, the amount entered on line 64 would be $22. The estimated annual labor cost for document retrieval is calculated by multiplying the average hourly wage on line 64 by the estimated number of retrieval hours, as previously entered on line 63. The result is entered on line 65.

### Lines 66, 67, 68, and 69

Lines 66 through 69 calculate annual print supply costs associated with document retrieval. The average number of document images printed per retrieval transaction is entered on line 66. Decimal values are permitted and may be appropriate in some situations. The value on line 66 is multiplied by the annual number of retrieval transactions, as previously entered on line 60. The result, to be entered on line 67, is the number of pages printed per year. The cost per page for print supplies (including, but not necessarily limited to, paper and toner) is entered on line 68. The estimated annual cost of printing supplies is calculated by multiplying the amount on line 68 by the value on line 67. The result is entered on line 69.

### Line 70

The total annual variable cost for document retrieval is the sum of annual costs for labor (line 65) and printing supplies (line 69). The total is entered on line 70.

### Line 71

Based on the worksheet entries described above, the total annual cost of an electronic document imaging system is the sum of the annualized value of fixed start-up costs (line 10), annual fixed costs (line 20), annual media costs (line 31), annual labor costs for document conversion (line 46), annual labor costs for indexing and data entry (lines 53 and 59), and annual retrieval costs (line 70). That total is entered on line 71.

### Example of Completed Worksheet

Table 5-4 illustrates completed worksheets for a hypothetical but realistic electronic document imaging implementation involving a master file of research and product development reports maintained by the technical information center of a pharmaceutical company. The reports, which average ten pages in length, consist entirely of letter-size pages. Produced by typewriters, laser printers, and other devices, they are in good condition and can be legibly digitized at a scanning resolution of 200 pixels per horizontal and vertical inch. The following explanations apply:

### Part A

Start-up costs are based on a two-workstation, microcomputer-based electronic document imaging system purchased as a turnkey configuration of hardware and software for $75,000. One of the workstations will be used for document scanning and index data entry, the other for data base searching and image retrieval. Each workstation includes a 5.25-inch, 650MB rewritable optical disk drive. Media recorded on the drive connected to the scanning workstation will be read by an identical drive connected to the retrieval workstation. The vendor, a value-added reseller, was paid an additional $2,500 to assist with data base definitions. The customer also incurred a charge of $500 for electrical improvements to the installation site. The customer has decided to limit the system's scope to new documents, leaving its paper backfiles unconverted. Two microcomputers, supplied by the customer, will access the turnkey system via an existing local area network. The two microcomputers are valued at $1,500 each. Principally intended for word processing, they will be used 10 percent of the time for imaging-related operations, principally data base searching to determine the existence of potentially relevant document images. The estimated useful life of the system is four years. The annualized value of start-up costs is $19,575.

### Part B

The customer must pay an annual license renewal fee of $500 for electronic document imaging software. That fee is the equivalent of a software lease payment. Charges for maintenance contracts on turnkey system components, or comparable funds set aside to pay for repairs on a per-incident basis, equal 12 percent of the purchase price of the covered components, or $9,360 for a system valued at $78,000. Maintenance contracts for the customer-supplied microcomputers total $350 per year. A network printer, leased for $2,000 per year, is used 10 percent of the time for imaging-related operations. Equipment dedicated to electronic document imaging occupies 100 square feet of floor space valued at $20 per square foot per year. The shared workstations occupy 25 square feet of floor space valued at $20 per square foot per year. The total of annual fixed costs is $12,145.

### Part C

Double-sided recording capacity of the rewritable optical disk cartridges used for document image storage is 650MB. Letter-size pages will be scanned at 200 pixels per horizontal and vertical inch with Group IV compression. Approximately thirty page-images can be stored per megabyte. Estimated cartridge capacity is 19,500 images. The anticipated annual input load is 125,000 pages (an average of 500 pages per workday). Seven optical disk cartridges will consequently be required. The media cost is $200 per cartridge. A duplicate set of cartridges will be produced for backup purposes.

### Part D

The document preparation rate is 1,000 pages per hour. Document preparation, as discussed in Chapter Two, involves removal of documents from cabinets and folders, removal of staples and paper clips, and other operations necessary to make pages "scanner-ready". Based on an annual workload of 125,000 pages, the time required for document preparation is 125 hours per year. The wage rate for document preparation is $10 per hour, which is equivalent to an annual salary of $16,000 per year plus fringe benefits at the 25-percent level. The document scanning rate is 600 pages per hour. Based on an annual workload of 125,000 pages, the time required for document scanning is 208 hours per year. As with document preparation, the wage rate for scanner operation is $10 per hour. It is assumed that 100 percent of digitized images will be inspected. At a rate of 1,000 images per hour, the time required for image inspection is 125 hours per year. The wage rate is $10 per hour.

### Part E

The electronic document imaging system is installed in the technical information center of a pharmaceutical company. Documents recorded on optical disk cartridges consist of brief technical reports which range from five to twenty-five pages in length. As noted above, the average number of pages per report is ten. Each report will be indexed by date, author, originating department, and an average of three subject terms consisting of names of chemical compounds. The document collection contains 12,500 indexable items. Required index values invariably appear in an abstract on the first page of the document and are easily determined by data entry personnel. It takes approximately two minutes to read the abstract and determine the index values for a given document. The estimated time required for document indexing is 417 hours per year. At an hourly wage of $16, which is equivalent to an annual salary of $24,000 plus fringe benefits at the 25-percent level, the annual cost of document indexing labor is $6,672.

The average number of characters to be entered per data base record is 100, including commands and control characters. Based on 12,500 indexable items, the annual data entry workload is 1,250,000 keystrokes. Data entry throughput is conservatively estimated at 6,500 keystrokes per hour to allow time for sight verification of entered values and correction of detected errors. The hourly wage for data entry personnel is $16, as noted above. The estimated annual cost of data entry is $3,088.

### Part F

An average of four retrieval transactions is performed each hour for a total of thirty-two transactions per workday and 8,000 transactions per year. The average time per retrieval transaction is seven minutes, including data base searching, display of document images, and printing of selected images. The retrieval time per year is 934 hours. Retrieval operations are performed by various employees, including chemists, laboratory technicians, and clerical support personnel. The average wage rate of persons performing retrieval is $25 per hour, which is equivalent to an annual salary of $37,500 plus fringe benefits at the 25-percent level. The estimated annual cost of retrieval labor is $23,350.

**Table 5-4: Cost Calculation Example**

PART A: Start-Up Costs

| | | | |
|---|---|---|---|
| 1. | Purchase price of hardware and software used exclusively for electronic document imaging | 1. | $ 75,000 |
| 2. | System-related charges not included in line 1 | 2. | $ 2,500 |
| 3. | Cost of site preparation for system installation | 3. | $ 500 |
| 4. | Cost of backfile conversion and related services | 4. | $ — |
| 5. | Purchase price of hardware and software shared with other applications | 5. | $ 3,000 |
| 6. | Percentage of amount on line 6 attributable to electronic document imaging | 6. | 0.10 |
| 7. | Amount on line 6 multiplied by decimal value on line 7 | 7. | $ 300 |
| 8. | Total of amounts on lines 1, 2, 3, 4, and 7 | 8. | $ 78,300 |
| 9. | Estimated useful life of imaging system, in years | 9. | 4 |
| 10. | Amount on line 9 divided by value on line 11; this is the annualized value of start-up costs for electronic document imaging | 10. | $ 19,575 |

PART B: Annual Fixed Costs

| | | | |
|---|---|---|---|
| 11. | Lease or rental payments for hardware and software used exclusively for electronic document imaging | 11. | $ 500 |
| 12. | Cost of maintenance contracts for electronic document imaging hardware and software | 12. | $ 9,360 |
| 13. | Annual value of floor space occupied by hardware used exclusively for electronic document imaging | 13. | $ 2,000 |
| 14. | Lease or rental payments for hardware and software shared with other applications | 14. | $ 2,000 |
| 15. | Cost of maintenance contracts for hardware and software shared with other applications | 15. | $ 350 |
| 16. | Annual value of floor space occupied by hardware shared with other applications | 16. | $ 500 |

17. Total of amounts on lines 14, 15, and 16     17. $ __2,850__

18. Percentage of amount on line 14 attributable to electronic document imaging     18. __0.10__

19. Amount on line 17 multiplied by decimal value on line 18     19. $ __285__

20. Total of amounts on lines 11, 12, 13, and 19; this is the annual fixed cost for electronic document imaging     20. $ __12,145__

PART C: Annual Variable Costs — Image Storage Media

21. Capacity of one unit of image storage media in megabytes     21. __650__

22. Number of images per megabyte (from table 5-2)     22. __30__

23. Value on line 21 multiplied by value on line 22; this is the image capacity of one unit of document storage media     23. __19,500__

24. Number of pages to be converted to document images per year     24. __125,000__

25. Value on line 24 divided by value on line 23; this is the number of media units required     25. __7__

26. Cost per unit for image storage media     26. $ __200__

27. Value on line 25 multiplied by amount on line 26     27. $ __1,400__

28. Number of back-up or distribution copies to be produced for each medium     28. __7__

29. Cost per unit for back-up or distribution copies     29. $ __200__

30. Value on line 28 multiplied by amount on line 29     30. $ __1,400__

31. Total of amounts on line 27 and line 30; this is the annual cost of image storage media, including back-up and distribution copies     31. $ __2,800__

PART D: Annual Variable Costs — Document Conversion Labor

32. Document preparation rate in pages per hour     32. __1,000__

33. Value on line 24 divided by value on line 32     33. __125__

34. Hourly wage rate for document preparer     34. $ __10__

35. Value on line 33 multiplied by amount on line 34; this is the annual labor cost for document preparation

35. $ __1,250__

36. Document scanning rate in pages per hour

36. __600__

37. Value on line 24 divided by value on line 36

37. __208__

38. Hourly wage rate for scanner operator

38. $ __10__

39. Value on line 37 multiplied by amount on line 38; this is the annual labor cost for scanner operation

39. $ __2,080__

40. Percentage of document images to be inspected (if 100 percent, enter 1.00)

40. __1.00__

41. Value on line 24 multiplied by decimal value on line 40; this is the number of pages to be inspected

41. __125,000__

42. Image inspection rate in pages per hour

42. __1,000__

43. Value on line 41 divided by value on line 42

43. __125__

44. Hourly wage rate for document image inspector

44. $ __10__

45. Value on line 43 multiplied by amount on line 44; this is the annual labor cost for document image inspection

45. $ __1,250__

46. Total of amounts on line 35, line 39, and line 45; this is the annual labor cost for document conversion

46. $ __4,580__

PART E: Annual Variable Costs — Document Indexing and Data Entry

47. Average number of pages per document (decimal values permitted)

47. __4__

48. Value on line 24 divided by value on line 47; this is the number of indexable documents per year

48. __12,500__

49. Average time, in minutes, required to index a document

49. __2__

50. Value on line 49 multiplied by value on line 48

50. __25,000__

51. Value on line 50 divided by 60; this is the document indexing time per year in hours

51. __417__

52. Hourly wage rate for document indexer

52. $ __16__

53. Amount on line 52 multiplied by value on line 51; this is the annual labor cost for document indexing

53. $ __6,672__

54. Average number of characters per database record     54.    100

55. Value on line 48 multiplied by value on line 54; this is the annual keystroking workload     55.    1,250,000

56. Data entry rate in keystrokes per hour     56.    6,500

57. Value on line 55 divided by value on line 56; this is the annual data entry workload in hours     57.    193

58. Hourly wage rate for data entry clerk     58.   $    16

59. Value on line 57 multiplied by amount on line 58; this is the annual labor cost for entry of database records     59.   $   3,088

PART F: Annual Variable Costs — Document Retrieval

60. Number of retrieval transactions per year     60.    8,000

61. Average time per retrieval transaction, in minutes     61.    7

62. Value on line 61 multiplied by value on line 60     62.    56,000

63. Value on line 61 divided by 60; this is the retrieval time per year in hours     63.    934

64. Hourly wage rate for retrieval personnel     64.   $    25

65. Value on line 63 multiplied by amount on line 64; this is the annual labor cost for document retrieval     65.   $   23,350

66. Average number of images printed per retrieval transaction (decimal values permitted)     66.    10

67. Value on line 66 multiplied by value on line 60     67.    80,000

68. Cost per print for paper and other supplies     68.   $   0.02

69. Amount on line 68 multiplied by value on line 67; this is the annual cost of print supplies     69.   $   1,600

70. Total of amounts on line 65 and line 69; this is the total annual cost for document retrieval     70.   $   24,950

PART G: Total Annual Cost Calculation

71. Total of amounts on lines 10,
20, 31, 46, 53, 59, and 70; this is the
total annual cost of an electronic document
imaging system

71.  $ __73,810__

---

Retrieved document images are usually printed for reference purposes. Documents, as previously discussed, average ten pages in length. The printing workload consequently totals 80,000 pages per year. At a supply cost of two cents per page, the annual cost of printing is $640. The total annual cost of retrieval operations is $24,950.

### Part G

Annual fixed and variable costs for the hypothetical electronic document imaging system discussed in this example total $73,810.

### Cost Justification

Electronic document imaging systems are implemented to achieve one or more information management objectives which presumably yield benefits to the implementing organization. Typical objectives, previously delineated in Chapter One, include faster retrieval of documents needed to perform specific tasks; the ability to retrieve documents that cannot be effectively retrieved by other means; automated routing of documents associated with particular transaction processing activities; reductions in space required for document storage; simplified file maintenance; and protection of documents against loss or damage. The benefits associated with such objectives may be tangible or intangible. Examples of the latter include improved output quality, improved employee morale, and increased customer satisfaction. Intangible benefits are important but, by definition, unquantifiable. As such, they fall outside the scope of this discussion.

Table 5-5 summarizes quantifiable benefits associated with particular electronic document imaging system objectives. Such benefits include reduced costs (or cost avoidance in the case of costs not yet incurred) and increased revenues through productivity improvements or the development of new products or services. Greater availability of information is sometimes cited as a benefit of electronic document imaging systems, but its value is difficult to quantify. Presumably, greater availability of information enhances employee productivity, permits faster completion of specific tasks, or has other desirable effects which can be measured. Adopting a reductionist attitude, some systems analysts contend that greater avaiability of information is not a distinct benefit but a means of reducing costs or increasing revenues.

In any case, the objectives and benefits presented in the accompanying table provide the foundation for cost justifying electronic document imaging implementations. Broadly defined, cost justification is an analytical procedure which evaluates the costs associated with a particular activity in order to determine whether such costs are defensible in terms of the benefits to be derived from them. The most common and, from the business standpoint, most persuasive approach to cost justification is cost-effectiveness analysis. As applied to electronic document imaging, a cost-effective system is one that fully addresses the requirements of a given application at a cost lower than that of other document management technologies or methodologies. As a cost-justification procedure, cost-effectiveness analysis involves the preparation of realistic, reliable comparisons between a proposed electronic document imaging system and alternative document storage and retrieval methodologies. In most cases, the proposed electronic document imaging system is compared to a paper-based or microfilm system that it will replace. In such situations, cost-effectiveness analysis seeks to demonstrate that the costs associated with a proposed electronic document imaging system are lower than those of an existing document storage and retrieval methodology.

**Table 5-5: Selected Objectives and Cost-benefits in Electronic Document Imaging Implementations**

| Objective | Cost-Benefit | How Achieved |
|---|---|---|
| Compact storage | Reduced cost, cost avoidance | Floor space savings; minimize purchase of new filing equipment and supplies |
| Faster retrieval | Reduced cost, cost avoidance | Reduction in staff required to perform given number of retrieval operations; ability to perform increased number of retrieval operations without corresponding increase in staff |
| More complex retrieval | Greater availability of information | Computer-based document indexing |
| Improved work-flow | Reduced cost, cost avoidance, increased revenue | Reduction in time and labor required to complete given number of transactions; ability to complete more transactions in given time; expansion of fee-based customer services |
| Simplified file maintenance | Greater availability of information, cost reduction, cost avoidance | Elimination of mis-files and clerical time spent on mis-file detection; documents never out of file; simultaneous access to documents; elimination of time wasted waiting for documents in use by others |
| Online access | Greater availability of information, cost reduction, cost avoidance | Reference to documents from remote workstations, fax machines; eliminate copying of documents for distribution |
| Protection of documents | Greater availability of information | Document images not subject to wear and tear through repeated use |

As an illustration, assume that the hypothetical electronic document imaging system used as an example in the preceding cost calculation will replace a paper-based system for storage and retrieval of research reports maintained by the technical information center of a pharmaceutical company. The company's master file of technical reports is stored in four-drawer, vertical-style file cabinets. The reports are grouped by the department which originated them. Within each departmental grouping, reports are filed alphabetically by the name of the principal author. Multiple reports by a given author are sequenced by a report number that is assigned by the technical information center. Individual reports are inserted into folders that are labelled with the name of the originating department, the author's name, and the report number.

To provide subject access to technical reports, a cross-reference file is arranged alphabetically by chemical compound name. Each report is indexed by an average of three chemical compounds. Photocopies of the reports' title pages are filed under pertinent compound names. Each title page indicates the originating department and author's name, which serve as entry points to the master file where complete copies of reports are maintained.

Retrieval is performed by information scientists on the technical information center staff who receive requests for reports from researchers, managers, and authorized employees. Requests may be received in person, by phone, or by fax. Desired reports are identified by author or compound name. The identification is conclusive for approximately 25 percent of retrieval requests. In the remaining cases, discussion with requestors is necessary to distinguish similar reports by a given author, to determine exact compound names, or to otherwise clarify the retrieval requirement. Browsing through reports is sometimes necessary to identify desired documents. An average of twelve minutes per transaction is spent clarifying retrieval requirements and locating reports. To maintain file integrity, the technical information center does not circulate master copies of reports. Instead, a photocopy is produced for the requestor.

Table 5-6 delineates costs associated with this hypothetical paper-based filing system. The following explanations apply.

### Part A

The annual accumulation of 12,500 reports totalling 125,000 pages necessitates the purchase of twelve file cabinets per year. The subject file, which accumulates at a rate of 37,500 pages per year, requires an additional four cabinets per year. File cabinets cost $250 each for an annual total of $3,750. The sixteen cabinets purchased each year occupy 115 square feet of office-quality floor space valued at $20 per square foot per year. Each year's accumulation of cabinets consequently occupies floor space valued at $2,300. Floor space consumption, however, increases from year to year as previously purchased cabinets are joined by new ones. For comparison with electronic document imaging costs presented in Table 5-4, floor space costs are averaged over a four-year period. Four-year cumulative floor space costs are based on the following annual amounts:

| Year | Number of Cabinets | Square Feet | Annual Cost |
|------|--------------------|-------------|-------------|
| 1 | 16 | 115 | $2,300 |
| 2 | 32 | 230 | $4,600 |
| 3 | 48 | 345 | $6,900 |
| 4 | 64 | 460 | $9,200 |

The four-year total of $23,000 yields an average cost of $5,750 per year based on an annualized average of 287.5 square feet. The total annual cost of document storage, including file cabinet purchases and floor space, is $9,500.

### Part B

The determination of originating department, author name, and chemical compound names for filing purposes is the counterpart of document indexing in an electronic document imaging implementation. The originating department and author are identified on the title page of each report. Chemical compounds are contained in an abstract and are easily identified. At two minutes per report, the annual time requirement is 417 hours based on a workload of 12,500 reports. At an hourly wage of $16, which is equivalent to an annual salary of $24,000 plus fringe benefits at the 25-percent level, the annual cost of labor to determine the originating department, author, and chemical compounds for filing purposes is $6,672.

Copies of title pages for inclusion in the cross-reference file are made on a photocopier that is shared with other activities. Users are charged 4

**Table 5-6: Annual Operating Costs for a Paper-based Filing System for Technical Reports**

PART A: Document Storage

1. Purchase of 16 file cabinets       $3,750
   at $250 each
2. Floor space: annualized over       5,750
   a four-year period: 287.5
   square feet at $20 per square foot

PART B: Document Filing

1. Determination of department,       6,672
   author, and compound names
   for each document: 417 hours
   at $16 per hour
2. Photocopying of title pages
   for cross-reference file
      a. Equipment and supplies:       1,500
        37,500 pages at .04 per page
      b. Labor: 417 hours at $10       4,170
        per hour
3. Preparation of file folder labels
      a. Purchase of 12,500       125
        labels at .01 each
      b. Typing of labels: 208       2,080
        hours at $10 per hour
4. Placement of reports and       6,250
   photocopied title pages in
   cabinets: 625 hours at $10
   per hour

PART C: Document Retrieval

1. Retrieval labor: 1,334 hours       40,000
   at $25 per hour
2. Photocopying of reports
      a. Equipment and supplies:       3,200
        80,000 pages at .04 per page
      b. Labor: 667 hours at $10       6,670
        per hour

   Total Annual Cost       $80,167

cents per page to cover equipment amortization, maintenance, and supplies. Based on a workload of 37,500 copies (three copies each for 12,500 title pages), equipment-related costs and supply costs total $1,500 per year. The photocopying itself is performed by a clerical employee at an hourly rate of $10, which is equivalent to an annual salary of $16,000 per year plus fringe benefits at the 25-percent level. Assuming that copying time averages two minutes per report, including transit time to and from the photocopier, the annual labor requirement is 417 hours. The annual labor cost for photocopying is $4,170.

Preparation costs for file folders for 12,500 reports involve the purchase and typing of labels. Adhesive labels are priced at 1 cent each. Labels contain an average of 50 characters each. Assuming that one minute is required to type each label and affix it to a folder, the required folder preparation time is 208 hours per year. At a clerical wage of $10 per hour including fringe benefits, the annual labor cost for folder preparation is $2,080.

Actual document filing involves the placement of reports and photocopied title pages into file cabinets. At an average of three minutes per report, the required filing time is 625 hours. At a clerical wage of $10 per hour including fringe benefits, the annual labor cost for placing reports and title pages into file cabinets is $6,250. The total annual cost of document filing, encompassing all cost components listed in Part B, is $20,797.

### Part C

Document retrieval, as noted above, is performed by information scientists who will locate desired documents based on identifying parameters supplied by researchers or other requestors. As noted above, an average of twelve minutes is spent on each retrieval transaction, including the time required to clarify requests and locate desired documents. Based on an annual retrieval workload of 8,000 transactions, the labor for document retrieval totals 1,600 hours per year. At an hourly wage of $25, which is equivalent to an annual salary of $37,500 plus fringe benefits at the 25-percent level, the estimated annual cost of retrieval labor is $40,000.

As noted above, reports are photocopied for requestors. Based on on average of ten pages per report, the annual photocopying workload is 80,000 pages. Photocopying charges total 4 cents per page, including equipment amortization and supply costs. Assuming that photocopying time averages five minutes per report, including transit time to and from the photocopier as well as the time to return reports to their file cabinets following copying, the annual labor requirement is 667 hours. At an hourly wage of $10 including fringe benefits, the cost of photocopying labor for document retrieval is $6,670. The total cost of document retrieval for all items included in Part C is $49,780.

The annual total for cost components enumerated in Table 5-5 is $80,167. As presented in Table 5-4, the total annual cost of an electronic document imaging system for the same application is $73,810. In this hypothetical example, electronic document imaging yields a cost reduction of $6,357 per year or $25,428 over a four-year period. The cost reduction is principally attributable to savings in labor associated with document filing and retrieval. Savings will also be realized from avoidance of file cabinet purchases and floor space consumption associated with storage of paper documents.

As a comparative analysis emphasizing cost reduction, the foregoing discussion necessarily ignored functional enhancements and special capabilities offered by electronic document imaging technology that have no counterparts in paper-based filing systems. Often characterized as "added value" features, such functional enhancements and special capabilities contribute to cost justification, although their impact may prove difficult to quantify in the context of a cost-effectiveness analysis. As an example, the powerful data base search capabilities offered by electronic document imaging systems may permit retrieval of potentially relevant documents that could not have been retrieved in a paper-based filing installation, but the value of such enhanced retrieval performance may not be measurable. In some cases, however, added value can be quantified. In the application cited above, for instance, electronic document imaging offers backup protection—in the form of duplicate optical disk cartridges—that is not present in the paper-based system. If an annual accumulation of 125,000 pages were to be recorded on 16mm microfilm reels by a service bureau for backup purposes without regard to retrievability of filmed images, the cost would be $3,125 based on a microfilming rate of $25 per 1,000 pages. When the value of this functional enhancement is added to the cost reduction cited above, the electronic document imaging implementation offers an annual advantage of $9,482 when compared to the paper-based filing system it is designed to replace.

## References

Andrews, H. (1990). Redefining document management: whither electronics, micrographics? Inform 4/6: 41-43.

_____. (1990a). When document systems are truly "media transparent". IMC Journal 26/3: 7-9.

Ashford, J. and Matkin, D. (1982). Studies in the Application of Free Text Package Systems. London: Library Association.

Banks, R. (1985). Optical disk storage and microfilm systems find separate applications. Computer Technology Review 5/4: 95-99.

Black, D. (1989). The new breed of mixed-media image management systems. IMC Journal 25/1: 9-13.

Blake, J. (1990). War over optical disk or microfilm ends; future contains multiple media. International Journal of Micrographics and Optical Technology 8/3: 141-43.

Blumer, A. et al. (1987). Complete inverted files for efficient text retrieval and analysis. Journal of the Association for Computing Machinery 34: 578-95.

Bogue, T. (1985). Document processing: surmounting the myth of a paperless office. Journal of Information and Image Management 18/10: 11-14, 27.

Burger, A. (1990). Integrating optical disk, microfilm in electronic imaging applications. IMC Journal 26/2: 6-8.

Colvin, G. (1986). The current state of text retrieval. In CD-ROM: The New Papyrus. Redmond, WA: Microsoft Press, pp. 131-36.

Croft, W. and Pezarro, M. (1981). Text retrieval techniques in the automated office. In Office Information Systems: Proceedings of the Second International Workshop. Amsterdam: North-Holland, pp. 565-76.

Dubois, C. (1987). Free text versus controlled vocabulary: a reassessment. Online Review 11: 243-53.

Gallenberger, J. (1989). EIM: electronic image micrographics? Inform 3/4: 14-17.

Gallenberger, J. and Batterton, J. (1989). Kodak optical disk and microfilm technologies carve niches in specific applications. Optical Information Systems 9/3: 127-130.

Geller, S. (1983). Care and Handling of Computer Magnetic Tape Storage Media. Washington, DC: Institute for Computer Science and Technology, National Bureau of Standards.

Gill, J. and Woll, T. (1986). Full text management. In CD-ROM: The New Papyrus. Redmond, WA: Microsoft Press, pp. 137-42.

Jones, K. and Bell, C. (1984). Automatic extraction of words from texts especially for input into information retrieval systems based on inverted files. In Research and Development in Information Retrieval: Proceedings of the Third Joint BCS and ACM Symposium. Cambridge: Cambridge University Press, pp. 409-20.

Kalthoff, R. (1983). A look at document-based optical mass memory systems for the 1980s. IMC Journal 19/1: 18-20.

_____. (1985). Document-based optical mass memories. Information Management 19/8: 1, 11, 13, 22, 27.

Meth, C. (1986). Microimage methods. Administrative Management 47/4: 23-27.

Newman, D. (1985). Document management: software is the link. The Office 101/5: 109-10.

Rowland, I. (1987). Text Retrieval: An Introduction. London: Taylor Graham.

Saffady, W. (1988). Optical Disks vs. Micrographics as Document Storage and Retrieval Technologies. Westport, CT: Meckler Corporation.

_____. (1989). Text Storage and Retrieval Systems: A Technology Survey and Product Directory. Westport, CT: Meckler Corporation.

_____. (1991). Stability, care, and handling of microforms, magnetic media and optical disks. Library Technology Reports 27: 5-116.

_____. (1986). Optical disk and micrographic document management systems: pros, cons, and draws. Journal of Information and Image Management 19/9: 15-17.

_____. (1992). Optical Disks vs. Micrographics as Document Storage and Retrieval Technologies, 2nd edition. Westport, CT: Meckler Corporation.

Smith, L. et al. (1986). Prediction of the Long Term Stability of Polyester-Based Recording Media. Gaithersburg, MD: National Bureau of Standards.

Skupsky D. (1989). Recordkeeping Requirements. Denver: Information Requirements Clearinghouse.

_____. (1991). Legal Requirements for Microfilm, Computer and Optical Disk Records: Evidence, Regulation, Government, and International Requirements. Denver: Information Requirements Clearinghouse.

Williams, R. (1987). Legality of Optical Storage. Chicago: Cohasset Assocates.

Wolf, D. (1984). Microfilm is dead: long live photo/optical image recording. Journal of Information and Image Management 17/8: 25-30.

Zagami, R. (1987). State of the art report on micrographics and optical disks. Administrative Management 48/4: 24-29.

# Appendix: Vendor Addresses

This appendix contains names and addresses for equipment manufacturers, turnkey system vendors, systems integrators, software developers, service bureaus, and others involved in the design, development, and sale of electronic document imaging systems and related products and services.

ACCESS Corporation
1011 Glendale-Milford Road
Cincinnati, OH 45215

Acumen Systems Inc
2-4 Garber Square
Ridgewood, NJ 07450

Adaptive Information Systems
24461 Ridge Route Drive, Suite 200
Laguna Hills, CA 92653

Advanced Archival Products, Inc.
6595 S. Dayton Street, Suite 1300
Englewood, CO 80111

Advanced IDAS, Inc.
9550 Firestone Boulevard, Suite 210
Downey, CA 90241

Advanced Recognition
Hatch Lane
Windsor
Berkshire, SL4 3QP
U.K.

Advanced Technologies International
355 Sinclair-Frontage Road
Milpitas, CA 95050

AEG Corporation
Recognition Systems Division
1350 Connecticut Avenue NW
Washington, DC 20036

Agfa Corporation
Matrix Division
100 Challenger Road
Ridgefield Park, NJ 07660

Alacrity Systems, Inc
43 Newburg Road
Hacketstown, NJ 07840

ALE Systems
334 Kings Charter Drive
Ashland, VA 23005

Allen Products Company
180 Wampus Lane
Milford, CT 06460

Alliance INFONET
4675 MacArthur Court, Suite 600
Newport Beach, CA 92660

ALOS Micrographics Corporation
118 Bracken Road
Montgomery, NY 12549

Alpharel, Inc.
3601 Calle Tecate
Camarillo, CA 93012

Alphatronix, Inc.
2300 Englert Drive, Suite C
P.O. Box 13687
Research Triangle Park, NC 27709

AME
8 Ballymoss Road
Sandyford Industrial Estate
Dublin 18
Ireland

A.M. Electronics, Inc.
540 Weddell Drive, Suite 3
Sunnyvale, CA 94089

American Photo Systems, Inc.
Box 332
St. Johnsbury, VT 05819

Amitech Corporation
2721 E. Merrilee Drive
Fairfax, VA 22031

Amtronics Inc.
P.O. Box 24190
New Orleans, LA 70184

Anacomp, Inc.
One Buckhead Plaza, Suite 1700
3060 Peachtree Road N.W.
Atlanta, GA 30305

Anamet Laboratories, Inc.
3400 Investment Boulevard
Hayward, CA 94545-3811

Andersen Consulting
West Washington Street
Chicago, IL 60602

Anderson Microfilming Company
501-1/2 South McCoy Street
Granville, IL 61326

Androcles Engineering
4555 Auburn Boulevard, Suite 6
Sacramento, CA 95841

Apple Computer, Inc.
20525 Mariana Avenue
Cupertino, CA 95014

Applied Image, Inc.
1653 East Main Street
Rochester, NY 14609

Applied Programming Technologies, Inc.
One Hollow Lane, Suite 313
Lake Success, NY 11042

Apunix Computer Services
5575 Ruffin
San Diego, CA 92123

Aquidneck Systems International, Inc.
650 Ten Rod Road
North Kingstown, RI 02852

AT&T
Guilford Center
P.O. Box 20045
Greensboro, NC 27420

ATG Gigadisc
400 West Cummings Park
Woburn, MA 07801

ATLIS Technology & Integration Services
60111 Executive Boulevard
Rockville, MD 20852

AutoGraph International Inc.
181 Metro Drive, Suite 510
San Jose, CA 95112

Automated Records Management Systems, Inc.
23011 Moulton Parkway, J-10
Laguna Hills, CA 92653

Auto-trol Technology
12500 N. Washington Street
Denver, CO 80241-2404

Avision, Inc.
2nd Fl No. 2 Prosperity Road
Science-Based Industry Park
Hsinchu
Taiwan, R.O.C.

BancTec, Inc.
4435 Spring Valley Road
Dallas, TX 75244

Bell & Howell Document Systems Division
6800 McCormick
Chicago, IL 60645

Benson Computer Research Corporation
7926 Jones Branch Drive, Suite 260
Mclean, VA 22102

Blueridge Technologies, Inc.
Flint Hill Square
P.O. Box 430
Flint Hill, VA 22627-0430

Blue Water Systems, Inc.
48813 West Road
Wixom, MI 48393

Borett Automation Technology
31324 Via Colinas, Suite 106
Westlake Village, CA 91362

Boss Logic Inc.
505 N. 3rd St.
Fairfield, IA 52556

Boston Software Company
Grove Court Business Centre
Building B
Hatfield Road
Slough
Berkshire, SL1 1QU
U.K.

Bruka Service B.V.
Industrieweg II B 1613 KT
Grootebroek
The Netherlands

CAD-Capture Limited
Whitebirk Estate
Blackburn
Lancashire, BB1 5UD
U.K.

CAL-ABCO
6041 Variel Avenue
Woodland Hills, CA 91367

Calera Recognition Systems, Inc.
475 Potrero Avenue
Sunnyvale, CA 94086

Candi Technology, Inc.
2236 Camino Ramon
San Ramon, CA 94583

Candid Logic, Inc.
31681 Dequindre
Madison Heights, MI 48071

Canon U.S.A., Inc.
One Canon Plaza
Lake Success, NY 11042

Cardiff Software Inc.
531 Stevens Avenue, Building B
Solano Beach, CA 92075

Cimage Corporation
Centennial Court
Easthampstead Road
Bracknell
Berkshire, RG12 1JZ
U.K.

Cimage Corporation
3885 Research Park Drive
Ann Arbor, MI 48108

CIMLINC Inc.
1222 Hamilton Parkway
Itasca, IL 60143

Cincinnati Bell Information Systems Inc.
600 Vine Street
Cincinnati, OH 45202

CISD International, Inc.
3525 Hyland Avenue
Costa Mesa, CA 92626

Coastal Software
100 Commercial Street
Portland, ME 04101

Cognitronics Imaging Systems, Inc.
4780 Mission Gorge Place
San Diego, CA 92120

Compulink Management Center, Inc.
370 South Crenshaw Boulevard, Suite E-106
Torrance, CA 90503

CompuLits, Inc.
11911 North Meridian
Carmel, IN 46032

Computer Expressions
3833 Chestnut St.
Philadelphia, PA 19104

Computership
125 Village Boulevard
Princeton Forrestal Village, Suite 220
Princeton, NJ 084540-5703

Computron Technologies
301 Route 17 North
Rutherford, NJ 07070

Com Squared Systems, Inc.
1285 Corporate Center Drive
St. Paul, MN 55121-1256

Corel Systems Corporation
1600 Carling Avenue
Ottowa, Ontario, K1Z 8R7
Canada

Cornerstone Technology
1990 Concourse Drive
San Jose, CA 95131

Corporate Information Systems
2916 Chicago Drive, S.W.
Grandville, MI 49418

Courtland Group, Inc.
10480 Little Patuxent Parkway
Columbia, MD 21044

CPT Image Systems, Inc.
8100 Mitchell Road
Minneapolis, MN 55344

Cranel, Inc.
510-F East Wilson Bridge Road
Worthington, OH 43085

CTA, Inc.
25 Science Park
New Haven, CT 06511

Cuadra Associates, Inc.
11835 West Olympic Boulevard, Suite 855
Los Angeles, CA 90064

Cygnet Systems, Inc.
2560 Junction Avenue
San Jose, CA 95134

Dakota Graphics, Inc.
9655 West Colfax Avenue
Lakewood, CO 80215

Dallas Digital Corporation
624 Krona Suite 160
Plano, TX 75074

DASCOM
Memorex Telex house
424 Bath Road
Longford
West Drayton
Middlesex, UB7 ORX
U.K.

Datacap Inc.
Five West Main Street
Elmsford, NY 10523

Datagen
Unit 12, Pines Trading Estate
Broad Street
Guildford
Surrey, GU3 3BH
U.K.

DataImage, Inc
628 Hebron Avenue
Glastonbury, CT 06067

Data Management Services
P.O. Box 619285 MD 4303
Dallas/Ft. Worth, TX 75261

Data Retrieval Corporation
11801 West Silver Spring Drive
Milwaukee, WI 53225-3042

Data/Ware Development, Inc.
9449 Carroll Park Drive
San Diego, CA 92121

Dataware Technologies, Inc.
222 Third Street
Cambridge, MA 02142

Dataworks Inc.
45 N.E. Loop 410, Suite 875
San Antonio, TX 78216

Decision Management Company, Inc.
23121 La Cadena Drive, Suite H
Laguna Hills, CA 92653

DeltaTech Corporation
8700 Georgia Avenue
Silver Spring, MD 20910

Digital Equipment Corporation
Digital Drive
P.O. Box 9501
Merrimack, NH 03054

Digital Image Systems
3033 Kellway, Suite 110
Carrollton, TX 75006

DISCORP
290 Easy Street, Suite 5
Simi Valley, CA 93065

Docubase Systems
90 Hatch Street
New Bedford, MA 02745

Docucon, Inc
9100 IH-10 West
San Antonio, TX 78230

Docufile, Inc.
462 Stevens Avenue, Suite 102
Solana Beach, CA 92075

DocuMaster Systems Inc.
1420 N. Claremont Boulevard #103B
Claremont, CA 91711

Document Control Systems, Inc.
187 W. Orange Thorpe Avenue
Suite 101
Placentia, CA 92670

Document Imaging Systems Corporation
543 Weddell Drive
Sunnyvale, CA 94089

Document Technologies, Inc.
1300 Charleston Road
Mountain View, CA 94043

DocuPoint, Inc
2701 Bayview Drive
Fremont, CA 94538

Docutec
Apolonio Morales 1
28036 Madrid
Spain

Dorotech
5 Hithercroft Court
Lupton Road
Wallingford
Oxon, OX10 9 BT
U.K.

Drew Resource Corporation
1717 Fourth Street
Berkeley, CA 94710

DSK Technology Inc.
671 Via Alondra, #808
Camarillo, CA 93012

D Store
Murdock Road
Bicester
Oxon, OX6 7PW
U.K.

EA Systems Inc.
960 Atlantic Avenue
Alameda, CA 94501

Eastman Kodak Company
Worldwide Imaging Information Systems
343 State Street
Rochester, NY 14650

EDM International
2120 E. Paisano Drive, Suite 140
El Paso, TX 79905

Electronic Cottage, Inc.
700 South 800 East
Green River, UT 84525

Elsag Inc
375 Park Avenue
New York, NY 10152

Engineering Images
123 Lehigh Drive
Fairfield, NJ 07004

Enhancement Technology, Inc.
17532 Von Karman Avenue
Irvine, CA 92714

Exabyte Corp.
1685 38th St.
Boulder, CO 80301

Excalibur Technologies Corporation
2000 Corporate Ridge, Suite 1095
McLean, VA 22102

Executive Technologies, Inc.
2120 16th Avenue South
Birmingham, AL 35205

EXP Group, Inc
44063 Fremont Boulevard
Fremont, CA 94538

Eye Communication Systems, Inc.
455 E. Industrial Drive
Hartland, WI 53029

FACSTORE, Inc.
1450 Route 22 West
Mountainside, NJ 07092

Feith System and Software, Inc.
425 Maryland Drive
Fort Washington, PA 19034

FileMark Corporation
12 Huron Drive
Natick, MA 01760

FileNet Corporation
3565 Harbor Boulevard
Costa Mesa, CA 92626

FileTek, Inc.
6100 Executive Boulevard
Rockville, MD 20852

Filmdex, Inc.
15500 Lee Highway
Centreville, VA 22020

Florida Data Bank Group
1699 Hobbs Road
Winter Haven, FL 33883

FORMSCAN
Apex House, West End
Frome
Somerset, BA11 3AS
U.K.

FORMTEK, Inc.
661 Andersen Drive
Pittsburgh, PA 15220

Fuji Photo Film U.S.A., Inc.
555 Taxter Road
Elmsford, NY 10523

Fulcrum Technologies, Inc.
785 Carling Ave
Ottowa, ON, K1S 5H4
Canada

Gannon Technology, Inc.
11250 Roger Bacon Drive, Atrium 8
Reston, VA 22090

GeneSys Data Technologies Inc.
Four North Park Drive, Suite 400
Hunt Valley, MD 21030

GESCAN International, Inc.
P.O. Box 12599
Research Triangle Park, NC 27709

Graphics Technology International
28 Gaylord Street
South Hadley, MA 01075

Greengage Development Corporation
12 Midland Court, Central Park
Lutterworth
Leicestershire
U.K.

Greengage Development Corporation
1895 Park Avenue, Second Floor
San Jose, CA 95126

Grundig Business Systems
6 Shaftesbury Court
Chalvey Park
Slough, SL1 2ER
U.K.

GTE Vantage Solutions
15000 Conference Center Drive
Chantilly, VA 22021-3808

Gyro Information Services
ECSL House
7 York Road
Woking
Surrey, GU22 7XH
U.K.

Headway Computer Products
Headway House
Christy Estate, Ivy Road
Aldershot
Hants, GU12 4TK
U.K.

Hewlett-Packard Company
3000 Hanover Street
Palo Alto, CA 94304

HNC, Inc.
5501 Oberlin Drive
San Diego, CA 92121

Horizons Technology, Inc.
3990 Ruffin Road
San Diego, CA 92123

IA Corp
1301 Harbor Bay Parkway
Alameda, CA 94501

IBM Corporation
101 Orchard Ridge Drive
Gaithersburg, MD 20878

ICI Imagedata
P.O. Box 6
Shire Park, Bessemer Road
Welwyn Garden City
Hertz, Al7 1HD
U.K.

ICL
Observatory House
Windsor Road
Slough
Berkshire, SL1 2EY
U.K.

Ideal Scanners & Copiers
11810 Parklawn Drive
Rockville, MD 20852

IdentiTech, Inc.
1333 Gateway Drive
Melbourne, FL 32901

IDL
Olympic House
1960299 The Broadway
Wimbledon
London, SW19 1SL
U.K.

Image Business Systems Corporation
417 Fifth Avenue
New York, NY 10016

Image Data Corporation
11550 IH-10 West
San Antonio, TX 78230

Image Graphics, Inc.
917 Bridgeport Avenue
Shelton, CT 06484

Image Machines Corporation
590 Herndon Parkway
Herndon, VA 22070

Image Management Systems
Commercial House
7 Soundwell Road
Staple Hill
Bristol, BS16 4QG
 U.K.

Imagement, Inc
1313 Bay Street
Bellingham, WA

Image Network Technology
2550 Corporate Place, #C101
Monterey Park, CA 91754

Image Processing Technologies
8300 Boone Boulevard, Suite 500
Vienna, VA 22182

Image Processor
1744 Portland Avenue
Walla Walla, WA 99362

Image Scanning Services
Headway House
Christy Estate
Ivy Road
Aldershot
Hants, GU12 4TX
U.K.

Imagesolve International
1 Torrington Park
Finchley
London, N12 9TB
U.K.

Image Systems Europe Ltd.
Sheffield Technology Park
60 Shirland Lane
Sheffield, S9 3SP
U.K.

Image Systems Technology, Inc.
385 Jordan Road
Troy, NY 12180

ImageTech Corp.
29444 Northwestern Highway, Suite L500
Southfield, MI 48034

Image-X
Suite #B1
600 Ward Drive
Santa Barbara, CA 93111-2300

Imara Research Corporation
111 Peter Street, Suite 804
Toronto, Ontario M5V 2H1
Canada

Imasys
Imasys House
24 Exchange Quay
Salford, M5 3EQ
U.K.

I.M.A.T. srl
Viale Lucania 15
Milan, 20139
Italy

IMNET, Inc.
34 Maple Avenue
Pine Brook, NJ 07058

Improvision
5901 Christie Avenue, Suite 502
Emeryville, CA 94608

IMT Graphic Imaging
12456 Plaza Drive
Cleveland, OH 44130

Indus International, Inc.
340 South Oak Street
West Salem, WI 54669

InforGraphix Corporation
W250 N6741 Highway J
Sussex, WI 53089

Information Design Products Inc.
3291 Keller Street
Santa Clara, CA 95054

Information Dimensions, Inc.
5080 Tuttle Crossing Boulevard
Dublin, OH 43017

Information Management Consultants
7915 Westpark Drive
McLean, VA 22102

Informative Graphics
706 East Bell Road, Suite 200
Phoenix, AZ 85022

Informix Software
4100 Bohannon Drive
Menlo Park, CA 94025

INFOTRONIC S.p.A.
Viale Berbera, 49
Milan, 20162
Italy

INSCI
Salisbury House
Finsbury Circus
London, EC2M 5QQ
U.K.

Instar Systems, Inc.
120 West Illinois
Chicago, IL 60610

Intelligent Archive Systems
Fulwood House
12 Fullwood Road
London, WC1V 6HR
U.K.

Intelus
9210 Corporate Boulevard
Rockville, MD 20850

Intergraph Corporation
One Madison Industrial Park
Huntsville, AL 35807

InterLinear Technology
1320 Harbor Bay Parkway, Suite 120
Alameda, CA 94501

International Imaging,Inc
701 West Foothill Boulevard
Azusa, CA 91702

Intrafed Inc.
5185 MacArthur Boulevard, Suite 102
Washington, DC 20016

Investronica
Conway House, Conway Street
Long Eaton
Nottingham, NG10 2AE
U.K.

IS Solutions
Admiral Hawke House, Green Street
Sunbury-on-Thames
Middlesex, TW16 6RA
U.K.

J. B. Engineering
1714 California Avenue
Monrovia, CA 91016

JRL Systems, Inc.
8305 Highway 71 West
Austin, TX 78735

JVC Information Products
1990 Beach Boulevard, Suite I
Huntington Beach, CA 92648

Karmac B.V.
7 Bronsweg
P.O. Box 212
Lelystad
Holland

Keyfile Corporation
22 Cotton Road
Nashua, NH 03063

Kofax Image Products, Inc.
3 Jenner Street
Irvine, CA 92718

K2 Systems
4 Colonial Business Park
Colonial Way
Watford
Hertshire, WD2 4PR
U.K.

Lanier Worldwide Inc.
2300 Parklake Drive NE
Atlanta, GA 30345

LaserAccess Corporation
22122 20th Avenue SE, #157
Bothell, WA 98021

LaserCard Systems Corporation
2644 Bayshore Parkway
Mountain View, CA 94043

LaserData, Inc.
300 Vesper Park
Tyngsboro, MA 01879

Laser Magnetic Storage International
4425 ArrowsWest Drive
Colorado Springs, CO 80907

LaserMaster Corporation,Imaging Products
6900 Shady Oak Road
Eden Prairie, MN 55344

LaserTape Systems Inc.
51 East Campbell Avenue, Suite 110
Campbell, CA 95008

Law Cypress Distributing Company
560 Lincoln Avenue
San Jose, CA 95126

LightStore Company
1825 South Grant Street, Suite 550
San Mateo, CA 94402

LOCAR Imaging Systems
25 Burlington Mall Road, Suite 300
Burlington, MA 01803

3M Document Systems Group
3M Center
St. Paul, MN 55144-1000

MAP-USA
27402 Camino Capistrano, Suite 218
Laguna Niguel, CA 92677

Martec Imaging Limited
Steam Mill
Steam Mill Street
Chester, CH3 5AN
U.K.

Maxoptix Corp.
2520 Junction Avenue
San Jose, CA 95134

Mekel Engineering, Inc.
777 South Penarth Avenue
Diamond Bar, CA 91789

Meridian Data, Inc.
5615 Scotts Valley Drive
Scotts Valley, CA 95066

Metafile Information Systems
421 First Avenue, S.W.
Rochester, MN 55902

Metrologie UK
Rapid House
Oxford Road
High Wycombe
Buckinghamshire, HP11 2EE
U.K.

MICRO-DAF Ltd
Microdaf Building
2 Hashalom Road
Tel-Aviv 67892
Israel

Micro Design
6985 University Boulevard
Winter Park, FL 32792

Micro Dynamics, Ltd
8555 16th Street, 7th Floor
Silver Spring, MD 20910

Microseal Corporation
2000 Lewis Avenue
Zion, IL 60099

Micro Synergy
31938 US 19 N
Palm Harbor, FL 34684

Micro-Tech Services
Unit 2, Arley Industrial Estate
Spring Hill
Arley
N. Coventry, CV7 8FG
U.K.

MicroVue USA Corp.
31 Watermill Lane
Great Neck, NY 11021

Minolta Corporation
101 Williams Drive
Ramsey, NJ 07446

Mira Computer Imaging Systems
9861 Copper Hill Road
St. Louis, MO 63124

National Computer Systems, Inc.
4401 West 76th Street
Edina, MN 55435

NCR Corporation
1700 S. Patterson Blvd
Dayton, OH 45479

Neotech Systems, Inc.
103 West 61st Street
Westmont, IL 60559

Network Computing Devices
350 North Bernardo Avenue
Mt. View, CA 94043

Network Express, Inc.
2200 Green Road
Ann Arbor, MI 48105

NNC Imaging Services
Booths Hall
Chelford Road
Knutsford
Cheshire, WA16 8QZ
U.K.

NKK Corporation
4-1-3 Kudankita, Chiyoda-Ku
Tokyo
Japan

NKK Electronics America, Inc.
2380 Oume Drive, Suite A
San Jose, CA 95131

Northern Telecom Inc.
200 Athens Way
Nashville, TN 37228

Novacad, Inc.
129 Middlesex Turnpike
Burlington, MA 01803

NYNEX Image Recognition Systems
565 Taxter Road
Elmsford, NY 10523

Ocron, Inc.
3350 Scott Boulevard, Building 36
Santa Clara, CA 95054

OCTO, Inc.
312 Laurel Avenue
Laurel, MD 20707

OMIC
6917 Woodley Avenue
Van Nuys, CA 91406

Open Image Systems
Longdene House
Haslemere
Surrey, GU27 2PH
U.K.

Optibase Inc.
7800 Deering Avenue
Canoga Park, CA 91304

Optical Laser, Inc.
315 3rd Street
Huntington Beach, CA 92648

Optigraphics Corporation
9339 Carroll Park Drive
San Diego, CA 92121

Optika Imaging Systems, Inc.
980 Enchanted Way, Suite 101
Simi Valley, CA 93065

Optisys, Inc
8620 North 22nd Avenue, Suite 109
Phoenix, AZ 85021

Optowand Inc.
3200 W. Story Road
Irving, TX 75038

Optivision, Inc.
4009 Miranda Avenue
Palo Alto, CA 94304

ORAC Information Systems
Molly Millar's Bridge
Wokingham
Berkshire, RG11 2WY
U.K.

Oracle Complex Systems Corporation
1110 North Glebe Road
Arlington, VA 22201

Pacific Image Communications, Inc.
1111 South Arroyo Parkway, Suite 430
Pasadena, CA 91105

Panasonic Communications & Systems Co.
2 Panosonic Way
Secaucus, NJ 07094

PaperClip Imaging Software
One University Plaza
Hackensack, NJ 07601

Paperless Corporation
1750 North Collins, Suite 104
Richardson, TX 75080

Paperlink
4 Dollis Park
Finchley
London, N2 1HG
U.K.

PCS Systems, Inc.
300 West Main Street
Northborough, MA 01532

PCWarehouse
1355 West 190 Street
Gardena, CA 90248

PDO Professional Media
1409 Foulk Road, Suite 200
Wilmington, DE 19803

Pegasus Disk Technologies, Inc.
55 Crest Avenue
Walnut Creek, CA 94595

PEPCO Division, Tappan Automation
Corporation
81 Hobart Street
Hackensack, NJ 07601

Personal Library Software
2400 Research Boulevard, Suite 350
Rockville, MD 20850

P.F.A., Inc.
9980 Glenoaks Boulevard, Suite F
San Valley, CA 91352

Phoenix Computers
Phoenix House
Oxwich Close
Brackmills
Northampton, NN4 OBH
U.K.

Photomatrix Corporation
5700 Buckingham Parkway
Culver City, CA 90230

Pinnacle Micro
19 Technology
Irvine, CA 92718

Pioneer Communications of America, Inc
600 East Crescent Avenue
Upper Saddle River, NJ 07458-1827

PI Technology, Inc.
1871 Tapo Street
Simi Valley, CA 93063

Pixel Magic
138 River Road
Andover, MA 01810

Plasmon Data Systems, Inc
1654 Centre Pointe Drive
Milpitas, CA 95035

Plexus Software, Inc.
5200 Great America Parkway
Santa Clara, CA 95054

PRC
1500 PRC Drive
McLean, VA 22102

Price Waterhouse
6500 Rock Spring Drive, Suite 500
Bethesda, MD 20817

Professional CAD/CAM Systems, Inc.
9145 Guilford Road
Columbia, MD 21046

QStar Technologies, Inc.
6707 Democracy Boulevard, Suite 202
Bethesda, MD 20817

RCI Image Systems
111 Main Street
El Segundo, CA 90245

Recognition Equipment Inc.
2701 East Grauwyler Road
Irving, TX 75061

Reflex Information Management
1 Effingham Road
Reigate
Surrey, RH1 7JN
U.K.

Ricoh Corporation
3001 Orchard Parkway
San Jose, CA 95134-2088

R Squared
11211 Arapahoe Road, Suite 200
Englewood, CO 80112

SAIC Imaging Solutions
10770 Wateridge Circle
San Diego, CA 92121

Satellite Image Systems, Inc.
990 West Atherton Drive #202
Salt Lake City, UT 84123

Saztec International, Inc.
6700 Corporate Drive
Kansas City, MO 64120

Scangraphics, Inc.
700 Abbott Drive
Broomall, PA 19008

Scanmedia
47 Bastwick Street
London, EC1V 3PS
U.K.

Scanning America
6700 Corporate Drive
Kansas City, MO 64120

Scan Text Corporation
12330 NE 8th Street, Suite 101
Bellevue, WA 98005

Scorpion Technologies
2010 North First Street, Suite 200
San Jose, CA 95131

Seaport Imaging
1340 Saratoga-Sunnyvale Road, Suite 104
San Jose, CA 95129

Security Engineered Machinery
Company, Inc.
5 Walkup Drive
P.O. Box 1045
Westboro, MA 01581

SEI, Inc.
100 Ashford Center North
Atlanta, GA 30338

Semaphore Image, Inc.
1400 Lincoln Village, #2331
Larkspur, CA 94939-2206

Severn Companies, Inc.
4640 Forbes Boulevard
Lanham, MD 20706

Sietec Open Systems
2235 Sheppard Avenue East, Suite 1800
Willodale, Ontario, M2J 5B5
Canada

Sigma Designs, Inc.
47900 Bayside Parkway
Fremont, CA 94538

Sigma Imaging Systems, Inc.
622 Third Avenue, 30th Floor
New York, NY 10017

Soda Creek Technologies, Inc.
72 Via Floreado
Orinda, CA 94563-1925

Software Alliance Corporation
2150 Shattuck Avenue, 11th floor
Berkeley, CA 94704

SoftwareFABRIK GmbH
Phorusgasse 8
A-1040 Vienna
Austria

Solutek Corporation
94 Shirley Street
Boston, MA 02119

Sony Corporation of America
3 Paragon Drive
Montvale, NJ 07645

South Bay Imaging
17424 Mt. Cliffwood
Foutain Valley, CA 92708

Southern Computer Systems, Inc.
2732 Seventh Avenue South
Birmingham, AL 35233

Spectrum Energy
56 Goldworth Road
Woking
Surrey, GU21 1LQ
U.K.

Spicer Corporation
221 McIntyre Drive
Kitchener, Ontario, N2R 1G1
Canada

Standard Platforms
Glenfield Park 2
Blakewater Road
Blackburn
Lancashire, BB2 5QH
U.K.

Staude Micrographics
2837 Walnut Boulevard
Walnut Creek, CA 94596

Summit Software Corporation
400 Colony Square, Suite 1960
Atlanta, GA 30361

Sun Microsystems
2550 Garcia Avenue
Mountain View, CA 94043

SunRise Imaging, Inc.
3439 Edison Way
Fremont, CA 94538

Sybex Computing
Strnmillis Embankment
Belfast
N. Ireland

Syntax, Inc.
11128 Harbor Court
Reston, VA 22091

Systems 2100
18 Woodside Road
Amersham
Bucks, HP6 6PA
U.K.

Talaris Systems Inc.
6059 Cornerstone Court West
San Diego, CA 92121

Tandem Computers
19191 Valleo Parkway
Cupertino, CA 95014

TASC
55 Walkers Brook Drive
Reading, MA 01867

Taywood Data Graphics
Greenford House
309 Ruislip Road East
Greenford
Middlesex, UB6 9BQ
U.K.

TEAMWorks Technologies, Inc.
65 Boston Post Road West
Marlboro, MA 01752

TechLaw Systems, Inc
14500 Avion Parkway, Suite 300
Chantilly, VA 22021-1101

TechView Corporation
2500 W. Higgins Road, Suite 1271
Hoffman Estates, IL 60195

Ten X Technology, Inc
4807 Spicewood Springs Road
Building 3, Suite 3200
Austin, TX 78759

Terminal Data Corporation
5898 Condor Drive
Moorpark, CA 93021-2606

TextWare Corporation
P.O. Box 3267
Park City, UT 84060

Thames Information Systems
1 David Mews
Greenwich South Street
London, SE10 8NW
U.K.

TIMS
ICL National House
Vanwall Road
Maidenhead
Berks
U.K.

TIS Tele Image Systems
25 Mall Road, Suite 300
Burlington, MA 01803

TMS, Inc.
110 West Third
Stillwater, OK 74074

TOSOH USA, Inc.
800 Gateway Boulevard, Suite C
South San Francisco, CA 94080

Tranmit
Microscribe House
Mitchell Close
West Portway, Andover
Hampshire, SO10 3TJ
U.K.

Triquest Corporation
210 Express Street
Plainview, NY 11803

Trimco Enterprises
84 Uxbridge Road
Easling
London, W13 8RA
U.K.

Troyton Computing Inc.
3807 Wilshire Boulevard, #1106
Los Angeles, CA 90010

TRW Financial Systems, Inc.
2001 Center Street
Berkeley, CA 94704

Tuscan Corporation
630 Dundee Road, Suite 425
Northbrook, IL 60062

Uni-Screen, Inc.
263 Kansas Street
Horicon, WI 53032

Unisys Corporation
P.O. Box 500
Blue Bell, PA 19424

United Systems & Software, Inc.
2301 Lucien Way, Suite 360
Maitland, FL 32751

University Microfilms International
300 North Zeeb Road
Ann Arbor, MI 48106

Verity, Inc.
1550 Plymouth Street
Mountain View, CA 94043

Viewpoint
Unit B, Progress House
Albert Road
Aldershot
Hants, GU11 1SZ
U.K.

ViewStar Corporation
5820 Shellmound Street
Emeryville, CA 94608

Visionshape
1434 W. Taft Avenue
Orange, CA 92665

Visual Access
Astec Centre, Astec West
Almonsbury
Bristol, BS12 4TD
U.K.

Visual Technology
Unit B, Progress House
Albert Road
Aldershot
Hants, GU11 1SZ
U.K.

Wang Laboratories, Inc.
One Industrial Avenue
Lowell, MA 01851

Westbrook, Technologies Inc
22 Pequot Park Rd
P.O. Box 910
Westbrook, CT 06498-0910

West Coast Information Systems, Inc.
1901 Olympic Boulevard
Walnut Creek, CA 94596

Westinghouse Electric Corporation
Civil Systems
P.O. Box 1693, MS# 5855
Walnut Creek, CA 94596

Wicks and Wilson Ltd.
Morse Road
Basingstoke
Hampshire, RG22 6PQ
U.K.

Wicks and Wilson USA Inc.
College Business Park, Suite D
707 South State College Blvd
Fullerton, CA 92631

The Woodin Group, Inc.
200 Bedford Street
Manchester, NH 03101

Xerox Corporation
100 Clinton Avenue South
Rochester, NY 14644

Xerox Engineering Systems
Xerox Square
Rochester, NY 14644

Xerox Imaging Systems
9 Centennial Drive
Peabody, MA 01960

Xionics Inc.
Two Corporation Way
Peabody, MA 01960

X-Ray Scanner Corporation
4030 Spencer Street, Suite 101
Torrance, CA 90503

Yeonjoo Systems, Inc.
4-F Okshin B/D
838-8 Yeoksam, Kangnam
Seoul, 135-080
Korea

Zuma Corporation
12016 Wilshire Boulevard #1
Los Angeles, CA 90025

# Index

WILLIAM SAFFADY is a long-time writer and researcher in the fields of computer science, mass storage technology, and optical imaging media. He is author of the annual *Optical Storage Technology: A State of the Art Review* and editor of the monthly industry newsletter, *Document Image Automation Update*. Recent books include *Electronic Document Imaging Systems* and *Optical Disks vs. Micrographics* (both Meckler, 1993). He is a professor at the School of Information Science and Policy at the State University of New York at Albany.

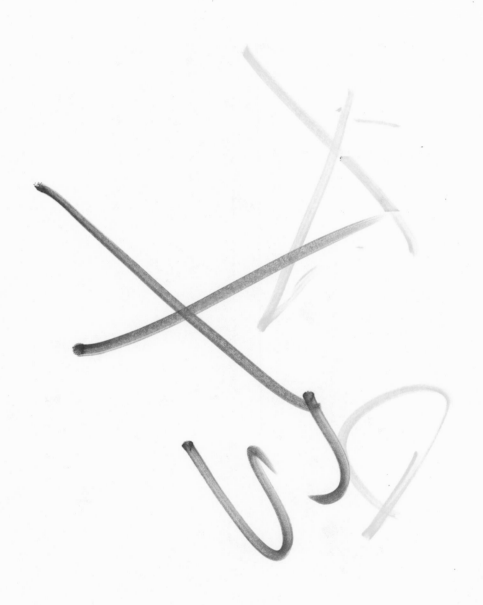